AN IMPROVED GRAMMAR
OF THE
ENGLISH LANGUAGE

AN IMPROVED GRAMMAR
OF THE
ENGLISH LANGUAGE

NOAH WEBSTER

GYAN

Published by

Gyan Publishing House
5, Ansari Road
Daryaganj, New Delhi-110002
Phone: 011-47034999, 9811692060
E-mail: books@gyanbooks.com

Distribution Network
gyanbooks.com
India, USA, Canada, UK, Australia

ISBN: 978-93-6780-421-6 (PB)

First Published, 1839

2nd Impression 2025

Printed at: Gyan Press, Delhi.

AN IMPROVED GRAMMAR OF THE ENGLISH LANGUAGE
Author: NOAH WEBSTER

AN

IMPROVED GRAMMAR

OF THE

ENGLISH LANGUAGE.

BY NOAH WEBSTER, LL. D.

NEW HAVEN:

PUBLISHED BY SIDNEY BABCOCK.

1839.

PREFACE.

The British Grammars of the English language appear to me to be very imperfect, and, in some particulars, very erroneous. Since the publication of the grammars of Lowth and Priestley, who added most of the improvements, which have been made since the days of Wallis, some important discoveries have been made in the origin of words and in the construction of sentences, which have not been introduced into any grammar published in Great Britain; at least as far as my knowledge extends.

Grammar is a difficult subject, especially to the young student; and the difficulties that belong to the subject, have been increased by the use of terms merely technical in designating the parts of speech. On entering upon the subject, the young student meets with the words *noun*, *pronoun*, *adjective*, *verb*, *adverb*; words he never saw or heard of before, as they are no part of the common language which he has been accustomed to use; and words which he does not understand. To remedy, as far as possible, this evil, I have, in this work, not only explained the technical terms, but have used other terms, with them, which serve as interpreters of the words commonly used. These interpreting words are more easily understood, and some of them are more strictly correct, or better adapted to express their true signification. Thus for *noun*, the English word *name* is often used; a word which every child understands. This accords with the practice of the nations on the continent of Europe. For *pronoun*, the word *substitute* or *representative* is sometimes used; for several of the words called *pronouns* are often used in the place of *sentences*, or they refer to them. *Attribute* is a word better understood than *adjective*; though it were to be wished, we could find a more familiar term for that class of words. For *adverb*, I often use *modifier*; a term much wanted to denote certain words which have the uses of different parts of speech. Thus *most* and *very*, which are adjectives, are often used as adverbs; as in the phrases *most* wise, *very* good. If we call the words, in such phrases, *adverbs*, then we call them by the same name as we do *mostly* and *verily*. In like manner, *up*, *over*, *to*, which are prepositions, are used to modify verbs, in such phrases as to *give up*, to *give over*, to *come to*; and it seems very unnatural to call them, in these and similar forms of speech, *prepositions*.

The terms used to express the tenses of English verbs, are borrowed from the Latin; but some of them are improperly applied. Thus, he *created* is called the *imperfect* tense, denoting *unfinished* action; but this is not correct: the imperfect tense in English is, he *was creating*. The words *pluperfect* and *preter-pluperfect*, which signify *more than finished, beyond more than finished*, are very awkward terms. For which reason I call the tense which they designate, the *prior-past*, which denotes an act past prior to another act, event or time. In like manner, the term *prior-future* is used to denote an act past prior to a future time or event specified.

In this work, I have given a complete exhibition of the English verb, in all its forms or combinations, declarative, interrogative and negative. This will show foreigners, as well as our own youth, the proper place of the auxiliaries, and of the sign of negation *not*, in all the various combinations.

In all or most English Grammars, *an* or *a* is said to be an *indefinite* article. This is not true; it is used before *definite* nouns, as well as before those which are *indefinite*. It is also said, that *a* becomes *an* before a vowel; but the fact is directly the reverse: *an* is the original word, and loses the *n* before a consonant. It is the same word as *one*, but in Saxon orthography.

Grammars also tell us, *that* is sometimes a *conjunction*. This is not true; it is always a pronoun or substitute: when it is called a function, it refers to a sentence.

In most grammars, *notwithstanding* is called a *conjunction*. This is not true; it is a compound of *not* and the participle *withstanding*, and with *that* expressed or understood, or with a sentence, constituting the case absolute, like *non obstante* in Latin.

Provided is also called, in certain cases, a *conjunction*. This is not true; it is a participle forming the case absolute, as above stated, in regard to *notwithstanding*.

If is called also a *conjunction*. This is not true; it is always a verb, being only a contracted form of *give*. The fact is the same with *though*; it is a verb, but defective.

To the syntax, I have added several new rules and illustrations; the British Grammars, in this particular, being very defective. Indeed, so defective and erroneous are the British Grammars, and the compilations in the United States, formed on their principles, that without some further helps, the construction of many established and legitimate phrases and sentences in our language, cannot be explained.

The term *mood* I have discarded. *Mode* is the proper translation of the Latin *modus*; and the orthography *mood* confounds this grammatical term with a word of different origin, denoting *temper* or *state of the mind*.

AN

IMPROVED GRAMMAR, &c.

OF LANGUAGE.

LANGUAGE, in its most extensive sense, is the instrument or means of communicating ideas and affections of the mind and body, from one animal to another. In this sense, brutes possess the powers of language; for by various inarticulate sounds, they make known their wants, desires and sufferings. Thus the neighing of the horse, the lowing of the ox, the cackling and chirping of birds, constitute the language of those animals; and each respective species understand instinctively their own peculiar language. The signs made by deaf and dumb people form also a kind of imperfect language; and even the looks, when made to express ideas and affections, speak an intelligible language.

As brutes have few affections or ideas, and little necessity for communicating them, their language consists in a few *inarticulate* sounds. But man, being a rational animal, capable of acquiring, and of learning to communicate numberless ideas, is furnished with suitable organs for uttering an indefinite variety of sounds to express his ideas; and the modulations of his voice, in the distinct utterance of sounds, by opening and closing the organs, constitute what are denominated *articulate* sounds.

DIVISION OF LANGUAGE.

Language is of two kinds, *spoken* and *written*. The elements of spoken language are articulate sounds, uttered by the voice, which is formed by the air issuing through the glottis, a small aperture in the wind pipe, and modulated by articulations of the throat, tongue, palate, teeth, and lips. This is the original and proper sense of the word *language*.

But as sounds are fleeting, and not capable of being communicated to a great distance, if men had no other means of communicating their thoughts, their intercourse would be limited to a small compass, and their ideas would be entrusted to memory and tradition only; by which they would soon be obscured, perverted, or forgotten. Hence the invention of characters to represent sounds, exhibit them to the eye, and render them durable. This was the origin of *written* language. The elements of this language are letters or characters, which, by consent of men, and common usage, are combined into words, and made to represent the articulate sounds uttered by the voice. These characters being easily inscribed or engraved upon durable substances, as paper, parchment, wood and stone, render language permanent, and capable of being transmitted from age to age, and of being communicated over the habitable globe. Of this art, it is not easy to decide which deserves to be most admired, the difficulty, the ingenuity, or the usefulness of the invention.

OF GRAMMAR.

Grammar, as a science, treats of the natural connection between ideas, and words which are the signs of ideas, and develops the principles which are common to all languages. These principles are not arbitrary, nor subject to change, but fixed and permanent; being founded on facts and distinctions established by nature. Thus the distinction between the sexes; between things and their qualities; between the names of substances and of their actions or motions; between unity and plurality; between the present, past and future time, and some other distinctions, are founded in nature, and give rise to different species of words, and to various inflections in all languages.

The grammar of a particular language is a system of *general principles*, derived from natural distinctions of words and of *particular rules*, deduced from the customary forms of speech, in the nation using that language. These usages are mostly arbitrary, or of accidental origin; but when they become common to a nation, they are to be considered as established, and received as rules of the highest authority.

A *rule*, therefore, is an established form of construction in a particular class of words. Thus the usual addition of *s* or *es*, to a noun, to denote plurality, being a general practice, constitutes a rule.

An *exception* to a rule, is the deviation of certain words from the common construction. Thus *man*, if regularly formed in the plural, would be *mans;* but custom having established the use of *men* as its plural, the word is an *exception* to the general rule.

Grammar is commonly divided into four parts—orthography, etymology, syntax and prosody.

Orthography treats of the letters, their powers and combinations in syllables; or, it teaches the true manner of writing words, called spelling.

Etymology treats of the derivation of words from their radicals or primitives, and of their various inflections and modifications to express person, number, case, sex, time and mode.

Syntax explains the true mode of constructing sentences.

Prosody treats of the quantity or accent of syllables and the laws of versification.

NOTE.—In this compilation, the only subjects treated are, a part of etymology, and syntax and prosody.

OF LETTERS.

The elements, or first principles of language, are articulate sounds, and letters or characters, which represent them.

There are in the English language twenty-six letters, which represent sounds or articulations: A. a.—B. b.—C. c.—D. d.—E. e.—F. f.—G. g.—H. h.—I. i.—J. j.—K. k.—L. l.—M. m.—N. n.—O. o.—P. p.—Q. q.—R. r.—S. s.—T. t.—U. u.—V. v.—W. w.—X. x.—Y. y.—Z. z. Of these, J and X represent a combination of articulations.

Letters are of two kinds—vowels and consonants; or, more strictly, of three kinds—vowels, consonants and aspirates.

A vowel is a vocal or open sound; or a simple sound, uttered by opening the mouth in a particular manner. A simple sound is one which is begun and continued at pleasure, with the same position of the organs, as—*a*, *e*, *o*, and the broad *a* or *aw*; the Italian *a* as in father, and *oo*, which in English represents the Italian *u* and French *ou*.

An articulation is the forming of a joint—a jointing or closing of the organs of speech; by which the voice is wholly or partially intercepted.*

A close articulation entirely and instantly interrupts the utterance of sound, as—*k*, *p*, *t*, in the syllables, *ek*, *ep*, *et*.

* Latin *articulatio*, from *articulus*, a joint.

These letters are therefore called *pure mutes.* A less close articulation admits a small prolongation of sound, as *b, d, g,* as in the syllables, *eb, ed, eg.* These are called *impure mutes.*

Imperfect articulations do not completely interrupt all sound. Some of them admit a kind of hum ; others of a hissing sound ; others of a breathing, which may be continued at pleasure. Of this kind are the following letters : *ef, el, em, en, er, es, ez, esh, eth.* These are therefore called *semi-vowels.*

H is a mark of breathing, and may be called an *aspirate.*

Articulations or consonants precede or follow vowels, as in *at, go, blush.* They therefore determine the manner of beginning and ending vocal sounds. But even when they produce no sound, they so modify the manner of uttering vowels, as to aid in forming distinct words. Thus in *bat, gap, cap,* we hear the same vowel, but the articulations which precede or follow that sound, form with it different words, that may be distinguished as far as the voice can be heard.

An *articulate* sound is properly a sound which is preceded or followed by a closing of the organs ; but we extend the signification to sounds formed by organs capable of articulation, that is, by the human organs of speech.

The great difference between men and brutes, in the utterance of sound by the mouth, consists in the power of articulation in man, and the entire want of it in brutes.

On articulation, therefore, depends the formation of syllables and words. It is the basis of human speech or language, and the faculty of articulation is the distinguishing characteristic and privilege of man.

All men, having similar organs of speech, use nearly the same articulations. Hence the same simple letters, or letters with the same powers, occur, with slight differences, in all languages. The compound letters, or combinations of sound, are subject to greater variety.

Articulations formed by the lips are called *labial* letters, or *labials,* lip-letters, from the Latin *labium,* a lip. Such are *b, l, m, p, v.* Those formed by the tongue and teeth, are called *dental letters,* or *dentals,* from the Latin *dens,* a tooth. Such are *d, t, th, s* and *z.* The two latter are also denominated *sibilant letters,* or *sibilants,* from the Latin *sibilo,* to hiss. Letters formed by the tongue and palate, are called *palatal letters*, or *palatals*, as *g*, *k*, *l*, *r*. The two former, when they represent a deep utterance of sound from the throat, may be called *gutturals*.

When an articulation occasions a sound through the nose, it is called a *nasal* letter. Such are *m*, *n*, and *ng*, in *ing*.

J, in English, represents the sounds of *d* and soft *g*. X represents the sound of *k* and *s*.

A diphthong is the union of two vowels, which are so rapidly uttered in succession, as to be considered as forming one syllable, as *oi*, and *oy*, in *voice*, *joy*.

A triphthong is the union of three vowels in a syllable.

ETYMOLOGY.—CLASSIFICATION OF WORDS.

Words are naturally divided into two CLASSES, PRIMARY and SECONDARY.

The *first class* consists of words which are essential to the language of men; on which other words depend, or to which they are added as auxiliaries. In this class are included the *Noun* or *Name*, and the *verb*. These two species of words are so necessary to a communication of ideas, that no complete sentence or proposition can be formed without the use of both, unless when a substitute is used for a name. Thus, the *sun shines*, is a complete sentence, containing a name and a verb; but remove either of them, and the proposition is destroyed. From the importance of these words, they are here denominated *Primary*, or the PRIMARY PARTS OF SPEECH.

The *second class* consists of words of secondary or subordinate use, or of such as are dependent on other words in construction. Of these there are several species.

1st. Words which supply the place of other words and of sentences, which are here called *pronouns* or *substitutes*.

2d. Words which express the qualities of things, and which therefore are attached to the names of those things. These are here called *adjectives*, *attributes* or *attributives*. These are *primary* words in point of importance; but being necessarily dependent on other words in construction, they are here ranked with the *secondary*.

3d. Words which modify the sense of other words by expressing the manner of action, or degree of quality. These are here called *adverbs* or *modifiers*.

4th. Words which are *placed before* other words, and show the relation between them and those which precede. These are called *prepositions*.

5th. Words which join together the parts of a sentence or of a discourse, in a regular construction. These are called *connectives* or *conjunctions*.

These five species of subordinate or dependent words are denominated *secondary*.

There are therefore *two classes* of words containing *seven species* or *parts of speech*. The first class contains two species.

I. *Nouns* or *Names* which are the signs of our ideas of whatever we conceive to exist, material and immaterial.

II. *Verbs* which express affirmation, motion, action or being.

The *second class* contains five species.

III. *Pronouns* or *Substitutes*, words which are used in the place of other words or of sentences.

IV. *Adjectives* or *Attributes*, which express the qualities of things, and qualify the action of verbs, or the sense of other attributes and modifiers.

V. *Adverbs* or *Modifiers*, which qualify the action of verbs, and the sense of attributes.

VI. *Prepositions*, which show the relation between words, and also the condition of things.

VII. *Connectives* or *Conjunctions*, which unite sentences in construction.

Note.—Participles are, by some grammarians, considered as a distinct part of speech; and they certainly have some claims to be so considered; but I have chose to follow the common arrangement which is attended with no inconvenience.

NOUNS OR NAMES.

A noun or name is that by which a thing is called; and it expresses the idea of that which exists, material or immaterial.—Of material substances, as man, horse, tree, table—of immaterial things, as faith, hope, love. These and similar words are, by customary use, made the *names* of things which exist, or the symbols of ideas, which they express without the help of any other word.

DIVISION OF NAMES OR NOUNS.

Names are of two kinds; *common*, or those which represent the idea of a whole kind or species; and *proper* or *appropriate*, which denote individuals. Thus *animal* is a name common to all beings, having organized bodies and endowed with life, digestion, and spontaneous motion. *Plant* and *vegetable* are names of all beings which have organized bodies and life, *without* the power of spontaneous motion. *Fowl* is the common name of all feathered animals which fly; *fish*, of animals which live wholly in water.

On the other hand, Thomas, John, William, are *proper* or appropriate names, each denoting an individual of which there is no species or kind. London, Paris, Amsterdam, Rhine, Po, Danube, Massachusetts, Hudson, Patowmac, are also proper names, being appropriate to individual things.

Proper names however become common when they comprehend two or more individuals; as, the Capets, the Smiths, the Fletchers—" *Two Roberts* there the pagan force defy'd."
Hoole's Tasso, b. 20.

LIMITATION OF NAMES.

Proper names are sufficiently definite without the aid of another word to limit their meaning, as Boston, Baltimore, Savannah. Yet when certain individuals have a common character, or predominant qualities which create a similitude between them, this common character becomes in the mind *a species,* and the proper name of an individual possessing this character, admits of the definitives and of plural number, like a common name. Thus a conspirator is called *a* Catiline; and numbers of them Catilines or *the* Catilines of their country. A distinguished general is called *a* Cesar; an eminent orator *the* Cicero of his age.

But names, which are common to a whole kind or species, require often to be limited to an individual or a certain number of individuals of the kind or species. For this purpose the English language is furnished with a number of words, as *an*, or *a, the, this, that, these, those,* and a few others, which define the extent of the signification of common names, or point to the particular things mentioned. These are all adjectives or *attributes,* having a dependence on some noun expressed or implied; but some of them are used also as substitutes. Of these *an* or *a* and *the* are never employed as substitutes, but are constantly attached to some name, or an equivalent word; and from their peculiar use, have obtained the distinctive appellation of *articles.* But *definitive* is a more significant and appropriate term; as they are *definitive attributes*, and have, grammatically considered, the like use as *this, that, some, none, any.*

An is simply the Saxon *ane*, or *an*, one. It was formerly written *an* before a consonant;* but for the ease and rapidity of utterance, it is written and pronounced *a* before a consonant, and before a vowel which includes the sound of a consonant; as, a pen, a union: also before *h* aspirate; as, a house. It retains its primitive orthography *an*, before a vowel, and a silent consonant; as, an eagle, an hour.

The is used before vowels and consonants; but in poetry, *e*, for the sake of measure, may be omitted, and *th* made to coalesce with a succeeding vowel; as, "th'embroidered vest."

RULE I.

A noun or name, without a preceding definitive, is used either in an unlimited sense, extending to the whole species, or, in an indefinite sense, denoting a number or quantity, but not the whole.

"The proper study of mankind is *man*." *Pope.*

Here *man* comprehends the whole species.

"In the first place, *woman* has, in general, much stronger propensity than *man* to the perfect discharge of parental duties."—*Life of Cowper.*

Here *woman* and *man* comprehend each the whole species of its sex.

"From whom also I received *letters* to the brethren."—*Acts*, xxii. 5.

"The men were overwhelmed by the waves, and absorbed by the eddies. *Horses, baggage,* and *dead bodies,* were seen floating together."

In these passages, letters, horses, and dead bodies, without a definitive, denote *some*, an *indefinite number*, but no *all.* So in the following sentence:

A house is consumed by *fire*—*fire* is extinguished by *water.*

---

* "And thæs geares wœrun ofslegene IX eorlas and *an* cyning.' And this year were slain nine earls and *one* king.—*Saxon Chron. p.* 82.

NOTE.—The rule laid down by Lowth, and transcribed implicitly by his followers, is general. "A substantive without any article to limit it, is taken in its *widest sense;* thus *man* means *all mankind.*" The examples already given prove the inaccuracy of the rule. But let it be tried by other examples.

"There are *fishes* that have wings, and are not strangers to the airy regions."—LOCKE, b. 3. ch. 6. 12. If the rule is just, that *fishes* is to be "taken in its widest sense," then *all fishes* have wings!

"When ye shall see Jerusalem compassed with *armies*"—What! *all* armies? "There shall be *signs* in the sun"—What! *all* signs? "*Nation* shall rise against *nation*"—What! every nation? How the rule vanishes before the test!

RULE II.

The definitive *an* or *a*, being merely *one*, in its *English* orthography, and precisely synonymous with it, limits a common name to an individual of the species—its sole use is to express *unity*, and with respect to number, is the most definite word imaginable—as *an* ounce, *a* church, *a* ship, that is, *one* ship, *one* church. It is used before a name, which is indefinite, or applicable to any one of a species; as,

"He bore him in the thickest troop,
As doth *a* lion in *a* herd of neat." *Shakspeare.*

Here *a* limits the sense of the word *lion*, and that of *herd* to *one*—but does not specify the particular one—"As *any* lion does or would do in *any* herd."

This definitive is used also before names which are definite and as specific as possible; as, "Solomon built *a* temple." "The Lord God planted *a* garden eastward in Eden." London is *a* great commercial city. *A* decisive battle was fought at Marengo. The English obtained *a* signal naval victory at the mouth of the Nile.*

---

* "*A* respects the primary perception and denotes individuals as *unknown*—*the* respects our secondary perceptions and denotes individuals as *known*. *A* leaves the individuals unascertained, whereas the article *the* ascertains the individual also."—*Harris' Hermes*, 215, 217.

"*A* has an indefinite signification and means *one*, with some reference to more."—*Johnson's Dict. Grammar.*

"*A* is used in a vague sense to point out one single thing of the kind, in other respects *indeterminate*"—"*a* determines it to be one, single thing of the kind, leaving it still *uncertain which*."

Lowth's Introduction.

But let us try this rule. Harris wrote, or rather compiled from Greek grammarians, "*A* Philosophical Inquiry concerning Universal Gram

2

NOTE.—When the sense of words is sufficiently certain, by the construction, the definitive may be omitted; as, "*Duty* to your majesty, and *regard* for the preservation of ourselves and our posterity, require us to entreat your royal attention."

It is also omitted before names whose signification is general, and requires no limitation—as, "*wisdom* is justified of her children"—"*anger* resteth in the bosom of fools."

The definitive *a* is used before plural names, preceded by *few* or *many*—as, *a* few days, *a* great many persons.* It is also used before any collective word, as, *a* dozen, *a* hundred, even when such words are attached to plural nouns; as, *a* hundred years.

It is remarkable that *a* never precedes *many* without the intervention of *great* between them—but follows *many*, standing between this word and a name—and what is equally

---

mar."—Johnson compiled "*A* Dictionary of the English Language."—Lowth wrote "*A* Short Introduction to English Grammar."—David left *a* flourishing kingdom to Solomon. Now I request some of the gentlemen, who teach the rules of these Grammars, to inform the world whether *a*, in the passages recited, denotes *one* thing of the kind, in other respects *indeterminate*.

Chares erected *a* huge Colossus at Rhodes—Romulus built *a* city in Italy and called it *Rome*—Great Britain has *a* navy superior to any on the ocean—Love to God is *an* indispensable duty—Virgil composed *an* epic poem—The Earl of Chatham was *an* eminent statesman—Oxygen is *a* substance which forms acids—the carbonic acid is *a* combination of oxygen and carbon—The air is *an* invisible elastic fluid—Lisbon was destroyed by *an* earthquake in 1755—that is, according to our grammars, *any earthquake, uncertain which*.

The history of this wŏrd is briefly this. *An* and *one* are the same word—*an*, the Saxon or English orthography, and *one* a corruption of the French *un* or *une*. The Greek *en*, the Latin *unus*, that is, *un* with the usual ending of adjectives, and the Saxon *an* or *ane*, are mere dialectical differences of orthography, as are the German *ein* and the Dutch *een*. Before the Conquest, *an* was used in computation or numbering—an, twa, threo—one, two, three, &c.; and the *n* was used before articulations, as well as before vowels—" Ac him sæd hyra *an*"—But to him said one of them.—*Alfred Orosius, lib.* 6. 30. "*An* cyning"—one king. *Sax. Chron. p.* 82. This word was also varied to express case and gender, like the Latin *unus*. " And thæs ymb *anne* monath"—And within this one month.—*Sax. Chron.* 82. " The on tham *anum* scipe wæron" —Who were in that one ship.—*ibm.* 98. *An* therefore is the original English adjective or ordinal number *one;* and was never written *a* until after the Conquest.

* The origin of this use of *a* before *many* is to be sought in the primitive character of *many*, which was a noun in the Gothic and Saxon, synonymous with *multitude*. *A many* was therefore correct. Its use as an attribute is secondary or derivative; but this use carries with it the definitive *a*, in anomalous phrases.

singular, *many*, the very essence of which is to mark plurality, will, with *a* intervening, agree with a name in the singular number; as,

"Full *many a gem* of purest ray serene." *Gray.*

"Where *many a rose* bud rears its blushing head." *Beattie.*

RULE III.

The definitive *the* is employed before names, to limit their signification to one or more specific things of the kind, discriminated from others of the same kind. Hence the person or thing is understood by the reader or hearer; as, *the* twelve Apostles, *the* laws of morality, *the* rules of good breeding.

This definitive is also used with names of things which exist alone, or which we consider as single; as, the Jews, the Sun, the Globe, the Ocean; and also before words when used by way of distinction; as, the Church, the Temple.

RULE IV.

The is used rhetorically before a name in the singular number, to denote the whole species, or an indefinite number; as, "*the fig-tree* putteth forth her green figs."—*Sol. Songs.*

"*The almond-tree* shall flourish, and *the grasshopper* shall be a burden."—"Or ever *the silver cord* shall be loosed—or *the golden bowl* be broken," &c.—*Ecclesiastes.*

"There loaded camels move in solemn state,
And *the huge elephant's* unwieldy weight."
Hoole's Tasso, b. 15.

"For here the splendid treasures of *the mine*,
And richest offspring of *the field* combine."
Lusiad, 2.

"*The Christian*, who, with pious horror, avoided the abominations of the circus or the theatre, found himself encompassed with infernal snares," &c.—*Gib. Rom. Emp.* ch. 15.

"*The heart* likes naturally to be moved and affected."—*Campbell's Rhet.* ch. 2.

NOTE 1.—This definitive is also used before names employed figuratively in a general sense; as,

"His mates their safety to *the waves* consign." *Lusiad*, 2.

Here *waves* cannot be understood of any particular *waves;* but the word is a metaphor for a particular thing, the *ocean.*

In addresses and exclamations, the definitive may be, and usually is, omitted; as, "Sink down, ye mountains, and, ye valleys, rise."

"Be smooth, ye rocks; ye rapid floods, give way." *Pope, Mes.*

"Granville commands; your aid, O Muses, bring." *Wind. Forest.*

Note 2.—The definitive *the* is used before an attribute, which is selected from others belonging to the same object; as, "The very frame of spirit proper for being diverted with *the laughable* in objects, is so different from that which is necessary for philosophizing on them."—*Campbell, Rhet.* 1. 2.

NUMBER.

As men have occasion to speak of a single object, or of two or more individuals of the same kind, it has been found necessary to vary the noun or name, and usually the termination, to distinguish plurality from unity. The different forms of words to express one or more are called in grammar, *numbers;* of which there are, in English, two, the *singular* and the *plural.* The *singular* denotes an individual, or a collection of individuals united in a body; as, a man, a ship, an office, a company, a society, a dozen. The *plural* denotes two or more individuals, not considered as a collective body; as, men, ships, offices, companies, societies. The plural number is formed by the addition of *s* or *es* to the singular.

Rule 1. When the terminating letter of a noun will admit the sound of *s* to coalesce with the name or the last syllable of it, *s* only is added to form the plural; as, sea, seas; hand, hands; pen, pens; grape, grapes; vale, vales; vow, vows.

2. When the letter *s* does not combine in sound with the word or last syllable of it, the addition of *s* increases the number of syllables; as, house, houses; grace, graces; page, pages; rose, roses; voice, voices; maze, mazes.

3. When the name ends in x, ss, sh, or ch with its English sound, the plural is formed by adding *es* to the singular; for a single *s* after those letters cannot be pronounced; as, fox, foxes; glass, glasses; brush, brushes; church, churches. But after *ch* with its Greek sound, like *k*, the plural is formed by *s* only; as monarch, monarchs.

4. When a name ends with *y* after a consonant, the plural is formed by dropping *y* and adding *ies;* as, vanity, vanities. *Alkali* has a regular plural, *alkalies.*

But after *ay*, *ey*, and *oy*, *s* only is added; as delay, delays; valley, valleys; joy; joys; money, moneys.

NOTE 1.—We sometimes see valley, chimney, money, journey, and a few others, with like terminations, written in the plural with *ies*—vallies, chimnies, &c. But this irregularity is not to be vindicated. Either the singular number should be written *vally*, or the plural *valleys*. The latter is preferable.*

NOTE 2.—A few English nouns deviate from the foregoing rules in the formation of the plural number:—

CLASS 1. In some names, *f* in the singular is, for the convenience of utterance, changed into *v*; as,

life	lives	self	selves	sheaf	sheaves
knife	knives	half	halves	shelf	shelves
wife	wives	beef	beeves	wolf	wolves
leaf	leaves	elf	elves	wharf	wharves
calf	calves	loaf	loaves	thief	thieves

CLASS 2. The second class consists of words which are used in both numbers, with plurals irregularly formed; as,

child	children	hypothesis	hypotheses
foot	feet	brother	brothers or brethren
tooth	teeth	penny	pennies or pence
man	men	die	dies or dice
woman	women	pea	peas or pease
ox	oxen	criterion	criterions or criteria
louse	lice	focus	focuses or foci
goose	geese	radius	radiuses or radii
beau	beaux	index	indexes or indices
thesis	theses	calx	calxes or calces
emphasis	emphases	phenomenon	phenomena
antithesis	antitheses		

Pennies is used for real coins; *pence* for their value in computation.—*Dies* denotes stamps for coining; *dice*, pieces used in games.—*Peas* denotes the seeds as distinct objects; *pease* the seeds in a mass.—*Brothers* is the plural used in

* The change of *y* into *ies* to form the plural number, may seem to a foreigner an odd irregularity; but the cause is very obvious. Formerly the singular number of this class of words ended with *ie*; as, glorie, vanitie, energie, and the addition of *s* made the plural *glories*. But whether from caprice, negligence, or a desire to simplify the orthography, the termination *ie* was laid aside for *y* in the singular, while the old plural *ies* was retained. A strange inconsistency, but by no means the only one which the progress of our language exhibits.

common discourse; *brethren*, in the scripture style, but is not restricted to it.

Cherubim and *seraphim* are real Hebrew plurals; but such is the propensity in men to form regular inflections in language, that these words are used as in the singular, with regular plurals, cherubims, seraphims. In like manner, the Hebrew singulars, *cherub* and *seraph*, have obtained regular plurals.

The influence of this principle is very obvious in other foreign words, which the sciences have enlisted into our service; as may be observed in the words radius, focus, index, &c. which now begin to be used with regular English plural terminations. This tendency to regularity is, by all means, to be encouraged; for a *prime excellence in language is the uniformity of its inflections*. The facts here stated will be evinced by a few authorities.

"Vesiculated corallines are found adhering to rocks, shells and *fucuses*."—*Encyc. art. Corallines.*

"Many *fetuses* are deficient at the extremities."—*Dar. Zoon. Sect.* 1, 3, 9.

"Five hundred *denariuses*."—*Baker's Livy*, 4. 491.

"The radiations of that tree and its fruit, the principal *focuses* of which are in the Moldavia islands."—*Hunter's St. Pierre*, vol. 3.

"The reduction of metallic *calxes* into metals."—*Ency. art. Metallurgy.*

See also *Mediums*, Campbell's Rhetoric, 1, 150; *Calyxes*, Darwin's Zoon. 1 74; *Caudexes*, Phytologia, 2, 3; *Irises*, Zoon. 1. 444; *Reguluses* and *residuums*.—*Encyc. art. Metal.*

In authorities equally respectable, we find *stamens*, *stratums*, *funguses;* and in pursuance of the principle, we may expect to see *lamens* for laminæ; *lamels* for lamellæ; *baryte* for barytes; *pyrite* for pyrites; *strontite* for strontites; *stálactites* for the plural *stalactites*. These reforms are necessary to enable us to distinguish the singular from the plural number.

Class 3. The third class of irregulars consists of such as have no plural termination; some of which represent ideas of things which do not admit of plurality; as, rye, barley, flax, hemp, flour, sloth, pride, pitch, and the names of metals, gold, silver, tin, zink, antimony, lead, bismuth, quicksilver. When, in the progress of improvement, any thing, considered as not susceptible of plurality, is found to have varieties, which are distinguishable, this distinction gives rise to a plural of the term. Thus. in early ages our ancestors took no notice of different varieties of *wheat*, and the term had no plural. But modern improvements in agriculture have recognized varieties of this grain, which have given the name a plural form. The same remark is applicable to fern, clay, marl, sugar, cotton, &c. which have plurals, formerly unknown. Other words may hereafter undergo a similar change.

Other words of this class denote plurality, without a plural termination; as, cattle, sheep, swine, kine, deer, hose; trout, salmon, carp, perch, and many other names of fish. *Fish* has a plural, but is used in the plural sense without the termination; as,

"We are to blame for eating *these fish*."

Anacharsis, 6. 272.

"The *fish* reposed in seas and crystal floods,
The beasts retired in covert of the woods."

Hoole, T. 2. 726.

Cannon, shot and *sail*, are used in a plural sense; as,

"One hundred *cannon were* landed from the fleet."

Burchett, Naval Hist. 732.

"*Several shot* being fired."—*Ibm.* 455.

"*Several sail* of ships."—*Ibm.* 426.

In the sense in which these words are here used, they hardly admit of a plural ending.

Under this class may be noticed a number of words, expressing time, distance, measure, weight and number, which, though admitting a plural termination, are often, not to say generally, used without that termination, even when used with attributes of plurality; such are the names in these expressions, two year, five mile, ten foot, seven pound, three tun, hundred, thousand, or million, five bushel, twenty weight, &c. Yet the most unlettered people never say, two minute, three hour, five day, or week, or month; nor two inch, yard or league; nor three ounce, grain, dram, or peck.

We observe this practice in the Saxon Chronicle. "He heold that Arcebisceop-rice 18 year."—p. 59. He held that archbishopric *eighteen year.* In that work, *winter* is used in the same manner; *forty-one winter*—p. 41. Yet *year* and *winter* had, in the Saxon, plural terminations. But this use is considered as vulgar.

A like singularity is observable in the Latin language. "Tritici quadraginta millia modium."—*Liv. lib.* 26. 47. Forty thousand modium of wheat. "Quatuor millia pondo auri," four thousand pound of gold.—*Ibm.* 27. 10.

Here we see the origin of our *pound.* Originally it was merely *weight*—four thousand of gold *by weight.* From denoting weight generally, *pondo* became the term for a certain division or quantity; retaining however its signification of unity, and becoming an indeclinable in Latin. *Twenty pound* then, in strictness, is twenty divisions *by weight*; or, as we say, with a like abbreviation, *twenty weight.*

The words *horse, foot* and *infantry,* comprehending bodies of soldiers, are used as plural nouns, and followed by verbs in the plural. *Cavalry* is sometimes used in like manner.

Class 4. The fourth class of irregular nouns consists of words which have the plural termination only. Some of these, denoting plurality, are always joined with verbs in the plural; as the following:

Annals	drawers	lees	customs
archives	downs	lungs	shears
ashes	dregs	matins	scissors
assets	embers	mallows	shambles
bitters	entrails	orgies	tidings
bowels	fetters	nippers	tongs
compasses	filings	pincers or	thanks
clothes	goods	pinchers	vespers
calends	hatches	pleiads	vitals
breeches	ides	snuffers	victuals

Letters, in the sense of literature, may be added to the foregoing list. *Manners,* in the sense of *behavior,* is also plural.

Other words of this class, though ending in *s*, are used either wholly in the singular number, or in the one or the other, at the pleasure of the writer.

Amends	wages	conics	economics
alms	billiards	catoptrics	mathematics
bellows	fives	dioptrics	mechanics
gallows	sessions	acoustics	hydraulics
odds	measles	pneumatics	hydrostatics
means	hysterics	statics	analytics
pains	physics	statistics	politics
news	ethics	spherics	
riches	optics	tactics	

Of these, *pains*, *riches*, and *wages** are more usually considered as plural—*news* is always singular—*odds* and *means* are either singular or plural—the others are more strictly singular; for *measles* is the name of a disease, and, in strictness, no more plural than gout or fever. Small *pox*, for *pocks*, is sometimes considered as a plural, but it ought to be used as singular. *Billiards* has the sense of *game*, containing unity of idea; and *ethics*, *physics* and other similar names, comprehending each the whole system of a particular science, do not convey the ideas of parts or particular branches, but of a whole collectively, a unity, and hence seem to be treated as words belonging to the singular number.

Authorities.

Pre-eminent by so *much odds*.—*Milt. P. L.* 4. 474.

With *every odds* thy prowess I defy.—*Hoole, Tas.* 6. 19. 40.

Where the *odds is* considerable.—*Camp. Rhet.* ch. 5.

The *wages* of sin *is* death.—*Bible.*

Much pains has been taken.—*Enfield, Hist. Phil.* ch. 2.

Let *a gallows* be made of fifty cubits high.—*Bible.*

Here he erected a fort and *a gallows*.—*Lusiad*, 1. 134.

The *riches* we had in England *was* the slow result of long industry and wisdom, and *is* to be regained, &c.—*Davenant*, 2. 12.

Mathematics informs us.—*Encyc. art. Strength of Materials.*

Politics is the art of producing individual good by general measures.—*Beddoes' Hygeia*, 2. 79.

Politics contains two parts.—*Locke*, vol. 2. 408.

Locke however uses a plural verb with ethics. "The ideas that *ethics are* conversant about."—*B.* 4. 12. 8.

---

* Originally *wagis*, and really singular.

Pains, when preceded by *much*, should always have a singular verb.

Means is so generally used in either number, (every means, all means, this means, and these means,) that authorities in support of the usage are deemed superfluous.

GENDER.

Gender, in grammar, is a difference of termination, to express distinction of sex.

There being two sexes, *male* and *female*, words which denote males are said to be of the *masculine* gender; those which denote females, of *feminine* gender. Words expressing things without sex, are said to be of neuter gender. There are therefore but *two* genders; yet for convenience, the neuter is classed with the genders; and we say there are *three*, the masculine, feminine and neuter. The English modes of distinguishing sex are these:

1. The regular termination of the feminine gender is *ess;* which is added to the name of the masculine; as, lion, lioness. But when the word ends in *or*, the feminine is formed by retrenching a vowel, and blending two syllables into one; as, actor, actress. In a few words, the feminine gender is represented by *ix;* as, testatrix, from testator; and a few others are irregular. The following are most of the words which have a distinct termination for the feminine gender:

Actor	actress	deacon	deaconess
abbot	abbess	duke	duchess
adulterer	adultress	embassador	embassadress
baron	baroness	emperor	empress
benefactor	benefactress	tiger	tigress
governor	governess	songster	songstress
hero	heroine	seamster	seamstress
heir	heiress	viscount	viscountess
peer	peeress	jew	jewess
priest	priestess	lion	lioness
poet	poetess	master	mistress
prince	princess	marquis	marchioness
prophet	prophetess	patron	patroness
shepherd	shepherdess	protector	protectress
sorcerer	sorceress	executor	executrix
tutor	tutoress	testator	testatrix
instructor	instructress	elector	electress
traitor	traitress	administrator	administratrix
count	countess		

2. In many instances, animals, with which we have most frequent occasions to be conversant, have different words to

express the different sexes; as, man and woman; brother and sister; uncle and aunt; son and daughter; boy and girl; father and mother; horse and mare; bull and cow.

Man however is a general term for the whole race of mankind; so also, *horse* comprehends the whole species. A law to restrain *every man* from an offence would comprehend *women* and *boys;* and a law to punish a trespass committed by *any horse*, would comprehend all mares and colts. In like manner, *goose*, though originally the name of the female, is used generally for the whole species; as is the plural *geese*.

3. When words have no distinct termination for the female sex, the sexes are distinguished by prefixing some word indicating sex; as, a male rabbit, a female opossum; a he goat, a she goat; a man servant, a maid servant; a male coquet; a female warrior; a cock-sparrow, a hen-sparrow.

4. In all cases, when the sex is sufficiently indicated by a separate word, names may be used to denote females without a distinct termination. Thus, although females are rarely soldiers, sailors, philosophers, mathematicians, or chimists, and we seldom have occasion to say, she is a soldier, or an astronomer; yet there is not the least impropriety in the application of these names to females, when they possess the requisite qualifications; for the sex is clearly marked by the word *she* or *female*, or the appropriate name of the woman; as, "Joan of Arc was a warrior." "The Amazons were a nation of female warriors."—*Ency. art. Amazons.**

5. Although the English language is philosophically correct in considering things without life as of neither gender, yet by an easy analogy, the imagination conceives of inanimate things as animated and distinguished by sex. On this fiction, called *personification*, depends much of the descriptive force and beauty of poetry.

"Indus or Ganges rolling *his* broad wave." *Akenside.*

"There does the soul
Consent *her* soaring fancy to restrain." *Ibm.*

---

* The termination *or* in Latin is a contraction of *ver*, a man; as *er* in English is of *wer*, the same word in Saxon. But in common understanding, the idea of gender is hardly attached to these terminations; for we add *er* to words to denote an agent without life; as, grater, heater.

"Now morn, *her* rosy steps in th' eastern clime
Advancing—" *Milton, P. L.* b. 5.

"The north-east spends *his* rage." *Thomson.*

CASE.

Case in grammar denotes a variation of words to express the relation of things to each other. In English, most of the relations are expressed by separate words; but the relation of property, ownership or possession, is expressed by adding *s* to a name, with an apostrophy; thus, John's book; which words are equivalent to "the book of John." This is called the ***Possessive Case.*** In English therefore names have two cases only, the *nominative* or simple name, and the *possessive.* The *nominative* before a verb, and the *objective* after a verb, are not distinguished by inflections, and are to be known only by position or the sense of the passage.

When the letter *s*, added as the sign of the possessive, will coalesce with the name, it is pronounced in the same syllable; as, *John's.* But if it will not coalesce, it adds a syllable to the word; as, Thomas's bravery, pronounced as if written *Thomasis*—the church's prosperity, *churchis* prosperity. These examples show the impropriety of retrenching the vowel; but it occasions no inconvenience to natives.

When words end in *es* or *ss*, the apostrophy is added without *e;* as, on eagles' wings; for righteousness' sake.

PRONOUNS OR SUBSTITUTES.

Substitutes or pronouns are of two kinds; those which are used in the place of the names of persons only, and may be called *personal;* and those which represent names, attributes, a sentence or part of a sentence, or a series of propositions.

The pronouns which are appropriate to persons, are, I, thou, you, he, she, we, ye, and who.

I is used by a speaker to denote himself, and is called the *first person* of the singular number.

When a speaker includes others with himself, he uses *we.* This is the *first person* of the plural number.

Thou and *you* represent the person addressed—*thou* in solemn discourse, and *you*, in common language.* These are the *second person*. In the plural, *ye* is used in solemn style, and *you* in familiar language.

He represents the name of a male, and *she*, that of a female, who is the subject of discourse, but not directly addressed. These are called the *third person*.

---

*As *you* was originally in the plural number, grammarians insist that it must still be restricted to that number. But national usage rejects the arbitrary principle. The true principle, on which all language is built, rejects it. What fundamental rule have we to dispose of words, but this, that when a word signifies *one*, or *unity*, it belongs to the singular number? If a word, once exclusively plural, becomes, by universal use, the sign of individuality, it must take its place in the singular number. That this is a fact with *you*, is proved by national usage. To assign the substitute to its verb, is to invert the order of things. The verb must follow its nominative—if that denotes unity, so does the verb.

"When *you was* at Athens, you attended the schools of the philosophers."—*Cicero, Tusc. Quest. Trans.* b. 2.

"On that happy day when you *was* given to the world."—*Dodd's Massillon, Serm.* 1.

"Unless you *was* ill."—*Boswell's Life of J. Æ.* 68.

"You *was* on the spot where your enemy was found killed."—*Guthrie's Quinctilian*, b. 2.

"*You was* in hopes to have succeeded to the inheritance."—*Ibm.* b. 5.

"When *you was* here comforting me"—*Pope's Let.*

"I am as well as when *you was* here."—*Gay's Let. to Swift.*

"Why *was you* glad?"—*Boswell's Life of Johnson.*

These writers did not commit mistakes in the use of the verb after *you*—they wrote the language as established by national usage—the foundation of all language. So is the practice in the United States—not merely popular usage, though this, when general, is respectable authority; but the practice of men of letters.

"Where *was you* standing during the transaction?"

"How far *was you* from the defendant?"

"How far *was you* from the parties?"—*Judge Parker. Trial of Selfridge*, p. 58.

"*Was you* acquainted with the defendant at college?"—*Mr. Dexter. Ibm.* p. 60.

"*Was you* there when the pistol was fired?"—*Mr. Gore. Ibm.* 60.

"*Was you* in the office?"—*Att. Gen. Ibm.* 68.*

* This use of *was* is from the Gothic dialect; but it is primitive and correct.

It is a substitute for the name of any thing of the neuter gender in the third person, and for a sentence.

They is a substitute for the names of persons or things, and forms the third person of the plural number.

Who is a relative or a personal pronoun, used to introduce a new clause or affirmation into a sentence, which clause has an immediate dependence on the preceding one.* *Who* is also used to ask questions, and hence it is called an interrogative.

Which is also a relative, but is of neuter gender. It is also interrogative.

These pronouns have two cases; the nominative which precedes a verb, and the objective which follows it. They are inflected in the following manner:

	Sing.	*Plu.*		*Sing.*	*Plu.*
Nominative	I†	we	Nom. - -	she	they
Objective	me	us	Obj. - -	her	them
Nom. - - -	thou	ye	Nom. - -	it	they
Obj. - - -	thee	you	Obj. - -	it	them
Nom. - - -	you	you	Nom. - -	who	who
Obj. - - -	you	you	Obj. - -	whom	whom
Nom. - - -	he	they			
Obj. - - -	him	them			

NOTE.—*Mine, thine, his, hers, yours* and *theirs*, are usually considered as the *possessive case*. But the three first are either attributes, and used with nouns, or they are substitutes. The three last are always substitutes, used in the place of names which are understood, as may be seen in the note below.‡

---

* *Who* is called a *relative*, because it *relates* to an antecedent. But this is also true of *he, she, they*, and most of the substitutes. They all *relate* to the words which they represent.

† *Me* is also used in the nominative, in popular practice—*it is me*. This is condemned as bad English; but in reality is an original idiom of the language, received from the primitive Celtic inhabitants of England and France, in whose language *mi* was the nominative case of the first personal pronoun. The French language retains the same word, from the same original, in the phrase *c'est moi*—it is I.

‡ That *mine, thine, his, yours, hers* and *theirs*, do not constitute a possessive case, is demonstrable; for they are constantly used as the nominatives to verbs, and as the objectives after verbs and prepositions, as in

Its and *whose* have a better claim to be considered as a possessive case; but as they equally well fall under the denomination of attributes, I have, for the sake of uniformity, assigned them a place with that part of speech.

But it must be observed, that although *it* and *who* are real substitutes, never united to names, like attributes—it day—who man; yet *its* and *whose* cannot be detached from a name expressed or implied; as, *its* shape—*its* figure—*whose* face—*whose* works—*whose* are they? that is, *whose* works? These are therefore real attributes.

In the use of substitutes, it is to be remarked, that *I, thou, you, ye* and *we* are generally employed without an antecedent name. When *I* and the name of the person are both employed, as they are in formal writings, oaths and the like,

---

the following passages: "Whether it could perform its operations of thinking and memory out of a body organized as *ours is*.—*Locke*, b. 2. 27. "In referring our ideas to those of other men called by the same name, *ours may be false*."—"It is for no other reason but that *his* agrees not with *our ideas*."—*Ibm.* ch. 32. 9 *and* 10.

"You may imagine what kind of faith *theirs was*."—*Bacon. Unity in Religion.*

"He ran headlong into his own ruin whilst he endeavored to precipitate *ours*."—*Bolingbroke. Let. to Windham.*

"The reason is, that his subject is generally things; *theirs*, on the contrary, *is* persons." *Camp. Rhet. b.* I. *ch.* 10.

"Yours of the 26th Oct. I have received, as I have always done *yours*, with no little satisfaction."—*Wycherley to Pope.*

"Therefore leave your forest of beasts for *ours* of brutes, called men." —*Ibm.*

"These return so much better out of your hands than they went from *mine*."—*Ibm.*

"Your letter of the 20th of this month, like the rest of *yours*—tells me with so much more wit, sense and kindness than *mine* can express," &c.—*Ibm.*

"Having good works enough of your own besides to ensure *yours* and their immortality."—*Ibm.*

"The omission of repetitions is but one, and the easiest part of *yours* and of *my design*."—*Pope to Wycherley.*

"My *sword* and *yours* are kin."—*Shakspeare.*

It is needless to multiply proofs. We observe these pretended *possessives* uniformly used as nominatives or objectives. To say that, in these passages, *ours, yours, theirs*, and *mine* form a possessive case, is to make the possessive perform the office of a nominative case to verbs, and an objective case after verbs and prepositions—a manifest solecism.

Should it be said that a noun is understood; I reply, this cannot be true, in regard to the grammatical construction: for supply the noun for which the word is a substitute, and the pronoun must be changed into

the pronouns precede the name; as, "I, Richard Roe, of Boston." In similar language, *you* and *we* also precede the name; as, "You, John Doe, of New York." "We, Richard Roe, and John Doe, of Philadelphia."

You is used by writers very indefinitely, as a substitute for any person who may read the work—the mind of the writer *imagining* a person addressed.

He and *they* are used in the same indefinite manner; as, "*He* seldom lives frugally, *who* lives by chance." "Blessed are *they* that mourn, for *they* shall be comforted."

He and *they*, in such sentences, represent any persons who fall within the subsequent description.

Who and *whom* are always substitutes for *persons*, and never for things or brutes. *Whose* is equally applicable to persons as to things.†

---

an adjective. "*Yours* of the 26th of October," becomes *your letter*—"he endeavored to precipitate *ours*," becomes *our ruin*. This shows that the words are *real* substitutes, like *others*, where it stands for *other men* or *things*.

Besides, in three passages, just quoted, the word *yours* is joined by a connective to a name in the same case: "To ensure *yours* and *their immortality*." "The easiest part of *yours* and of *my design*." "My sword and *yours* are kin." Will any person pretend that the connective here joins different cases?

Another consideration is equally decisive of this question. If *yours*, *ours*, &c. are real possessives, then the same word admits of two different signs of the case; for we say correctly, "an acquaintance of *yours*, *ours*, or *theirs*"—*of* being the sign of the possessive; but if the words in themselves are possessives, then there must be two signs of the same case, which is absurd.*

Compare these words with a name in the possessive case—"*My* house is on a hill; my father's is on a plain." Here *father's* is a real possessive case; the word *house* being understood; and the addition of the noun makes no alteration in the word *father's*; "my father's is," or "my father's house is."

* This case does not compare with that of names. We say, "a soldier of the king's"—or a soldier of the king's soldiers—but we cannot say, "an acquaintance of your's acquaintance."

† "*Whose* is rather the poetical, than the regular genitive of *which*." —*Johnson*. Lowth also condemns the use of *whose*, in the neuter gender, citing, at the same time, the most respectable authorities for this use—*Dryden*, *Milton* and *Addison*. "The question *whose* solution I require"—"the tree *whose* mortal taste."—But these critics seem not to have penetrated to the bottom of this usage. The truth is, *who* and its inflections are a part of the primitive language. The Latin *qui*, *cui*, *quo*, *qua*, are the English *who*—*quem* and *quod* are *whom* and *what*—*cujus* is *whose*. The Scots formerly wrote *quha*, *quhat*; the Saxons, *hwa*.—

Whoever is often employed as the nominative to two verbs; as, "*Whoever expects* to find in the scriptures a specific direction for every moral doubt that arises, *looks* for more than he will meet with."—*Paley, Phil. ch.* 4.

Mine, thine and *his* are equally well used as substitutes, or as attributes. "The silver is *mine*, and the gold is *mine*." —*Hag*. 2. 8. "The day is *thine*, the night also is *thine*."—*Ps*. 74. 16. "The Lord knoweth them that are *his*."—2 *Tim*. 2. 19. In these examples, the words *mine, thine, his*, may be considered as substitutes.—"The silver is mine," that is, *my silver*.

In this character, the words usually follow the verb; but when emphatical, they may precede it; as, "*His* will I be." —2 *Sam*. 16. 18. "*Thine*, O Lord, is the greatness, the power and the glory."—1 *Ch*. 29. 11. "*Thine is the kingdom*."*

These words are also used as attributes of possession; as, "Let not *mine* enemies triumph." "So let *thine* enemies perish." "And Abram removed *his* tent." *Mine* and *thine* are however not thus used in familiar language; but in solemn and elevated style, they are still used as attributes.

"*Mine* eyes beheld the messenger divine."—*Lusiad, b*. 2.

The Germans still use *wer, wessen, wem;* the Dutch, *wie, wiens, wien*. In a fragment of the Laws of Numa, *cujus* is spelt *quoius*—We have this word in *whose*. From the time of Numa, at least, this genitive has been of *all genders*, and I believe, remains so, in all branches of the Teutonic. It is better classed with adjectives or attributes, like *his*.

* In addition to the proofs already alleged, that these words are not a possessive case, according to the usual acceptation of the word, we may remark, that *mine, thine* and *his*, in the passages used in the text, do not stand in the place of, *of me, of thee, of him*. The silver is *of me*, the gold is *of me*, the day is *of thee*, the Lord knoweth them that are *of him*, do not convey the same ideas, as the present form of expression. *Of*, in these expressions, would rather imply *proceeding from*.

Besides, the same words admit the sign of the possessive; as, "And the man *of thine*, whom I shall not cut off from mine altar."—1 *Sam*. 2. 33. "Sing to the Lord, all ye saints *of his*."—*Ps*. 30. 4. "He that heareth these sayings *of mine*."—*Matt*. 7. When we say, "a soldier of the king's," we mean *one* of the king's soldiers; and in the passage here cited from Samuel, "the man of thine" has a like sense—"the man of thy men," that is, any one of them. But in the passages from Psalms and Matthew, the words "all ye saints of his," "these sayings of mine," are evidently meant to include the whole number. It is therefore impossible to resolve these passages, without considering *mine, thine* and *his* as substitutes, in the same case, as the nouns would be, which they represent.

There is another class of substitutes, which supply the place of names, attributes, sentences or parts of a sentence.

It.

In the following sentence, *it* is the substitute for a name. "The sun rules the day; *it* illumines the earth;" here *it* is used for *sun*, to prevent a repetition of the word.

In the following passage, *it* has a different use: "The Jews, *it* is well known, were at this time under the dominion of the Romans."—*Porteus, Lect.* 8. Here *it* represents the whole of the sentence, except the clause in which it stands. To understand this, let the order of the words be varied. "The Jews were at this time under the dominion of the Romans, *it* [all that] is well known."

"*It* is a testimony as glorious to his memory, as *it* is singular, and almost unexampled in his circumstances, *that he loved the Jewish nation*, and *that* he gave a very decisive proof of *it*, by building them a synagogue."—*Ibm.*

To discover what is represented by the first *it*, we must inquire, What is a glorious testimony? Why, clearly, that he loved the Jewish nation, and gave them a decisive proof of *it*, by building them a synagogue. *It* then is a substitute for those clauses of the sentence. The second *it* refers to the same clauses. In the latter part of the sentence, he gave a magnificent proof of *it*—of what? of what is related in a preceding clause—*he loved the Jewish nation*—of *that* he gave a decisive and magnificent proof. Here *it* represents that member of the sentence.

"As for *the pulling of them down*, if the affairs require *it*."—*Bacon on Ambition.* Require what? "The pulling of them down"—for which part of the sentence *it* is a substitute.

"Shall worldly glory, impotent and vain,
That fluctuates like the billows of the main;
Shall this with more respect thy bosom move
Than zeal for crowns that never fade above?
Avert *it*, heaven!"—*Hoole's Tasso,* 6. 5.

Avert what? All that is expressed in the four preceding lines, for all which *it* is a substitute.

"And how could he do this so effectually, as by performing works, which *it* utterly exceeded all the strength and ability of men to accomplish."—*Porteus, Lect.* 5.

What utterly exceeded? To what does *it* refer? Let us invert the order of the words—"as by performing works, *to accomplish* which exceeded all the strength of men." Here we find *to accomplish*, a verb in the infinitive, is the nominative to *exceeded*, and for that verb, *it* is a substitute.

This inceptive use of *it* forms a remarkable idiom of our language, and deserves more particular illustration. It stands as the substitute for a subsequent member or clause of a sentence, and is a sort of pioneer to smooth the way for the verb. Thus, "*It* is remarkable, *that* the philosopher Seneca makes use of the same argument."—*Porteus, Lect.* 6. If we ask, What is remarkable? the answer must be, The fact stated in the last clause of the sentence. That this is the real construction, appears from a transposition of the clauses, "The philosopher Seneca makes use of the same argument, *that* is remarkable." In this order we observe the true use of *that*, which is also a substitute for the preceding clause of the sentence, and *it* becomes redundant. The use then of the inceptive *it*, appears to be to enable us to begin a sentence, without placing a verb as the introductory word; and by the use of *it* and *that* as substitutes for subsequent members of the sentence, the order is inverted without occasioning obscurity.

It is to be noticed also that this neuter substitute *it*, is equally proper to begin sentences, when the name of a *person* is afterwards used; as, "*It* was John who exhibited such powers of eloquence." But if we transpose the words, and place *who* or *that*, the substitute which begins a new clause, next after the inceptive word, we must use *he* for the inceptive—"*He, who* or *that* exhibited such powers of eloquence, was John."

In interrogative sentences, the order of words is changed, and *it* follows the verb. Who is *it* that has been thus eloquent?

There is a sentence in Locke, in which the inceptive *it*, is omitted, "Whereby comes to pass, that, as long as any uneasiness remains in the mind."—*B. ch.* 21. In strictness, this is not a defective sentence, for *that* may be considered as the nominative to *comes*—Whereby *that* comes to pass which follows. Or the whole subsequent sentence may be considered as the nominative—for all that comes to pass. But the use of the inceptive *it* is so fully established as the true idiom of language, that its omission is not to be vindicated.

This and *that*, *these* and *those*.

This and *that* are either definite attributes or substitutes. As attributes, they are used to specify individuals, and distinguish them from others; as, "*This* my son was dead and is alive again." "Certainly *this* was a righteous man." "The end of *that* man is peace." "Woe to *that* man by whom the Son of man is betrayed." *This* and *that* have plurals, *these* and *those*.

The general distinction between *this* and *that*, is, *this* denotes an object to be present or near in time or place; *that*, to be absent. But this distinction is not always observed. In correspondence however with this distinction, when, in discourse, two things are mentioned, *this* and *these* refer to the last named, or nearest in the order of construction; *that* and *those* to the most distant; as,

"*Self-love* and *reason* to one end aspire,
Pain their aversion, pleasure their desire;
But greedy *that* [self love] its object would devour,
This [reason] taste the honey and not wound the flower."
Pope.

"Some place the bliss in action, some in ease,
Those call it pleasure, and contentment *these*."—*Ibm.*

The poets sometimes contrast these substitutes in a similar manner, to denote individuals acting or existing in detached parties; or to denote the whole acting in various capacities; as,

"'Twas war no more, but carnage through the field,
Those lift their sword, and *these* their bosoms yield."
Hoole's Tasso, b. 20.

"Nor less the rest, the intrepid chief retain'd;
These urged by threats, and *those* by force constrain'd."
Ibm.

There is a peculiarity in the use of *that;* for when it is an attribute, it is always in the singular number; but as a substitute for persons or things, it is plural as well as singular; and is used for persons as well as things more frequently than any word in the language; as,

"I knew a man *that* had *it* for a by-word, when he saw men hasten to a conclusion, 'Stay a little, that we may make an end the sooner.'"—*Bacon on Dispatch.*

Here *that* is the representative of *man*, and *it* stands for the last clause of the sentence or by-word.

"Let states *that* aim at greatness take heed how their nobility and gentlemen multiply too fast."—*Bacon.*

Here *that* is a substitute for a plural name. So also in the following. "They *that* are whole need not a physician, but they *that* are sick." "They *that* had eaten were about four thousand"—"they *that* are in the flesh"—"they *that* weep" —"bless them *that* curse you."

Another very common use of *this* and *that*, is to represent a sentence or part of a sentence; as,

"It is seldom known *that*, authority thus acquired is possessed without insolence, or *that*, the master is not forced to confess *that*, he has enslaved himself by some foolish confidence."—*Rambler, No.* 68.

In this sentence, the first *that* represents the next member—"Authority thus acquired is possessed without insolence, *that* is seldom known;" *it* represents the same clause. The second *that* represents all which follows, including two clauses or members; the third *that* is the substitute for the last clause. In strictness, the comma ought always to be placed after *that;* which punctuation would elucidate the use of the substitute and the true construction; but the practice is otherwise; for *that*, in this and like sentences, is either a nominative or an objective. The first *that* in the foregoing sentence is the nominative, coinciding with it, or in apposition to it; and when the clauses are transposed, the inceptive *it*, being redundant, is dropped, and *that* becomes the nominative. The same remark is applicable to the second *that;* the verb and first clause, *it is seldom known*, being understood. The third *that* is the objective after *confess.* "The master has enslaved himself by some foolish confidence—he is forced to confess *that*—all that is seldom known."

Such is the true construction of sentences—the definitive *that*, instead of being a conjunction, is the representative of a sentence or distinct clause, preceding that clause, and pointing the mind to it, as the subject which follows. And it is as definite or demonstrative in this application to sentences, as when it is applied to a name or noun.

The following sentence will exhibit the true use of *that* as a substitute: "He recited his former calamities; to which *was* now to be added *that* he was the destroyer of the man who had expiated him."—*Beloe's Herodotus, Clio*, 45.

According to our present grammars, *that* is a conjunction; if so, the preceding verb *was*, has no nominative word. But the sense is, "to which was to be added *that*" which is related in the following words.

The use and importance of this substitute are more clearly manifest, when it denotes purpose or effect; as in this passage, "And he came and dwelt in a city called Nazareth; *that* it might be fulfilled *which* was spoken by the prophets, He shall be called a Nazarene."—*Matt.* 2. 23. Here *that* is equivalent to *that purpose or effect*. He came and dwelt in Nazareth, *for the purpose expressed in what follows*. *It* and *which* represent the last clause in the sentence—"He shall be called a Nazarene." The excellence and utility of substitutes and abbreviations are strikingly illustrated by this use of *that*.

This substitute has a similar use in this introductory sentence, *That we may proceed*—*that* here refers to the following words. The true construction is, *But that we may proceed*—*but*, as will hereafter be shown, denoting *supply* or *something more* or *further*; so that the literal interpretation of the expression is—*More that*, or *further that*, *we may proceed*. It is the simple mode our ancestors used to express addition to what has preceded, equivalent to the modern phrase; *let us add*, or *we may add* what follows, by way of illustrating or modifying the sense of what has been related.

That, like *who* and *which*, has a connecting power, which has given to these words the name of *relative*; in which character, it involves one member of a sentence within another, by introducing a new verb; as, "He, that keepeth his mouth, keepeth his life." *Prov.* 13. 3.—In this passage, *that keepeth his mouth*, is a new affirmation, interposed between the first nominative and its verb; but dependant on the antecedent nominative.

"The poor of the flock, *that* waited upon me, knew *that it* was the word of the Lord."—*Zech.* 11. 11. In this passage, we have *that* in both its characters—the first *that* is a substitute for *poor* of the flock; the second, for the last clause of the sentence, *it was the word of the Lord*.

This exposition of the uses of *that* enables us to understand the propriety of *that that* joined in construction.

"Let me also tell you *that*, *that* faith, which proceeds from insufficient or bad principles, is but little better than infidelity." In this passage, the first *that* is a substitute for the whole subsequent part of the sentence; the second *that* is an attribute agreeing with *faith*—"That faith which proceeds from bad principles is little better than infidelity—let me tell you *that*." Hence it might be well always to separate the two words by a comma. We now distinguish these words by a stronger emphasis on the last.

"He, whom thou now hast, is not thy husband; in *that* saidst thou truly."—*John* 4. 16. That is, in that whole declaration.

From these passages and the explanation, we learn that *that* is a substitute—either for a single word or a sentence; nor has it any other character, except when an attribute.

This is much less frequently a substitute for sentences than *that*; but is used in this character, as well as in that of an attribute; as, "Let no prince measure the danger of discontents by *this*, *whether they be just or unjust;* for *that* were to imagine people to be reasonable, who do often spurn at their own good; nor yet by *this*, *whether the griefs whereupon they rise be in fact great or small*."

Bacon on Kingdoms.

Here *this*, in each part of the sentence, is the representative of the clause in italics succeeding.

"Can we suppose that all the united powers of hell are able to work such astonishing miracles, as were wrought for the confirmation of the Christian religion? Can we suppose that they can control the laws of nature at pleasure, and that with an air of sovereignty, and professing themselves the lords of the universe, as we know Christ did? If we can believe *this*, then we deny," &c. We observe, here, *this* represents a series of sentences.

In some cases, *this* represents a few words only in a preceding sentence, as in the following—"The rule laid down is in general certain, that the king only can *convoke a parliament*. And *this* by the ancient statutes of the realm, he is bound *to do*, every year, or oftener, if need be." *Blacks. Comment. B.* 1. *ch.* 2.

If we ask, What is the king bound to do? the answer must be, *Convoke a parliament;* for which words alone *this* is the substitute, and governed by *do*.

The plurals *these* and *those*, are rarely or never used as substitutes for sentences.

Which.

Which is also a substitute for a sentence, or part of a sentence, as well as for a single word; as, "if there can be any other way shown, how men may come to that universal agreement, in the things they do consent in, *which* I presume may be done."—*Locke on Und. B.* 1. 2.

Which, in this passage, represents all which precedes—*which* or *all that is above related*, may be done.

"Another reason that makes me doubt of any innate practical principles, is, that I think there cannot any one moral rule be proposed, whereof a man may not justly demand a reason; *which* would be perfectly ridiculous and absurd, if they were innate, or so much as *self-evident*, *which* every innate principle must needs be."—*Ibm. chap.* 3.

In this passage, the first *which* represents the next preceding part of the sentence, *a man may justly demand a reason*—which *power of demanding a reason* would be ridiculous. The second *which* is a substitute for *self-evident; which*, that is, *self-evident*, every principle must be.

"Judas declared him *innocent*, *which* he could not be, had he, in any respect, deceived the disciples."—*Porteus, Lect.* 2. Here *which* represents the attribute *innocent.*

That would equally well represent the same word, with a connective. "Judas declared him innocent, and *that* he could not be," &c.

"We shall find the reason of it to be the *end of language*, *which* being to communicate thoughts"—that is, *end of language;* and for those words, is *which* the substitute.

What.

This substitute has several uses. *First*—it has the sense of *that which;* as, "I have heard what has been alleged."

Secondly—*What* stands for any indefinite idea; as, "He cares not *what* he says or does." "We shall the better know *what* to undertake."—*Locke on Und.* 1. 6.

Thirdly—*What* is an attribute, either in the singular or plural number, and denotes something uncertain or indeterminate; as, "In *what* character, Butler was admitted into that lady's service, is unknown."—*Johnson's Life of Butler.*

"It is not material *what* names are assigned to them."
Camp. Rhet. 1. 1.

"I know not *what* impressions time may have made upon your person." *Life of Cowp. Let.* 27.

"To see *what* are the causes of wrong judgment."
Locke, 2. 21.

Fourthly—*What* is used by the poets preceding a name, for *the* or *that which*, but its place cannot be supplied by these words, without a name between them; as,

"*What time* the sun withdrew his cheerful light,
And sought the sable caverns of the night."
Hoole's Tasso, b. 7.

That is, *at the time when* or *in which.*

Fifthly—A principal use of *what* is to ask questions; as, "What will be the consequence of the revolution in France?"

This word has the singular property of containing *two cases;* that is, it performs the office of a word in the nominative, and of another in the objective case; as, "I have, in *what goes* before, been engaged in physical inquiries farther than I intended."—*Locke*, 2. 8. Here *what* contains the object after *in*, and the nominative to *goes.*

What is used with a name as an attribute and a substitute; as, "It was agreed that *what goods* were aboard his vessels, should be landed."—*Mickle's Discovery of India*, 89. Here *what goods* are equivalent to the *goods which;* for, *what goods* include the nominative to two verbs, *were* and *should be landed.* This use of the word is not deemed elegant.

As.

As primarily signifies *like, similar;* the primary sense of which is *even*, equal. It is used adverbially in the phrases, *as* good, *as* great, *as* probable. The sense of which is, *like* or *equally* good, great or probable. Hence it frequently follows *such.* "Send him such books *as* will please him." But in this and similar phrases, *as* must be considered as the nominative to *will please;* or we must suppose an ellipsis of several words. "Send him such books as *the books which* will please him, or as *those which* will please him." So in the following sentences:

"We have been accustomed to repose on its veracity with such humble confidence *as* suppresses curiosity."

Johnson's Life of Cowley.

"All the punishment which God is concerned to see inflicted on sin, is only such *as answers* the ends of government."

"Many wise men contented themselves with such probable conclusions, *as* were sufficient for the practical purposes of life." *Enfield, Hist. Phil.* 2. 11.

"The malcontents made such demands *as* none but a tyrant could refuse." *Bolingbroke on Hist. Let* 7.

In the last example, if *as* is to be considered as a pronoun or substitute, it is in the objective case.

These and similar phrases are anomalous; and we can resolve them only by supplying the ellipsis, or by considering *as* in the nature of a pronoun, and the nominative to the verb.

In the following form of expression, we may supply *it* for the nominative: "Do every thing *as* was said about mercury and sulphur."—*Encyc.*

"As *it* was said."

In poetry, *as* supplies the place of *such*, or *such as.*

"From whence might contest spring and mutual rage,
As would the camp in civil broils engage."

Hoole's Tasso.

In prose, we should say, "*such* contest and rage *as.*"

As sometimes refers to a sentence or member of a sentence, and sometimes its place may be supplied by *which.* "On his return to Egypt, *as* I learned from the same authority, he levied a mighty army." *Beloe, Herod.*

Which I learned. "On his return to Egypt, he levied a mighty army, *which* [fact] I learned from the same authority."

As often begins a sentence. "*As* to the three orders of pronouns already mentioned, they may be called pre-positive, *as* may indeed all substantives."—*Harris.* That is, *concerning*, *respecting* the three orders, or to explain that which respects the three orders, &c.

Both.

Both is an adjective of number; but it is a substitute also for names, sentences, parts of sentences, and for attributes.

"Abraham took sheep and oxen, and gave them to Abimelech, and *both* of them made a covenant."
Genesis, 21. 27.

Here *both* is the representative of *Abraham* and *Abimelech.*

"If the blind lead the blind, *both* shall fall into the ditch."
Matt. 15. 14.

"A certain creditor had two debtors—and when they had nothing to pay, he frankly forgave them *both*."—*Luke* 7.

"He will not bear the *loss of his rank*, because he can bear *the loss of his estate;* but he will bear *both*, because he is prepared for *both*."—*Boling. on Exile.*

In the last example, *both* represents the parts of the sentence in italics.

When it represents two attributes, it may and usually does precede them; as, "he endeavored to render commerce *both* disadvantageous and infamous."—*Mickle, p.* 159.

As an attribute, it has a like position before names; as, "Tousa confessed he had saved *both* his life and his honor."
Ibm. 160.

"It is *both* more accurate, and proves no inconsiderable aid to the right understanding of things, to discriminate by different signs such as are truly different."
Campbell's Rhet. 1. 33.

In this passage, *both* represents *more accurate*, and the following member of the sentence; but the construction is harsh.

"The necessity which a speaker is under, of suiting himself to his audience, *both that* he may be understood by them, and *that* his words may have an influence upon them."—*Camp. Rhet. Ch.* 10.

Here *both* represents the two following clauses of the sentence. The definitive *the* is placed between *both* and its noun; as, "To *both* the preceding kinds, the term *burlesque* is applied."—*Camp. Rhet.* 1. 2.

Same.

The adjective *same* is often used as a substitute for persons and sentences or parts of a sentence; as, "Nothing appears so clearly an object of the mind or intellect only, as the *future* does, since we can find no place for its existence any where else. Not but the *same*, if we consider, is equally true of the *past*."—*Hermes, p.* 112.

In this ill-constructed sentence, *same* has reference to all which is predicated of the future tense—that is, *that it is an object of intellect only, since we can find no place for its existence any where else*—The *same, all this*, is true of the *past* also.

"For *brave* and *generous* ever are the *same*." *Lusiad.* 1.

Many, few, all, any.

These words we often find used as substitutes for names; "For *many* shall come in my name, saying, I am Christ, and shall deceive *many*."—*Matt.* 24. 5. "*Many* are called, but *few* chosen." 20. 16. "*All* that come into the tent, and *all* that is in the tent, shall be unclean seven days."—*Num.* 19. 14. "If a soul shall sin against *any* of the commandments."—*Lev.* 4. 2. "Neither is there *any*, that can deliver out of my hand."—*Deut.* 32, 39.

First, last, former, latter, less, least, more, most, are often used as substitutes.

"The victor's laurel, as the martyr's crown,
The *first* I hope, nor less the *last* I prize."
Hoole's Tasso, 6. 8.

"The *last* shall be *first*, and the *first last*.—*Matt.* 20. 16.

"It will not be amiss to inquire into the cause of this strange phenomenon; *that*, even a man of discernment should write without meaning, and not be sensible that he hath no meaning; and *that* judicious people should read what hath been written in this way, and not discover the defect. *Both* are surprising, but the *first* much more than the *last*."—*Camp. Rhet.* 2. 7.

Here *both* represents the two clauses of the sentence, preceded by *that*—*both* of those propositions are surprising. *First* and *last* stand in the place of the same clauses.

"Sublimity and vehemence are often confounded, the *latter* being considered as a species of the *former*."—*Camp. Rhet.* 1. 1.

Here *latter* and *former* are used for names which are near in construction, and no obscurity is occasioned by the substitutes. But these words, when placed far from the words which they represent, obscure the sense, and compel the reader to peruse a sentence the second time, which is always a fault in style. For example: "As to the Ætolian, it is frequently confounded with the Doric; and as this union takes place also in other essential points, it is only between the Dorians and Ionians that a kind of parallel can be drawn. This I shall not undertake to perform; I shall only make one general observation; the manners of the *former* have ever been severe, and the characteristics of their architecture, language and poetry, are grandeur and simplicity. The *latter* more early made a progress in refinement."—*Anarch. ch.* 72.

In every case, where the antecedent word or sentence is not obvious, so that the mind instantly applies the substitute to its principal, the use of a substitute is a fault. For example: "When a speaker addresseth himself to the understanding, he proposes the instruction of his hearers, and that *by explaining* some doctrine unknown or not distinctly comprehended by them, or *by proving* some position disbelieved or doubted by them. In other words, he proposes to dispel ignorance or to vanquish error. In the *one*, his aim is their *information;* in the other, their *conviction.* Accordingly, the predominant quality of the *former* is *perspicuity;* of the *latter, argument.* By *that*, we are made to know; by *this*, to believe."—*Camp. Rhet.* 6. 1. *ch.* 1.

To what antecedent words or clauses, do all these substitutes refer? In the *one*—and the *other* what? Doubtless, the antecedents must be the two parts of the sentences, beginning with, *by explaining* and *by proving*. That is, in explaining an unknown doctrine, his aim is instruction—in proving a doubted point, his aim is conviction. The predominant quality of the *former*—former what? unquestionably, the same sentences are the antecedents to the *former* and *latter*. These words cannot refer to *information* and *conviction;* for although *perspicuity* may be predicated of *information*, yet it cannot be a *predominant* quality of it; and *argument* cannot be predicated of *conviction*. But the whole passage is perplexed and obscure.*

---

* This criticism is the more necessary, as the use of *former* and *latter* in our best writers, is indulged to a fault. There are few places in which it is not better to repeat the antecedents than to use *former* and *latter*. The injudicious use of these and other substitutes is a great blemish in Campbell's Philosophy of Rhetoric.

"Leonis refused to go thither with *less* than the appointed equipment."—*Mickle*, 1. 181. Here *less* supplies the place of *equipment*, and prevents the necessity of its repetition.

"To the relief of these, Noronha sent some supplies, but while he was preparing to send *more*, an order from Portugal arrived."—*Mickle*, 1. 180.

Here *more* is sufficiently intelligible without a repetition of the name—*supplies*.

"And the children of Israel did so, and gathered, some *more*, some, *less*."—*Exod*. 16. 17.

"I cannot go beyond the word of the Lord, my God, to do *less* or *more*.—*Numb*. 22. 18.

"Then began he to upbraid the cities wherein *most* of his mighty works were done."—*Matt*. 11. 20.

"Was not this love indeed ?
We men say *more*, swear *more*, but indeed
Our shews are more than will." *Shaks. Twelfth Night.*

Such.

"Jabal was the father of *such* as dwelt in tents."—*Gen*. 4.
"Thou shalt provide able men, *such* as fear God."—*Ex*. 18.

"Objects of importance must be portrayed by objects of importance ; *such* as have grace, by things graceful."—*Camp Rhet*. 1. 2.

Such here supplies the place of a name or noun, but it retains its attributive sense, and the name may be added.

Self and *own*.

Self is said to have been originally an attribute ; but is now used as an intensive word to give emphasis to substitutes and attributes.* Sometimes it is used as a noun. In the plural, it forms *selves*. It is added to the attributes *my*, *your*, *own* ; as, myself, yourself,† ourselves ; and to *him*, *her*,

---

* *Self* has the force of the Latin *ipse*, and was in Saxon, added to all cases ; *he-self*, *his-self*, *him-self*. So in Latin *tu*, *te*, *ipse*, was used in the nominative.

† In this compound, we have a strong confirmation of what I have alledged respecting the arrangement of *you* in the singular number, when used of a single person. *Self* is invariably in the singular—*selves* in

them; as, himself, herself, themselves. And though annexed to substitutes in the objective case, these words are indifferently in the nominative or objective. *Self* is never added to *his*, *their*, *mine*, or *thine*.

The compounds *himself*, *herself*, *thyself*, *ourselves*, *themselves*, may be placed immediately after the personal substitute; as, *He himself* wrote a letter to the minister; or immediately after the following verb or its object; as, "He wrote a letter *himself*,"—"he went *himself* to the admiralty." In such phrases, *himself* not only gives emphasis to the affirmation, but gives to an implied negative, the force of one expressed. "He went himself to the minister," carries with it a direct negation that another person went. In negative sentences, it has a different effect. "He did not write the letter himself," implies strongly that he wrote it by an agent, or had an agency in procuring it to be written.

These compound substitutes are used after verbs when reciprocal action is expressed; as, "They injure themselves."

Itself is added to names for emphasis; "this is the book *itself*."

Own is an attribute denoting property, used with names to render the sense emphatical; as, "this book is my *own*."

Own is sometimes a substitute; as, "He came unto his *own*, and his *own* received him not."—*John* 1. 11.

"This is an invention of his *own*."

One, *other*, *another*, *none*.

The attribute *one* is very often a substitute—*other* is used in the same manner, and often opposed to *one*. "All rational or deductive evidence is derived from *one* or the *other* of these two sources."—*Camp. Rhet. ch.* 5. To render these words more definite, and the specification of the alternative

---

the plural. Now if *you* is to be classed with plurals in *all* cases, we must, to be consistent, apply *yourselves* to a single person. Yet we make the proper distinction—*yourself* is applied to one person—*yourselves* to more.. But upon the principle of our grammars, that *you* must *always* be joined to a verb in the plural, we are under the necessity of saying, "*You yourself were*," when we address a single person—which is false construction. Whatever verb therefore is used with *you* when applied to an individual, it must be considered as a verb in the singular number.

more explicit, the definitive *the* is placed before them; as, "either he will hate *the one*, and love *the other*."

Another has sometimes a possessive case; as, "the horse is another's;" but this form of speech is but little used.

Another is the Saxon *an*, one, and *other—one other*. It is an attribute; but often used as a substitute. "Let *another* praise thee, and not thine own mouth."—*Prov.* 27. 2.

None [no one] is often a substitute; as, "Ye shall lie down and *none* shall make you afraid."—*Lev*. 26. 6. It is used in the plural as well as the singular number.

The cardinal numbers are all used as substitutes, when the things to which they refer are understood by the train of discourse, and no ambiguity is created by the omission of the name; as, "The rest of the people also cast lots, to bring *one* of *ten* to dwell in Jerusalem."—*Neh.* 11. 1.

One has sometimes the possessive form; "One's person is to be protected by law;" and frequently the plural number; as, "I have commanded my sanctified *ones*, and I have called my mighty *ones*."—*Isa.* 13. 9.

One, when contrasted with *other*, sometimes represents plural names, and is joined with a plural verb, as in this passage; "The reason why *the one are* ordinarily taken for real qualities, and the *other*, only for bare powers, seems to be," &c.—*Locke, b.* 2. *ch.* 8. 25.

One and *another* have a peculiar distributive use in the following and the like expressions; "Brethren, let us love *one another*." The effect of these words seems to be, to separate an act affirmed of a number collectively, and distribute it among the several individuals—"Let us love—let each one love the other." "If ye have love one to another" —"by love serve one another." *One another*, in this phraseology, have the comprehensive sense of *every one*. "By love serve"—every one serve the other. *Each* is used in a like sense—They love each other—that is—they love —each love the other.

Several.

Several is an attribute, denoting originally one thing *severed* from others. But this sense seems to be now confined to technical law language; as, "a joint and *several* estate." In common use, it is always plural, expressive of an indefinite number, not very large. It is frequently a substitute;

as, "*Several* of my unknown correspondents."—*Spectator*, 281.

Some.

The attribute *some* is often used as a substitute ; as, "*Some* talk of subjects they do not understand ; others praise virtue who do not practice it."—*Johnson.*

Each, every, either, neither.

Each is a distributive attribute, used to denote every individual of a number, separately considered ; as, "The king of Israel and the king of Judah sat *each* on his throne." "Thou also and Aaron, take *each* of you his censer." "The *four* beasts had *each* of them six wings."

In these passages, *each* is a substitute for the name of the persons or objects, one separate from the other.*

Every denotes all the individuals of a number considered separately ; it is therefore a distributive attribute, but sometimes a substitute, chiefly in the law style ; as, "*every* of the clauses and conditions." It is generally followed by the name to which it belongs, or by the cardinal number *one*.

We sometimes see *every* separated from its name by the definitive *the* and an attribute of the superlative degree ; as, "every the least variation."—*Locke.*

Either and *neither* are usually classed with the conjunctions ; but in strictness, they are always attributes or substitutes. Their correlatives *or* and *nor*, though considered as conjunctions, belong to the latter class of words—*or* being merely an abbreviation of *other*, and *nor* being the same word with the Saxon negative prefixed, as will be hereafter shown.

Either and *or* denote an alternative ; as, "I will take *either* road at your pleasure." That is, I will take one road or the other. In this use, *either* is an attribute.

Either is also a substitute for a name ; as, "*Either* of the roads is good." It also represents a sentence or a clause of a sentence ; as, "No man can serve two masters, for *either* he will hate the one and love the other, or else," &c. *Matt.* 6. 2. To understand the true import of *either*, let *or* be also reduced back to its original orthography ; "for *either* he will hate the one and love the other ; *other* else he will

* Each is as applicable to a *hundred* or *thousand* as to *two*. "The prince had a body-guard of a thousand men, *each* of whom was six feet high."

hold to the one and despise the other." Here we are presented with the sentence as it would have stood in the Saxon; and we see two distinct affirmations, to the first of which is prefixed *either*, and to the last *other*. These words then are substitutes for the following sentences, when they are intended to be alternative. *Either* and *or* are therefore signs of an alternative, and may be called *alternatives*.

Either is used also for *each*; as, "Two thieves were crucified—on *either* side one." This use of the word is constantly condemned by critics, and as constantly repeated by good writers; but it was the true original sense of the word, as appears by every Saxon author.

Either is used also to represent an alternative of attributes; as, "the emotion must be *either*, not violent *or* not durable."—*Camp. Rhet.* 1. 2.

Neither is *not either*, from the Saxon *ne-either*; and *nor* is *ne-other*, *not other*. As *either* and *or* present an alternative or a choice of two things; so *neither* and *nor* deny both or the whole of any number of particulars; as, "Fight *neither* with small *nor* great."—1 *Kings*, 22. 31. Which sentence, when resolved, stands thus; "Fight not either with small, not other with great." Such is the curious machinery of language!

Neither is also used as an attribute and as a substitute for a name; as, "*Neither* office is filled, but *neither* of the offices will suit the candidate."

NOTE.—*Or*, *either*, *nor* and *neither*, are here explained in their true original character; but when they stand for sentences, it is more natural to consider them as *connectives*, under which head I have arranged them.

In general, any attribute [adjective] which describes persons or things with sufficient clearness, without the name to which it strictly belongs, may be used as a substitute; as, "The *rich* have many friends"—"Associate with the *wise* and *good*"—"*The future* will resemble the *past*"—"Such is the opinion of the *learned*."

ATTRIBUTES OR ADJECTIVES.

Adjectives in grammar are words which denote the qualities inherent in, or ascribed to things, or defining them; as, a *bright* sun; a *splendid* equipage; a *miserable* hut; a *magnificent* house; an *honest* man; an *amiable* woman; *liberal* charity; *false* honor; a *quiet* conscience.

As qualities may exist in different degrees, which may be compared with each other, suitable modes of speech are devised to express these comparative degrees. In English, most attributes admit of *three* degrees of comparison, and a few admit of *four*. There are therefore *four* degrees of comparison.

The *first* denotes a slight degree of the quality, and is expressed by the termination *ish;* as, *reddish, brownish, yellowish.* This may be denominated the *imperfect* degree of the attribute.

The *second* denotes such a degree of the attribute as to constitute an absolute or distinct quality; as, *red, brown, great, small, brave, wise.* This is called the *positive* degree.

The *third* denotes a greater or less degree of a quality, than exists in another object, with which it is compared; as, *greater, smaller, braver, wiser.* This is called the *comparative* degree.

The *fourth* denotes the utmost or least degree of a quality; as, *bravest, wisest, poorest, smallest.* This is called the *superlative* degree.

The imperfect degree is formed by adding *ish* to an attribute; as, *yellow, yellowish.* If the attribute ends in *e*, this vowel is omitted; as *white, whitish.*

The comparative degree is formed by adding *r* to adjectives ending with *e;* as, *wise, wiser*—and by adding *er* to words ending with a consonant; as, *cold, colder*—or by prefixing *more* or *less;* as, *more just, less noble.*

The superlative degree is formed by adding *st* to attributes ending with *e;* as, *wise, wisest*—and *est* to those which end with a consonant; as, *cold, coldest*—or by prefixing *most* and *least*; as, *most brave, least charitable.*

Every attribute susceptible of comparison, may be compared by *more* and *most*, *less* and *least.*

All monosyllables admit of *er* and *est*, and dissyllables when the addition may be easily pronounced; as, *happy, happier, happiest; lofty, loftier, loftiest.* But few words of more syllables than one will admit of *er* and *est.* Hence most attributes of more syllables than one are compared by *more* and *most, less* and *least;* as, *more fallible, most upright, less generous, least splendid.*

When attributes end in *y* after a consonant, this letter is dropped, and *i* substituted before *er* and *est;* as, *lofty, loftier, loftiest.*

A few attributes have different words or irregular terminations for expressing the degrees of comparison; as, *good, better, best; bad* or *evil, worse, worst; fore, former, first; little, less* or *lesser, least; much, more, most; near, nearer, nearest* or *next; old, older, oldest* or *eldest; late, later, latest* or *last.*

When qualities are incapable of increase or diminution, the words which express them do not admit of comparison. Such are the numerals, *first, second, third,* &c., attributes of mathematical figures, as *square, spherical, rectangular*—for it will readily appear, that if a thing is *first* or *square,* it cannot be more or less so.

The sense of attributes however is not restricted to the modification, expressed by the common signs of comparison; but may be varied in an indefinite number of ways, by other words. Thus the attribute *very,* which is the French *vrai,* true, formerly written *veray,* is much used intensively to express a great degree of a quality, but not the greatest; as, *very wise* or *learned.* In like manner are used *much, far, extremely, exceedingly,* and most of the modifiers in *ly.*

Some adjectives, from particular appropriate uses, have received names, by which they are distinguished. But the usual classification is by no means correct. The following distribution seems to result from the uses of the words named.

An or *a, the, this, that, these, those, other, another, one, none, some,* may be called *definitives,* from their *office,* which is to limit or define the extent of the name to which they are prefixed, or to specify particulars.

My, thy, her, our, your, their; and *mine, thine, his,* when used as attributes, with names, are *possessive attributes,* as they denote possession or ownership. *Its* and *whose,* if ranked with attributes, belong to the same class.

Each and *every* are *distributives,* but they may be classed with the *definitives.*

Either is an *alternative,* as is *or,* which is now considered merely as a connective.

Own is an *intensive* adjective. The words to which *self* is affixed, *himself, myself, themselves, yourself, yourselves, ourselves, thyself, itself,* may be denominated *intensive substitutes,* or, for brevity, *intensives.* Or they may be called *compound substitutes.*

VERB.

The verb is a *primary* part of speech, and of the most importance. The uses of the verb are,

1st. To affirm, assert or declare; as, the sun shines; John loves study; God is just; and negatively, avarice is not commendable.

2d. To command, exhort or invite; as, go, attend, let us observe.

3d. To pray, request, entreat; as, O may the spirit of grace dwell in us.

4th. To inquire or question; as, does it rain? will he come?

From the various uses and significations of verbs, have originated several divisions or classes. The only one in English which seems to be correct, and sufficiently comprehensive, is into *transitive* and *intransitive*. To these may be added a combination of the verb *be*, with certain auxiliaries and participles, which is called a *passive verb*, or rather the passive form of the verb.*

1. A *transitive* verb denotes action or energy, which is exerted upon some object, or in producing some effect. In natural construction, the word expressing the object, follows the verb, without the intervention of any other word, though the order may be sometimes varied. Thus, "ridicule provokes anger," is a complete proposition—*ridicule* is the agent or nominative word, which causes the action—*provoke* is the verb, or affirmation of an act—*anger* is the object or effect produced, following the transitive verb *provoke*.

"The wind propels a ship," is the affirmation of an act of the wind exerted on a ship. *Wind* is the agent, *propels*, the verb, and *ship*, the object.

2. An *intransitive* verb denotes simple being or existence in a certain state; as, *to be, to rest;* or it denotes action, which is limited to the subject. Thus, "*John sleeps*," is an affirmation, in which *John*, the nominative to *sleeps*,

---

* The common distribution into *active*, *neuter* and *passive*, is very objectionable. Many of our neuter verbs imply action in a pre-eminent degree, as to *run*, to *walk*, to *fly;* and the young learner cannot easily conceive why such verbs are not called *active*.

is the subject of the affirmation; *sleeps* is a verb intransitive, affirming a particular thing of *John*, which extends to no other object.

3. The *passive* form of the verb in English, is composed of certain auxiliaries and participles with the verb *be*. It denotes passion or suffering; that is, that the subject of the affirmation or nominative is affected by the action affirmed; as, "John is convinced." "Laura is loved and admired."

In this form of the verb, the agent and object change places. In the transitive form, the agent precedes the verb, and the object follows; as, "John has convinced Moses." In the passive form, the order is changed, and the agent follows the verb, preceded by a preposition; as, "Moses is convinced by John."

To correspond with their nominatives, verbs are used in both numbers, and with the three persons in each.

As action and being may be mentioned as present, past or future, verbs have modifications to express time, which are called *tenses*. And as action and being may be represented in various ways, verbs have various modifications to answer these purposes, called *modes*. Hence to verbs belong person, number, tense and mode.

The persons which have been already explained, are, I, thou or you, he, she, it, in the singular number; in the plural, we, ye or you, they. The numbers have been before explained.

TENSES.

There are *six tenses*, modifications or combinations of the verb to express time. Each of these is divided into two forms, for the purpose of distinguishing the *definite* or *precise* time from the *indefinite*. These may be thus explained and exemplified:—

Present Tense, indefinite.

This form of the present tense affirms or denies action or being, in present time, without limiting it with exactness to a given point. It expresses also facts which exist generally, at all times, general truths, attributes which are permanent, habits, customary actions, and the like, without reference to a specific time; as, God *is* infinitely great and just; man *is* imperfect and dependent; plants *spring* from the earth; birds *fly*; fishes *swim*.

Present Tense, definite.

This form expresses the present time with precision; usually denoting action or being, which corresponds in time with another action; as, *I am writing*, while *you are waiting*.

Past Tense, indefinite.

This form of the past tense represents action which took place at a given time past, however distant, and completely past; as, "In six days, God *created* the heavens and the earth." "Alexander *conquered* the Persians." "Scipio *was* as virtuous as brave." "The Earl of Chatham *was* an eloquent statesman."

Past Tense, definite [imperfect.]

This form represents an action as taking place and unfinished in some specified period of past time; as, "I *was standing* at the door when the procession passed."

Perfect Tense, indefinite.

This form of the perfect tense represents an action completely past, and often at no great distance, but the time not specified; as, "*I have accomplished my design.*" But if a particular time is named, the tense must be the *past;* as, "I accomplished my design last week." "I have seen my friend last week," is not correct English. In this respect, the French idiom is different from the English; for, "J'ai vu mon ami hier," is good French, but "I have seen my friend yesterday," is not good English. The words must be translated, "I saw my friend yesterday." No fault is more common than a mistranslation of this tense.

It is to be noted however that this perfect indefinite tense, is that in which we express *continued* or *repeated* action. "My father *has lived* about eighty years." "The king *has reigned* more than forty years." "He *has been frequently heard* to lament."—*Life of Cowper*. We use it also when a specified past time is represented, if that time is expressed as a *part of the present period*. Thus, although we cannot say, "We have been together yesterday," we usually say, "We have been together this morning, or this evening." We even use this tense in mentioning events which happened at a greater distance of time, if we connect that time with the present; as, "His brother has visited him once within two years." "He has not seen his sister, since the year 1800."

Perfect Tense, definite.

This form represents an action as just finished; as, "I *have been reading* a history of the revolution in France."

Prior-Past Tense, indefinite [pluperfect.]

This form of the prior past tense expresses an action which was past at or before some other past time specified; as, "He *had received* the news before the messenger arrived."

Prior-Past, definite.

This form denotes an action to be just past, at or before another time specified; as, "I *had been reading* your letter when the messenger arrived."

Future Tense, indefinite.

This form of the future tense gives notice of an event to happen hereafter; as, "Your son *will obtain* a commission in the navy." "We *shall have* a fine season."

Future Tense, definite.

This form expresses an action which is to take place and be unfinished at a specified future time; as, "He *will be preparing* for a visit at the time you arrive."

Prior-Future, indefinite.

This form of the future tense denotes an action which will be past at a future time specified; as, "They *will have performed* their task, by the appointed hour."

Prior-Future, definite.

This form represents an action which will be just past at a future specified time; as, "We *shall have been making* preparations, a week before our friends arrive."*

---

* The common names and distribution of the tenses, are so utterly incorrect and incompetent to give a just idea of their uses, that I have ventured to offer a new division, retaining the old names, as far as truth will warrant. The terms *prior-past*, and *prior-future*, are so perfectly descriptive of the tenses arranged under them, that I cannot but think they will be well received. The distinction of indefinite and definite is not wholly new; but I have never seen the definite forms displayed, though they are as necessary as the indefinite forms. Indeed, I see not how a foreigner can learn our language, as the tenses are commonly distributed and defined.

In the use of the present tense, the following things are to be noticed.

1. The present tense is customarily used to express future time, when by any mode of expression, the mind is transported forward to the time, so as to conceive it present; as, "I cannot determine, till the mail *arrives*." "As soon as it *is* light, we shall depart." "When he *has* an opportunity, he will write." The words *till, when, as soon as,* carry the mind to the time of an event to happen, and we speak of it as present.

2. By an easy transition, the imagination passes from an author to his writings; these being in existence and present, though long after his decease, we substitute the writer's name for his works, and speak of him as living, or in the present tense; thus, Milton *resembles* Homer in sublimity and invention, as Pope *resembles* Virgil, in smoothness of versification. Plato *is* fanciful; Aristotle *is* profound.

3. It gives great life and effect to description, in prose or verse, to represent past events as present; to introduce them to the view of the reader or hearer, as having a present existence. Hence the frequent use of the present tense for the future, by the historian, the poet and the orator:—

"She spoke; Minerva *burns* to meet the war;
And now heaven's empress *calls* the blazing car;
At her command *rush* forth the steeds divine;
Rich with immortal gold, the trappings shine."

Iliad, 5.

The definite tenses, it will be observed, are formed by the participle of the present tense, and the substantive verb, *be*. This participle always expresses present time, even when annexed to a past or future tense; for *I was writing*, denotes, that, at the past time mentioned, the action was present; *I shall be writing*, denotes future time, but an action then to be present.

The past tense of every regular verb ends in *ed—d* being added to a verb ending in *e;* and *ed* to a verb with other terminations; as, hate, hated; look, looked.

The future tense is formed by the present tense of *shall* and *will;* for, I shall go, he will go, are merely an appropriate use of *I shall to go, I will to go*. See an explanation of these words under the head of auxiliaries.

There are other modes of expressing future time; as, "I am going to write"—"I am about to write." These have been called the *inceptive* future, as they note the commencement of an action, or an intention to commence an action without delay.

We have another mode of expression, which does not strictly and positively foretell an action, yet it implies a necessity of performing an act, and clearly indicates that it will take place. For example, "I *have to pay* a sum of money to-morrow." That is, I am under a *present* necessity or obligation to do a *future* act.

The substantive verb followed by a radical verb, forms another idiomatic expression of future time; as, "John *is to command* a regiment." "Eneas went in search of the seat of an empire which *was*, one day, *to command* the world." The latter expression is a future-past—that is, *past* as to the narrator; but *future* as to the event, at the time specified.

MODES.

Mode, in grammar, is the manner of representing action and being, or the wishes and determinations of the mind. This is performed by inflections of the verb, or by combinations of verbs with auxiliaries and participles, and by their various positions.

As there are scarcely two authors who are agreed in the number and denominations of the modes in English, I shall offer a distribution of the verbs, and a display of their inflections and combinations, somewhat different from any which I have seen.

1. The first and most simple form of the verb, is, the verb without inflections, and unconnected with persons. This form usually has the prefix *to;* as, *to love.*

This form of the verb, not being restricted to person or number, is usually called the *Infinitive Mode.*

2. Another use of the verb is to *affirm, assert* or *declare* some action or existence, either positively, as, *he runs*, or negatively, as, *you are not in health.* This form is called the *Indicative Mode.*

3. Another office of the verb is to command, direct, ask, or exhort; as, *arise, make haste, let us be content.* This is called the *Imperative Mode.*

4. Another use of verbs is to represent actions or events which are uncertain, conditional or contingent; as, *if he shall go; if they would attend.* This is called the *Subjunctive* Mode; but would better be denominated the *Conditional.* The indicative becomes *conditional,* by means of words used to express condition; as, *if, though, unless, whether.*

The MODES then are four—the Infinitive, the Indicative, the Imperative, and the Subjunctive.

It may also be observed that the combinations, and arrangements of our verbs and auxiliaries to express negative and interrogative propositions, are really *modes* of the verb, and a place might be assigned to the verb for each purpose, were it not for the inconvenience of having *modes* of *modes.* For the sake of distinction, I denominate these verbs *interrogative* and *negative,* and have exhibited the conjugation of each.

PARTICIPLES.

Participles are derivatives from *verbs,* formed by particular terminations, and having the sense of verbs, attributes or names.

There are two species of participles—one denoting present time, and formed by adding *ing* to the verb; as, *turn, turning:* or, when the verb ends with *e,* by dropping that letter and adding *ing;* as, *place, placing.* But *e* is retained in *dyeing,* from *dye,* to color, to distinguish it from *dying,* the participle of *die;* in which word, *y* is used to prevent the duplication of *i.* In *singeing,* from *singe, e* is retained to soften *g,* and to distinguish the word from *singing;* so also in *twingeing.*

This participle of the present tense is used, as before observed, to form the definite tenses. But it often loses the sense of the verb, and becomes an attribute; as, a *loving* friend, *lasting* friendship. In this use, it admits of comparison by *more* and *less, most* and *least;* as, *more lasting, less saving, most promising.*

This participle also becomes an adverb or modifier by receiving the termination *ly;* as, *lovingly, laughingly:* and this species of modifiers admits of comparison; as, *more lovingly, most charmingly.*

This participle also becomes a name and admits of the definitive; as, "the *burning* of London in 1666." In this capacity, it takes the plural form; as, "the *overflowings* of the Nile"—" He seeth all his *goings*." And sometimes the plural is used when a modifier is attached to the participle; as, "the *goings out*, the *comings in*."—*Ezek*. 43. 11. But this use of the participle is not esteemed elegant, nor is it common.

In a few instances, the participle in *ing* becomes a name by receiving the termination *ness;* as, *willingness*, from *willing*.

The other species of participle is formed from the verb, by adding *d* or *ed*, and in regular verbs, it corresponds exactly with the past time; as, *loved*, *preceded*. This may be called the participle of the *perfect* tense.

This participle, when its verb is *transitive*, may be joined with the verb *be*, in all its inflections, to form the passive form of a verb, and the participle, in such combination, is called *passive*. But

This participle, when formed from an *intransitive* verb, cannot, except in a few instances, be joined to the substantive verb, or used in a passive sense; but it unites with the other auxiliaries.

This participle often loses its verbal character, and becomes an attribute; as, a *concealed* plot, a *painted* house. In this character, it admits of comparison; as, "a more admired artist," "a most respected magistrate;" and a few of these verbal attributes receive the termination *ly*, and become modifiers; as, *pointedly*, *more conceitedly*, *most dejectedly*.

Those verbs, whose past tense and participle end in *ed*, are deemed regular. All which deviate from this rule, are deemed irregular, and their participles of the perfect tense end mostly in *t*, *n* and *g*. A list of them will be found in the sequel.

AUXILIARIES.

In English, a few monosyllabic verbs are chiefly employed to form the modes and tenses of other verbs, and from this use, are denominated *auxiliaries* or *helping verbs*. These are followed by other verbs, without the prefix *to;* as, "he may go;" though they were originally principal verbs, and some of them still retain that character, as well as that of auxiliaries.

The verbs which are always auxiliary to others, are *may*, *can*, *shall*, *must;* those which are sometimes auxiliaries, and sometimes principal verbs, are *will*, *have*, *do* and *be*. To these may be added *need* and *dare*.

May conveys the idea of *liberty* or permission; as, "he may go, if he will." Or it denotes *possibility*; as, "he may have written or not."*

Can has the sense of *to be able*.

Shall, in its primitive sense, denotes *to be obliged*, coinciding nearly with *ought*; which sense it retains in the German. But this signification, though evidently the root of the present uses of this word, is much obscured. The following remarks will illustrate the several uses of *will* and *shall*.

Will has a common origin with the Latin *volo*. Hence the German *wollen*, the old English *woll*, and the present contraction *won't*, that is, *woll-not*.†

This was originally a principal verb, and is still used as such in our language. It denotes the act of the mind in determining, or a determination; for he *wills to go*, and *he will go*, are radically of the same import.

When a man expresses his own determination of mind, *I will*, we are accustomed to consider the event, or act willed, as certain; for we naturally connect the power to act, with the intention; hence we make the declaration of *will* a ground of confidence, and by an easy association of ideas, we connect the declaration with an *obligation* to carry the determination into effect. Hence *will* expressed by a person himself, came to denote a *promise*.

But when a person declares the will of another, he is not supposed to possess the power to decide for him, and to carry his will into effect. He merely offers an opinion, grounded on information or probable circumstances, which give him more or less confidence of an event depending on another's will. Hence *will* in the second and third person simply *foretells*, or expresses an opinion of what will take place.

Shall, in many of its inflections, retains its primitive sense —*to be obliged* or *bound in duty*; but in many of its uses,

---

* The primitive idea expressed by *may* was *power*; Sax. *magan*, to be able.

† It is supposed that the Roman *v* was pronounced as our *w*, *wolo*.

its sense is much varied. In the first person, it merely foretells; as, "I shall go to New York to-morrow." In this phrase, the word seems to have no reference to *obligation;* nor is it considered by a second person as imposing an obligation on the person uttering it. But when *shall* is used in the *second* and *third* persons, it resumes its primitive sense, or one nearly allied to it, implying obligation; as, when a superior commands with authority, *you shall go;* or implying a right in the second and third person to expect, and hence denoting a promise in the speaker; as, "you *shall* receive your wages." This is radically saying, "you *ought* to receive your wages;" but this *right* in the second person to receive, implies an *obligation* in the person speaking to pay. Hence *shall* in the first person *foretells;* in the second, *promises, commands,* or *expresses determination.* When *shall,* in the second and third persons, is uttered with emphasis, it expresses *determination* in the speaker, and implies an authority to enforce the act. "You *shall* go."

Hence proceeds the impropriety of using *shall,* when the Supreme Being is supposed to be the person addressed or spoken of. The Lord *shall* fight for us—the Lord *shall* destroy them—the Lord *shall* comfort Zion. "Thou *shalt* not suffer thy Holy One to see corruption." Acts 13. 35. See Ps. 16. 10. Acts 2. 27.

No human being has a right to use words respecting God which imply authority or command. In the examples cited, *will* is the proper auxiliary, expressing prediction.

But when *shall* is preceded by another word, as by *when, while, whoever, if, provided,* &c. it ceases, in the second and third person, to express promise, command or determination; as, When you *shall* have read the books; while he *shall* be present; whoever *shall* put away his wife; if you *shall* see my friend; provided you or he *shall* receive information. In these and similar examples, *shall* refers to event merely, without implying obligation, promise or command.

Must expresses necessity, and has no variation for person, number or tense.

Do is a principal and a transitive verb, signifying *to act* or *make;* but is used in the present and past tenses as an auxiliary, to give emphasis to a declaration, to denote contrast, or to supply the place of the principal verb.

"It would have been impossible for Cicero to inflame the

minds of the people to so high a pitch against *oppression*, considered in the abstract, as he actually *did* inflame them against Verres the *oppressor*."—*Camp. Rhet.* 1. 10. Here *did* expresses emphasis.

"It was hardly possible that he should not distinguish you as he has done."—*Cowp. Let.* 40. Here *done* stands in the place of *distinguished you.* For it must be observed that when *do* is the substitute for another verb, it supplies the place not only of the *verb*, but of the *object* of the verb.

———" He loves not plays
As thou *dost*, Antony."

That is, as *thou lovest plays.*

Do is also used in negative and interrogative sentences; the present and past tenses of the indicative mode being chiefly formed by this auxiliary; as, "I *do* not reside in Boston." ***Does*** John hold a commission?

Have is also a principal and transitive verb, denoting to *possess;* but much used as an auxiliary; as, "He *has* lately been to Hamburg." It is often used to supply the place of a principal verb or participle, preventing a repetition of it, and the object after it; as, "I have not seen Paris, but my brother has"—that is, *has seen **Paris***.

Equally common and extensive is the use of ***be***, denoting existence, and hence called the *substantive* verb. Either in the character of a principal verb, or an auxiliary, it is found in almost every sentence of the language.

The inflection of a verb, in all the modes, tenses, numbers and persons, is termed *Conjugation.* The English verbs have few inflections, or changes of termination; most of the tenses and modes being formed by means of the auxiliaries.

NOTE.—In the following conjugations, a small *n* in an Italic character, is inserted in the place where *not* should stand in negative sentences. The same place is generally occupied by *never*, but not in every case. It is believed this letter will be very useful, especially to foreigners. The learner may conjugate the verb with or without *not*, at pleasure.

CONJUGATION OF THE AUXILIARIES.

MAY.

Present Tense.

	Singular.	*Plural.*
1st *Person,*	I may *n*	We may *n*

	Singular.	*Plural.*
2d *Person,*	{ Thou mayest *n* { You may *n**	{ Ye may *n* { You may *n*
3d *Person,*	{ *mas.* He may *n* { *fem.* She may *n*. { *neut.* It may *n*	They may *n*

Past Tense.

I might *n*	We might *n*
{ Thou mightest *n*	{ Ye might *n*
{ You might *n*	{ You might *n*
He might *n*	They might *n*

CAN.

Present Tense. *Singular.*	*Plural.*	Past Tense. *Singular.*	*Plural.*
I can *n*	We can *n*	I could *n*	We could *n*
{ Thou canst *n*	{ Ye can *n*	{ Thou couldst *n*	{ Ye could *n*
{ You can *n*	{ You can *n*	{ You could *n*	{ You could *n*
He can *n*	They can *n*	He could *n*	They could *n*

SHALL.

Present Tense.		Past Tense.	
I shall *n*	We shall *n*	I should *n*.	We should *n*
{ Thou shalt *n*	{ Ye shall *n*	{ Thou shouldst *n*	{ Ye should *n*
{ You shall *n*.	{ You shall *n*	{ You should *n*	{ You should *n*
He shall *n*	They shall *n*	He should *n*	They should *n*

WILL.

Present Tense.		Past Tense.	
I will *n*	We will *n*	I would *n*	We would *n*
{ Thou wilt *n*	{ Ye will *n*	{ Thou wouldst *n*	{ Ye would *n*
{ You will *n*	{ You will *n*	{ You would *n*	{ You would *n*
He will *n*	They will *n*	He would *n*	They would *n*

NOTE.—*Will*, when a principal verb, is regularly conjugated: I will, thou willest, he wills. Past tense, *I willed.*

MUST.

Must has no change of termination, and is joined with verbs only in the following tenses.

Present Tense.

I must *n* love	We must *n* love
{ Thou must *n* love	{ Ye must *n* love
{ You must *n* love	{ You must *n* love
He must *n* love	They must *n* love

---

* It may be remarked once for all, that *thou* and *ye* are the second person used in the sacred style; and sometimes in other grave discourses. In all other cases, *you* is the second person of the singular number, as well as of the plural. It is not one of the most trivial absurdities which the student must now encounter at every step, in the study of English grammar, that he meets with *you* in the plural number only, though he finds it the reoresentative of an individual.

Perfect Tense.

Singular.	*Plural.*
I must *n* have loved	We must *n* have loved
Thou must *n* have loved	Ye must *n* have loved
You must *n* have loved	You must *n* have loved
He must *n* have loved	They must *n* have loved

DO.

Indicative Mode.

Present Tense.

I do *n* love	We do *n* love
Thou dost *n* love	Ye do *n* love
You do *n* love	You do *n* love
He does or doth *n* love	They do *n* love

Past Tense.

I did *n* love	We did *n* love
Thou didst *n* love	Ye did *n* love
You did *n* love	You did *n* love
He did *n* love	They did *n* love

Infinitive Mode.	Participles.
To do	*Doing, done, having done.*

NOTE.—In the third person singular of the present tense, *doth* is used in sacred and solemn language; *does* in common and familiar language. This verb, when principal and transitive, has all the tenses and modes; I have done, I had done, I will do, &c.

HAVE.

Infinitive Mode, Present Tense.—*To have.*

Perfect Tense.—*To have had.*

Participle of the Present Tense.—*Having.*

Of the Perfect Tense.—*Had.*

Compound.—*Having had.*

Indicative Mode.

Present Tense.		Past Tense.	
I have *n*	We have *n*	I had *n*	We had *n*
Thou hast *n*	Ye have *n*	Thou hadst *n*	Ye had *n*
You have *n*	You have *n*	You had *n*	You had *n*
He has or hath *n**	They have *n*	He had *n*	They had *n*

NOTE.—In the foregoing tenses, this verb is used either as a principal verb or an auxiliary.

Perfect Tense.

I have *n* had	We have *n* had
Thou hast *n* had	Ye have *n* had
You have *n* had	You have *n* had
He has or hath *n* had	They have *n* had

* *Hath* is used in the solemn style; *has* in the familiar.

The Conjugation of a Regular Verb.

LOVE.

Infinitive Mode, Present Tense—*To love.*
Perfect Tense—*To have loved.*
Participle of the Present Tense—*Loving.*
Of the Perfect—*Loved.*
Compound—*Having loved.*

Indicative Mode—Present Tense, indefinite.

Singular	Plural
I love *n*	We love *n*
{ Thou lovest *n*	{ Ye love *n*
{ You love *n*	{ You love *n*
He loveth or loves *n*	They love *n*

With the auxiliary *do.*

Singular	Plural
I do *n* love	We do *n* love
{ Thou dost *n* love	{ Ye do *n* love
{ You do *n* love	{ You do *n* love
He doth or does *n* love	They do *n* love

Definite.

Singular	Plural
I am *n* loving	We are *n* loving
{ Thou art *n* loving	{ Ye are *n* loving
{ You are *n* loving	{ You are *n* loving
He is *n* loving	They are *n* loving

---

tion—*if, though, unless, whether*—a rule which, without qualification, has a mischievous effect. On carefully examining the original state of the language, I find the common and true use of *were* in the singular number, is, to express *hypothesis* or *supposition*. Thus, *Sax. Chron. ad annum* 1017. On the third of the ides of December, at night, the moon appeared—"swylce he eall blodig wære"—*such, or, as, if, he all bloody were*—and the heaven was red, "swylce hit bryne wære"—as if it *were* on fire. This use of *were*, in the singular number, is legitimate, and is still retained by good writers—but its use to express a mere uncertainty respecting a past event, after a sign of condition, is obsolete or not legitimate. The following examples will illustrate the distinction—"Whether the killing *were* malicious or not, is no farther a subject of inquiry," &c.—*Judge Parker, trial of Selfridge*, p. 161. Here *were* is improperly used. So also where the fact is admitted: "Though he *were* a son, yet learned he obedience."—*Heb.* 5. 8, where Lowth justly condemns the use of *were*—"Unless a felony *were* attempted or intended."—*Selfridge's Trial*, p. 125. It ought to be *was*.

The following is the true sense of *were* in the singular number—"*Were* it necessary for you to take your books with you?"—*Judge Parker, Ibm.* 159. "If it *were* possible, they would deceive the elect."—*Mat.* 24, 24. This is the only legitimate use of this tense. "It were easy." *Miller's Letters*, p. 281.—It would be easy.

Past Tense, indefinite.

Singular.	*Plural.*
I loved *n*	We loved *n*
Thou lovedst *n*	Ye loved *n*
You loved *n*	You loved *n*
He loved *n*	They loved *n*

With the auxiliary *did*.

I did *n* love	We did *n* love
Thou didst *n* love	Ye did *n* love
You did *n* love	You did *n* love
He did *n* love	They did *n* love

Definite.

I was *n* loving	We were *n* loving
Thou wast *n* loving	Ye were *n* loving
You was *n* loving	You were *n* loving
He was *n* loving	They were *n* loving

Perfect Tense, indefinite.

I have *n* loved	We have *n* loved
Thou hast *n* loved	Ye have *n* loved
You have *n* loved	You have *n* loved
He has or hath *n* loved	They have *n* loved

Definite.

I have *n* been loving	We have *n* been loving
Thou hast *n* been loving	Ye have *n* been loving
You have *n* been loving	You have *n* been loving
He has or hath *n* been loving	They have *n* been loving

Prior-Past, indefinite.

I had *n* loved	We had *n* loved
Thou hadst *n* loved	Ye had *n* loved
You had *n* loved	You had *n* loved
He had *n* loved	They had *n* loved

Definite.

I had *n* been loving	We had *n* been loving
Thou hadst *n* been loving	Ye had *n* been loving
You had *n* been loving	You had *n* been loving
He had *n* been loving	They had *n* been loving

Future Tense, indefinite.

The form of predicting.

I shall *n* love	We shall *n* love
Thou wilt *n* love	Ye will *n* love
You will *n* love	You will *n* love
He will *n* love	They will *n* love

The form of promising, commanding and determining.

I will *n* love	We will *n* love
Thou shalt *n* love	Ye shall *n* love
You shall *n* love	You shall *n* love
He shall *n* love	They shall *n* love

Definite.

Singular.	*Plural.*
I shall or will *n* be loving	We shall or will *n* be loving
Thou shalt or wilt *n* be loving	Ye shall or will *n* be loving
You shall or will *n* be loving	You shall or will *n* be loving
He shall or will *n* be loving	They shall or will *n* be loving

Prior-Future, indefinite.

I shall *n* have loved	We shall *n* have loved
Thou shalt or wilt *n* have loved	Ye shall or will *n* have loved
You shall or will *n* have loved	You shall or will *n* have loved
He shall or will *n* have loved	They shall or will *n* have loved

Definite.

I shall *n* have been loving	We shall *n* have been loving
Thou shalt or wilt *n* have been loving	Ye shall or will *n* have been loving
You shall or will *n* have been loving	You shall or will *n* have been loving
He shall or will *n* have been loving	They shall or will *n* have been loving

Imperative Mode.

Let me *n* love	Let us *n* love
Love *n*	Love *n*
Do *n* love	Do *n* love
Do thou *n* love	Do ye or you *n* love
Do you *n* love	

Subjunctive Mode.

Present Tense.

If, though, unless, whether, suppose, admit, &c.

I love *n*	We love *n*
Thou lovest *n**	Ye love *n*
You love *n*	You love *n*
He loveth or loves *n*	They love *n*

Some authors omit the personal terminations in the second and third persons—*if thou love, if he love.* With this single variation, which I deem contrary to the principles of our language, the subjunctive mode differs not in the least from the indicative, and to form it the learner has only to prefix a sign of condition, as, *if, though, unless,* &c. to the indicative, in its several tenses: With this exception, however, that in the future tense, the auxiliary may be and often is suppressed. Thus instead of

If I shall or will love	We shall or will love
Thou shalt or wilt love	Ye shall or will love
You shall or will love	You shall or will love
He shall or will love	They shall or will love

Authors write,

If, &c. I love	We love
Thou love	Ye love
You love	You love
He love	They love

It is further to be remarked, that *should* is very often used to form the conditional future—*if I should, thou shouldst,* &c. This tense is inflected like the past tense, but is probably more used for the conditional future than *shall* and *will.*

The other auxiliaries also in the past time are used in this conditional mode in a very indefinite sense.

I shall therefore offer a new tense in this mode composed of any principal verb, with *might, could, should,* and *would,* expressing, like the Greek aorists, time indefinite *present, past* or *future,* especially the *future.*

Subjunctive Mode, *indefinite* Tense.

If, though, unless, whether, lest, except, suppose, &c.

Singular.

I might, could, should, or would *n* love
Thou mightest, couldst, shouldst or wouldst *n* love
You might, could, should, would *n* love
He might, could, should, would *n* love

Plural.

We might, could, should, would *n* love
Ye or you might, could, should, would *n* love
They might, could, should, would *n* love

In the subjunctive mode, there is a peculiarity in the tenses which should be noticed. When I say, *if it rains,* it is understood that I am *uncertain* of the fact, at the time of speaking. But when I say, "*If it rained,* we should be obliged to seek shelter," it is not understood that I am uncertain of the fact; on the contrary, it is understood that I am certain, it *does not rain* at the time of speaking. Or if I say, "*if it did not rain,* I would take a walk," I convey the idea that it *does* rain at the moment of speaking. This form of our tenses in the subjunctive mode has never been the subject of much notice, nor ever received its due explanation and arrangement. For this hypothetical verb is actually a present tense, or at least indefinite,—it certainly does not belong to past time. It is further to be remarked, that a negative sentence always implies an affirmative—"if it did not rain," implies that it *does* rain. On the contrary, an affirmative sentence implies a negative—"if it *did* rain," implies that it does *not*.

In the past time, a similar distinction exists; for "if it rained yesterday," denotes uncertainty in the speaker's mind—but "if it had *not* rained yesterday," implies a certainty, that it *did* rain.

Passive form of the Verb.—*Indicative Mode.*

Present Tense.

Singular.	*Plural.*
I am *n* loved	We are *n* loved
Thou art *n* loved	Ye are *n* loved
You are *n* loved	You are *n* loved
He is *n* loved	They are *n* loved

Past Tense.

I was *n* loved	We were *n* loved
Thou wast *n* loved	Ye were *n* loved
You was or were *n* loved	You were *n* loved
He was *n* loved	They were *n* loved

Perfect Tense.

I have *n* been loved	We have *n* been loved
Thou hast *n* been loved	Ye have *n* been loved
You have *n* been loved	You have *n* been loved
He has or hath *n* been loved	They have *n* been loved

Prior-Past Tense.

I had *n* been loved	We had *n* been loved
Thou hadst *n* been loved	Ye had *n* been loved
You had *n* been loved	You had *n* been loved
He had *n* been loved	They had *n* been loved

Future Tense.

I shall or will *n* be loved	We shall or will *n* be loved
Thou shalt or wilt *n* be loved	Ye shall or will *n* be loved
You shall or will *n* be loved	You shall or will *n* be loved
He shall or will *n* be loved	They shall or will *n* be loved

Prior-Future Tense.

I shall *n* have been loved	We shall *n* have been loved
Thou shalt or wilt *n* have been loved	Ye shall or will *n* have been loved
You shall or will *n* have been loved	You shall or will *n* have been loved
He shall or will *n* have been loved	They shall or will *n* have been loved

Imperative Mode.

Let me *n* be loved	Let us *n* be loved
Be *n* loved	Be *n* loved
Be thou or you *n* loved	Be ye or you *n* loved
Do you *n* be loved*	Do you *n* be loved

* The *not* is usually placed after *do*, and contracted into *don't*.

Subjunctive Mode.

Present Tense.

Singular.	*Plural.*
If, &c. I am *n* loved	We are *n* loved
Thou art *n* loved	Ye are *n* loved
You are *n* loved	You are *n* loved
He is *n* loved	They are *n* loved

Or thus:

If, &c. I be *n* loved	We be *n* loved
Thou be *n* loved	Ye be *n* loved
You be *n* loved	You be *n* loved
He be *n* loved	They be *n* loved

Past Tense.

If, &c. I was *n* loved	We were *n* loved
Thou wast *n* loved	Ye were *n* loved
You was or were *n* loved	You were *n* loved
He was *n* loved	They were *n* loved

Or thus:

If, &c. I were *n* loved	We were *n* loved
Thou wert *n* loved	Ye were *n* loved
You were *n* loved	You were *n* loved
He were *n* loved	They were *n* loved

Perfect Tense.

If, &c. I have *n* been loved	We have *n* been loved
Thou hast *n* been loved	Ye have *n* been loved
You have *n* been loved	You have *n* been loved
He has or hath *n* been loved	They have *n* been loved

Prior-Past Tense.

If, &c. I had *n* been loved	We had *n* been loved
Thou hadst *n* been loved	Ye had *n* been loved
You had *n* been loved	You had *n* been loved
He had *n* been loved	They had *n* been loved

Future Tense.

If, &c. I shall, will or should *n* be loved	We shall, will or should *n* be loved
Thou shalt, wilt or shouldst *n* be loved	Ye shall, will or should *n* be loved
You shall, will or should *n* be loved	You shall, will or should *n* be loved
He shall, will or should *n* be loved	They shall, will or should *n* be loved

Prior-Future Tense.

If, &c. I shall or should *n* have been loved	We shall or should *n* have been loved
Thou shalt or shouldst *n* have been loved	Ye shall or should *n* have been loved
You shall or should *n* have been loved	You shall or should *n* have been loved
He shall or should *n* have been loved	They shall or should *n* have been loved

The future is often elliptical, the auxiliary being omitted. Thus, instead of *if I shall be loved,* &c. are used the following forms:

If, &c. I be *n* loved	We be *n* loved
Thou be *n* loved	Ye be *n* loved
You be *n* loved	You be *n* loved
He be *n* loved	They be *n* loved

An exhibition of the verb in the interrogative form, with the sign of the negative.

Indicative Mode.

Present Tense, indefinite.

Love I *n*?	Love we *n*?
Lovest thou *n*?	Love ye *n*?
Love you *n*?	Love you *n*?
Loveth or loves he *n*?	Love they *n*?

The foregoing form is but little used. The following is the usual mode of asking questions.

Do I *n* love?	Do we *n* love?
Dost thou *n* love?	Do ye *n* love?
Do you *n* love?	Do you *n* love?
Does or doth he *n* love?	Do they *n* love?

Definite.

Am I *n* loving?	Are we *n* loving?
Art thou *n* loving?	Are ye *n* loving?
Are you *n* loving?	Are you *n* loving?
Is he *n* loving?	Are they *n* loving?

Past Tense, indefinite.

Did I *n* love?	Did we *n* love?
Didst thou *n* love?	Did ye *n* love?
Did you *n* love?	Did you *n* love?
Did he *n* love?	Did they *n* love?

The other form of this tense, loved he? is seldom used.

Definite.

Was I *n* loving?	Were we *n* loving?
Wast thou *n* loving?	Were ye *n* loving?
Was or were you *n* loving?	Were you *n* loving?
Was he *n* loving?	Were they *n* loving?

Perfect Tense, indefinite

Have I *n* loved?	Have we *n* loved?
Hast thou *n* loved?	Have ye *n* loved?
Have you *n* loved?	Have you *n* loved?
Has or hath he *n* loved?	Have they *n* loved?

Definite.

Singular.	*Plural.*
Have I *n* been loving?	Have we *n* been loving?
Hast thou *n* been loving? / Have you *n* been loving?	Have ye *n* been loving? / Have you *n* been loving?
Has or hath he *n* been loving?	Have they *n* been loving?

Prior-Past, indefinite.

Had I *n* loved?	Had we *n* loved?
Hadst thou *n* loved? / Had you *n* loved?	Had ye *n* loved? / Had you *n* loved?
Had he *n* loved?	Had they *n* loved?

Definite.

Had I *n* been loving?	Had we *n* been loving?
Hadst thou *n* been loving? / Had you *n* been loving?	Had ye *n* been loving? / Had you *n* been loving?
Had he *n* been loving?	Had they *n* been loving?

Future Tense, indefinite.

Shall I *n* love?	Shall we *n* love?
Shalt or wilt thou *n* love? / Shall or will you *n* love?	Shall or will ye *n* love? / Shall or will you *n* love?
Shall or will he *n* love?	Shall or will they *n* love?

Definite.

Shall I *n* be loving?	Shall we *n* be loving?
Shalt or wilt thou *n* be loving? / Shall or will you *n* be loving?	Shall or will ye *n* be loving? / Shall or will you *n* be loving?
Shall or will he *n* be loving?	Shall or will they *n* be loving?

Prior-Future, indefinite.

Shall I *n* have loved?	Shall we *n* have loved?
Shalt or wilt thou *n* have loved? / Shall or will you *n* have loved?	Shall or will ye *n* have loved? / Shall or will you *n* have loved?
Shall or will he *n* have loved?	Shall or will they *n* have loved?

The definite form of this tense, is little used.

Will, in this tense, is not elegantly used in the first person. The interrogative form is not used in the imperative mode—a command and a question being incompatible.

Let the learner be instructed that in interrogative sentences, the nominative follows the verb when alone, or the first auxiliary when one or more are used; and the sign of negation *not*, (and generally *never*,) immediately follows the nominative.

The following combinations, with *can*, *may*, *could*, and *might*, are, by some writers, considered as forming a *mode*, called *Potential*. They may however be resolved, thus: *can* is a verb regularly followed by *have* in the Infinitive Mode, and *had*, the participle; these together constituting a tense, in the Indicative or Subjunctive Mode. But if any persons think it more correct or convenient, to call these combinations the *Potential Mode*, let them do so.

Present Tense.

I may or can *n* have	We may or can *n* have
{ Thou mayest or canst *n* have	{ Ye may or can *n* have
{ You may or can *n* have	{ You may or can *n* have
He may or can *n* have	They may or can *n* have

Perfect Tense.

I may *n* have had	We may *n* have had
{ Thou mayest *n* have had	{ Ye may *n* have had
{ You may *n* have had	{ You may *n* have had
He may *n* have had	They may *n* have had

In like manner with *can.*

Prior-Past Tense.

I might *n* have had	We might *n* have had
{ Thou mightest *n* have had	{ Ye might *n* have had
{ You might *n* have had	{ You might *n* have had
He might *n* have had	They might *n* have had

In like manner with *could, would,* and *should.*

IRREGULAR VERBS.

All verbs whose past tense and perfect participle do not end in *ed* are deemed irregular. The number of these is about one hundred and seventy-seven. They are of three kinds.

1. Those whose past tense and participle of the perfect are the same as the present; as, beat, burst, cast, cost, cut, hit, hurt, let, put, read, rid, set, shed, shred, shut, slit, split, spread, thrust, sweat, wet. *Wet* has sometimes *wetted; heat* sometimes *het;* but the practice is not respectable.

2. Verbs whose past time and participle are alike, but different from the present; as, *meet, met; sell, sold.*

3. Verbs whose present and past tenses and participle are all different; as, *know, knew, known.*

A few verbs ending with *ch, ck, x, p, ll, ess,* though regular, suffer a contraction of *ed* into *t,* as, snatcht for snatched, checkt for checked, snapt for snapped, mixt for mixed, dwelt for dwelled, past for passed. Others have a digraph shortened; as, dream, dreamt; feel, felt; mean, meant; sleep, slept; deal, dealt. In a few, *v* is changed into *f;* as, bereave, bereft; leave, left.

As some of the past tenses and participles are obsolete or obsolescent, it is deemed proper to set these in separate columns, in italics, for the information of the student.

IRREGULAR VERBS.

Infinitive.	*Past Tense.*	*Participle.*	*Past Tense obsolete.*	*Participle obsolete.*
Abide	abode	abode		
Am	was	been		
Arise, rise	arose, rose	arisen, risen		
Awake	awoke, awaked	awaked		
Bear	bore	borne	*bare*	
Beat	beat	beat, beaten		
Begin	begun, began	begun		
Bend.	bended, bent	bended, bent		
Bereave	bereaved, bereft	bereaved, bereft		
Beseech	besought	besought		
Bid	bid, bade	bid, bidden		
Bind	bound	bound		*bounden*
Bite	bit	bit, bitten		
Bleed	bled	bled		
Blow	blew	blown		
Break	broke	broke, broken	*brake*	
Breed	bred	bred		
Bring	brought	brought		
Build	builded, built	built		
Burst	burst	burst		
Buy	bought	bought		
Cast	cast	cast		
Catch	catched, caught	catched, caught		
Chide	chid	chid		*chidden*
Chuse, choose	chose	chose, chosen		
Cleave, to stick	cleaved	cleaved	*clave*	
Cleave, to split	cleft	cleft, clove, cloven		
Cling	clung	clung		
Clothe	clothed	clothed, clad		
Come	came, come	come		
Cost	cost	cost		
Crow	crowed	crowed	*crew*	
Creep	crept	crept		
Cut	cut	cut		
Dare	durst, dared*	dared		
Deal	dealt	dealt		
Dig	dug, digged	dug, digged		
Do	did	done		
Draw	drew	drawn		
Drive	drove	driven, drove	drave	
Drink	drank	drank		*drunken,* [*drunk*
Dwell	dwelt, dwelled	dwelt, dwelled		
Eat	ate	eat, eaten		
Engrave	engraved	engraven, engraved		
Fall	fell	fallen		
Feel	felt	felt		
Fight	fought	fought		

* When transitive, this verb is always regular; as, "he dared him."

Infinitive.	*Past Tense.*	*Participle.*	*Past Tense obsolete.*	*Participle obsolete.*
Find	found	found		
Flee	fled	fled		
Fling	flung	flung		
Fly	flew	flown		
Forget	forgot	forgot, forgotten	*forgat*	
Forsake	forsook	forsaken		
Freeze	froze	frozen, froze		
Get	got	got, gotten	*gat*	
Gild	gilded, gilt	gilded, gilt		
Gird	girded, girt	girded, girt		
Give	gave	given		
Go	went	gone		
Grave	graved	graved, graven		
Grind	ground	ground		
Grow	grew	grown		
Have	had	had		
Hang	hanged, hung	hanged, hung		
Hear	heard	heard		
Hew	hewed	hewed, hewn		
Hide	hid	hid, hidden		
Hit	hit	hit		
Hold	held	held		*holden*
Hurt	hurt	hurt		
Keep	kept	kept		
Knit	knit	knit		
Know	knew	known		
Lade	laded	laden		
Lay	laid	laid		
Lead	led	led		
Leave	left	left		
Lend	lent	lent		
Let	let	let		
Lie (down)	lay	lain		
Lose	lost	lost		
Make	made	made		
Meet	met	met		
Mow	mowed	mowed, mown		
Pay	paid	paid		
Put	put	put		
Read	read	read		
Rend	rent	rent		
Rid	rid	rid		
Ride	rode	rid		*ridden*
Ring	rung, rang	rung		
Rise	rose	risen		
Rive	rived	rived, riven		
Run	ran, run	run		
Saw	sawed	sawed, sawn		
Say	said	said		
See	saw	seen		
Seek	sought	sought		

Infinitive	*Past Tense.*	*Participle.*	*Past Tense obsolete.*	*Participle. obsolete.*
Sell	sold	sold		
Send	sent	sent		
Set	set	set		
Shake	shook	shaken, shook		
Shape	shaped	shaped		*shapen*
Shave	shaved	shaved		*shaven*
Shear	sheared	sheared, shorn		
Shed	shed	shed		
Shine	shone, shined	shone, shined		
Shew	shewn	shewn		
Show	showed	shown, showed		
Shoe	shod	shod		
Shoot	shot	shot		
Shrink	shrunk	shrunk		
Shred	shred	shred		
Shut	shut	shut		
Sing	sung	sung	*sang*	
Sink	sunk	sunk	*sank*	
Sit.	sat	sat		*sitten*
Slay	slew	slain		
Sleep	slept	slept		
Slide	slid	slid		*slidden*
Sling	slung	slung		
Slink	slunk	slunk		
Slit	slit, slitted	slit, slitted		
Smite	smote	smitten, smit		
Sow	sowed	sowed, sown		
Speak	spoke	spoke, spoken	*spake*	
Speed	sped	sped		
Spend	spent	spent		
Spill	spilled, spilt	spilled, spilt		
Spin	spun	spun		
Spit	spit	spit	*spat*	*spitten*
Spread	spread	spread		
Spring	sprung	sprung	*sprang*	
Stand	stood	stood		
Steal	stole	stole, stolen		
Sting	stung	stung		
Stink	stunk	stunk	*stank*	
Stride	strid, strode	strid		*stridden*
Strike	struck	struck		stricken
String	strung	strung		
Strive	strove	striven		
Strow	strowed	strowed strown		
Strew	strewed	strewed		
Swear	swore	sworn	*sware*	
Sweat	sweat	sweat		
Swell	swelled	swelled		swollen
Swim	swum, swam	swum		
Swing	swung	swung		
Take	took	taken		

Infinitive.	*Past Tense.*	*Participle.*	*Past Tense obsolete.*	*Participle obsolete*
Teach	taught	taught		
Tear	tore	torn		
Tell	told	told		
Think	thought	thought		
Thrive	thrived, throve	thrived		*thriven*
Throw	threw	thrown		
Thrust	thrust	thrust		
Tread	trod	trod, trodden		
Wax	waxed	waxed		*waxen*
Wear	wore	worn		
Weave	wove	woven, wove		
Weep	wept	wept		
Win	won	won		
Wind	wound	wound		
Work	worked, wrought	worked, wrought		
Wring	wrung, wringed	wrung, wringed		
Write	wrote	writ, written		

NOTE 1.—The old forms of the past tense, *sang*, *spake*, *sprang*, *forgat*, &c. are here placed among the obsolete words. They are entirely obsolete, in ordinary practice, whether popular or polite; and it seems advisable not to attempt to revive them. In addition to this reason for omitting them, there is one which is not generally understood. The sound of *a* in these and all other like cases, was originally the broad *a* or *aw;* which sound, in the Gothic and Saxon, as in the modern Scotch, corresponded nearly with *o* in *spoke, swore*. *Spoke* is therefore nearer to the original than *spake*, as we now pronounce the vowel *a* with its first or long sound, as in *sake*.

NOTE 2.—In the use of the past tense and participle of some of these verbs, there is a diversity of practice; some authors retaining those which others have rejected as obsolete. Many words which were in use in the days of Shakspeare and Lord Bacon, are now wholly laid aside; others are used only in books, while others are obsolescent, being occasionally used; and a few of the old participles, having lost the verbal character, are used only as attributes. Of the last mentioned species, are *fraught*, *drunken*, *molten*, *beholden*, *shorn*, *bounden*, *cloven*. *Holpen* is entirely obsolete. *Holden*, *swollen*, *gotten*, are nearly obsolete in common parlance. *Wrought* is evidently obsolescent.

Bishop Lowth has attempted to revive the use of many of the obsolescent past tenses and participles, for which he has, and I think deservedly, incurred the severe animadversions of eminent critics. "Is it not surprising (says Campbell on Rhetoric, b. ii. ch. 2.) that one of Lowth's penetration should think a single person entitled to revive a form of inflection in a particular word, which had been rejected by all good writers of every denomination, for more than a hundred and fifty years?"—This writer declares what Lowth has advanced on the use of the past tense and participle, to be inconsistent with the very first principles of grammar. He observes justly that authority is every thing in language, and that this authority consists in reputable, national, present usage.

Independent of authority, however, there are substantial reasons in the language itself for laying aside the participles ending with *en*, and for removing the differences between the past time and participle. In opposition to the opinion of Lowth, who regrets that our language has so few inflections, and maintains that we should preserve all we have, I think it capable of demonstration that the differences between the past time and participle of the past tense of our irregular verbs, is one of the greatest inconveniences in the language. If we used personal terminations to form our modes and tenses, like the Greeks, it would be desirable that they should be carefully retained. But as we have no other than about half a dozen different terminations, and are therefore obliged to form our modes and tenses by means of auxiliaries, the combination of these forms a part of the business of learning the language, which is extremely difficult and perplexing to foreigners. Even the natives of Scotland and Ireland do not always surmount the difficulty. This difficulty is very much augmented by the difference between the past tense and the participle. To remove this difference, in words in which popular usage has given a lead, is to obviate, in a degree, this inconvenience. This is recommended by another circumstance—it will so far reduce our irregular verbs to an analogy with the regular, whose past tense and participle of the perfect are alike.

In a number of words, the dropping of *n* in the participle will make a convenient distinction between the participle and the adjective; for in the latter, we always retain the *en*—we always say a written treatise, a spoken language, a hidden mystery—though the best authors write, a "mystery hid from ages;" "the language spoke in Bengal."

Defective Verbs.

Verbs which want the past time or participle, are deemed defective. Of these we have very few. The auxiliaries *may, can, will, shall, must,* having no participle, belong to this class. *Ought* is used in the present and past tenses only, with the regular inflection of the second person only—*I ought, thou oughtest, he ought, we, you, they ought.* *Quoth* is wholly obsolete, except in poetry and burlesque. It has no inflection, and is used chiefly in the third person, with the nominative following it, *quoth he.*

Wit, to know, is obsolete, except in the infinitive, to introduce an explanation or enumeration of particulars; as, "There are seven persons, *to wit,* four men and three women." *Wot* and *wist* are entirely obsolete.

Adverbs or Modifiers.

Adverbs are a secondary part of speech. Their uses are to enlarge, restrain, limit, define, and in short, to *modify* the sense of other words.

Adverbs may be classed according to their several uses.

1. Those which qualify the actions expressed by verbs and participles; as, "a good man lives *piously;*" "a room is *elegantly* furnished." Here *piously* denotes the *manner of living*—*elegantly* denotes the *manner of being furnished.* The words of this kind, which are very numerous, are really compound adjectives, formed by annexing the attribute *like*

to any other attribute—*pious-like, elegant-like.* The phrases mentioned, when expressed according to the primitive idiom, stand thus: "he lives pious-like;" "a room elegant-like furnished." So that the most numerous class of modifiers of verbs are really attributes or adjectives; but being used as the qualifiers of verbs and other attributes, and not to express the qualities of names, they may well take a different appellation.

In this class may be ranked a number of other words; as, *when, soon, then, where, whence, hence,* and many others, whose use is to modify verbs.

2. Another class of modifiers are words usually called prepositions, used with verbs to vary their signification; for which purpose they generally follow them in construction; as, *to fall on, give out, bear with, cast up;* or they are prefixed and become a part of the word; as, *overcome, underlay.* In these uses, these words *modify,* or change the sense of the verb; and when prefixed, are united with the verb in orthography.

A few modifiers admit the termination of comparison; as, *soon, sooner, soonest; often, oftener, oftenest.* Most of those which end in *ly,* may be compared by *more* and *most, less,* and *least;* as, *more justly, more excellently; less honestly, least criminally.*

Note.—The numerous distinctions of adverbs into those of time, place and quantity, casual, illative, adversative, &c. seem to be more perplexing than useful. We might as well make the definition of every word in our dictionaries the foundation of a class, as to recognize the divisions of this species of words, with which the ingenuity of authors has filled our grammars.

Prepositions.

Prepositions, so called from their being *put before* other words, serve to connect words and show the relation between them, or to show the condition of things. Thus, a man *of* benevolence, denotes a man who possesses benevolence. Christ was crucified *between* two thieves. Receive the book *from* John and give it *to* Thomas.

The prepositions most common are, *to, for, by, of, in, into, on, upon, among, between, betwixt, up, over, under, beneath, against, from, out, with, through, at, towards, before, behind, after, without, across.*

We have a number of particles, which serve to vary or modify the words to which they are prefixed, and which are sometimes called *inseparable prepositions,* because they are never used but as parts of other words—such are *a, be, con, mis, pre, re, sub*, in *abide, become, conjoin, mistake, prefix, return, subjoin*, &c. These may be called *prefixes*.

Connectives or Conjunctions.

Connectives are words which unite words and sentences in construction, joining two or more simple sentences into one compound one, and continuing the sentence at the pleasure of the writer or speaker. They also begin sentences after a full period, manifesting some relation between sentences in the general tenor of discourse.

The connectives of most general use, are, *and, or, either, nor, neither, but, than.*

And is supposed to denote an *addition;* as, "The book is worth four shillings *and* sixpence." That is, it is worth four shillings, *add* sixpence, or with sixpence *added.* "John resides at New-York, and Thomas at Boston." That is, John resides at New-York, *add* [add this which follows]. Thomas resides at Boston. From the great use of this connective in joining words of which the same thing is affirmed or predicated, it may be justly called the *copulative* by way of eminence.

The distinguishing use of the connective is to save the repetition of words; for this sentence, "John, Thomas and Peter reside at York," contains three simple sentences; "John resides at York"—"Thomas resides at York"—"Peter resides at York;" which are all combined into one, with a single verb and predicate, by means of the copulative.

Either and *or* have been already explained under the head of substitutes; for in strictness they are the representatives of sentences or words; but as *or* has totally lost that character, both these words will be here considered as connectives. Their use is to express an alternative, and I shall call them *alternatives.* Thus, "Either John *or* Henry will be at the Exchange," is an alternative sentence; the verb or predicate belonging to one or the other, but not to both; and whatever may be the number of names or propositions thus joined by *or*, the verb and predicate belong to one only.

One very common use of *or*, is to join to a word or sentence, something added by way of explanation or definition. Thus, "No disease of the mind can more fatally disable it from benevolence than ill-humor *or* peevishness." *Rambler, No.* 74. Here *peevishness* is not intended as a distinct thing from *ill-humor*, but as another term for the same idea. In this case, *or* expresses only an *alternative of words*, and not of signification.

As *either* and *or* are affirmative of one or other of the particulars named, so *neither* and *nor* are negative of all the particulars. Thus, "For I am persuaded that *neither* death, *nor* life, *nor* angels, *nor* principalities, *nor* powers, *nor* things present, *nor* things to come, *nor* height, *nor* depth, *nor* any other creature shall be able to separate us from the love of God."—*Rom.* 8. 38. Here *neither* is in fact a substitute for each of the following particulars—all of which it denies to be able to effect a certain purpose—*not either* of these which follow shall separate us from the love of God. It is laid down as a rule in our grammars, that *nor* must always answer to *neither;* but this is a great mistake, for the negation of *neither*, not either, extends to every one of the following alternatives. But *nor* is more generally used, and in many cases, as in the passage just recited, is far the most emphatical.

But is used for two Saxon words, originally by mistake, but now by established custom; *bet* or *bote*, the radical of our modern words *better*, *boot*, and denoting *sufficiency*, *compensation*, *more*, *further*, or *something additional*, by way of amendment; and *beuton* or *butan*, equivalent to *without* or *except*.

In the former sense, we have the word in this sentence; "John resides at York, *but* Thomas resides at Bristol." The primitive sense here is, John resides at York; *more*, *add* or *supply*, Thomas resides at Bristol. It does not always signify *opposition*, as is usually supposed, but some addition to the sense of what goes before.

In the latter sense, or that of *butan*, it is used in this passage, "He hath not grieved me, *but* in part."—2 *Cor*. 2. 5. That is, "He hath not grieved me, *except* in part." The first assertion is a complete negation; the word *but* (beutan) introduces an exception. "Nothing, *but* true religion, can give us peace in death." Here also is a complete negation; with a saving introduced by *but*. Nothing, except true religion.

These were the only primitive uses of *but*, until, by means of a mistake, a third sense was added, which is that of *only*. Not knowing the origin and true meaning of *but*, authors omitted the negation in certain phrases where it was essential to a true construction; as in the following passages: "Our light affliction, which is *but* for a moment."—2 *Cor.* 4. "If they kill us, we shall *but* die."—2 *Kings* 7.

The *but*, in these passages, is *buton*, be out, except; and, according to the true original sense, *not* should precede, to give the sentence a negative turn: "Our light affliction is not, but (except) for a moment." "We shall not, *but* die." As they now stand, they would in strictness signify, Our light affliction is *except* for a moment—We can *except* die, which would not be sense. To correct the sense, and repair the breach made in the true English idiom, by this mistake, we must give *but* a new sense, equivalent to *only*. Thus we are obliged to patch and mend, to prevent the mischiefs of innovation.

The history of this word *but* should be, as Johnson expresses the idea, "a guide to reformers, and a terror to innovators." The first blunder or innovation blended two words of distinct meanings into one, in orthography and pronunciation. Then the sense and etymology being obscured, authors proceeded to a further change, and suppressed the negation, which was essential to the *buton*. We have now therefore one word with three different and unallied meanings; and to these may be reduced the whole of Johnson's eighteen definitions of *but*.

Let us however trace the mischief of this change a little further. As the word *but* is now used, a sentence may have the same meaning *with* or *without* the negation. For example: "he hath *not* grieved me, but in part"—and "he hath grieved me, but in part," have, according to our present use of *but*, precisely the same meaning. Or compare different passages of scripture, as they now stand in our Bibles.

He hath *not* grieved me, *but* in part.

Our light affliction *is but* for a moment.

This however is not all; for the innovation being directed neither by knowledge nor judgment, is not extended to all cases, and in a large proportion of phrases to which *but* belongs, it is used in its original sense with a preceding negation, especially with *nothing* and *none*. "There is none good, *but* one, that is God."—*Matt.* 19. 17. This is correct—there is none good, except one, that is God. "He saw a fig-tree in the way, and found nothing thereon *but* leaves only."—*Matt.* 21. 19. This is also correct—"he found nothing, except leaves;" the *only* is redundant. "It amounts to no more but this."—*Locke, Und. b.* 1. 2. This is a correct English phrase; "It amounts to no more, *except* this;" but it is nearly obsolete.

Hence the propriety of these phrases; "They could not, *but* be known before."—*Locke,* 1. 2. "The reader may be, nay, cannot chuse *but* be, very fallible in the understanding of it."—*Locke,* 3. 9. Here *but* is used in its true sense—They could not, except this, be known before. That is, the contrary was not possible. The other phrase is frequently found in Shakspeare and other old writers, but is now obsolete. They *cannot chuse but*—that is, they have no choice, power or alternative, *except* to be very fallible.

But is called in our grammars, a *disjunctive conjunction,* connecting sentences, but expressing opposition in the sense. To illustrate the use of this word which *joins* and *disjoins* at the same time, Lowth gives this example: "You and I rode to London, *but* Peter staid at home." Here the bishop supposed the *but* to express an opposition in the sense. But let *but* be omitted, and what difference will the omission make in the sense? "You and I rode to London, Peter staid at home." Is the opposition in the sense less clearly marked than when the conjunction is used? By no means. And the truth is, that the opposition in the sense, when there is any, is never expressed by the connective at all, but always by the following sentence or phrase: "They have mouths, but they speak not; eyes have they, but they see not."—*Psalm* 115. 5. Let *but* be omitted—"They have mouths, they speak not; eyes have they, they see not." The omission of the connectives makes not the smallest alteration in the sense, so far as opposition or difference of idea in the members of the sentence is concerned. Indeed the bishop is most unfortunate in the example selected to illustrate his rule; for the copulative *and* may be used for *but,* without the least alteration in the sense: "You and I rode to London, *and* Peter staid at home." In this sentence the opposition is as completely expressed as if *but* was used; which proves that the opposition in the sense has no dependence on the connective.

Nor is it true that an opposition in the sense always follows *but:* "Man shall not live by bread alone, *but* by every word which proceedeth out of the mouth of God."—*Matt.* 4. 4. Here the last clause expresses no opposition, but merely an additional fact. The true sense of *but* when used for *bote*, is *supply*, *more*, *further*, *something additional*, to complete the sense—it may be in opposition to what has preceded or in continuation only. In general, however, the word *but* is appropriately used before a clause of a sentence, intended to introduce a new and somewhat different idea, by way of modifying the sense of the preceding clause. This use is very naturally deduced from the original sense of the word, something further which is to make complete or qualify what has preceded.

Than is a connective of comparison: "John is taller *than* Peter."

Because is a mere compound of *by* and *cause*—by cause. "It is the case of some to contrive some false periods of business, *because they* may seem men of dispatch."—*Bacon of Dispatch.* See also *Apoth.* 7. 6. This is a correct English idiom, Dr. Lowth's criticism to the contrary notwithstanding; but it is now obsolete.

Exclamations.

Exclamations are sounds uttered to express passions and emotions; usually those which are violent or sudden. They are called *interjections*, words *thrown in* between the parts of a sentence. But this is not always the fact, and the name is insignificant. The more appropriate name is *exclamations;* as they are mere irregular sounds, uttered as passion dictates, and not subject to rules.

A few of these sounds however become the customary modes of expressing particular passions and feelings in every nation. Thus in English, joy and surprise and grief are expressed by *oh*, uttered with a different tone and countenance. *Alas* expresses grief or great sorrow—*pish*, *pshaw*, express contempt. Sometimes verbs, names, and attributes are uttered by way of exclamation in a detached manner; as, Hail! Welcome! Bless me!

In two or three instances, exclamations are followed by names and substitutes in the nominative and objective—as, *O thou* in the nominative—*ah me* in the objective. Sometimes *that* follows *O*, expressing a wish—"O that the Lord would guide my ways." But in such cases, we may consider *wish* or some other verb to be understood.

25. Names ending in *ite* from other names, and denoting salts formed by the union of acids with other bodies; as, sulphite, from sulphur.

26. Names ending in *ret* formed from other names, and denoting a substance combined with an alkaline, earthy or metallic base; as, sulphuret, carburet, from sulphur and carbon.

27. Names formed from other names by adding *cy;* as, ensigncy, captaincy, from ensign, captain.

Words are also formed by prefixing certain syllables and words, some of them significant by themselves; others never used but in composition: as, *re*, *pre*, *con*, *mis*, *sub*, *super;* and great numbers are formed by the union of two words; as, bed-room, ink-stand, pen-knife.

Syntax.

Syntax teaches the rules to be observed in the construction of sentences.

A sentence is a number of words arranged in due order, and forming a complete affirmation or proposition. In philosophical language, a sentence consists of a subject and a predicate, connected by an affirmation. Thus, "God is omnipotent," is a complete proposition or sentence, composed of *God*, the subject, *omnipotent*, the predicate or thing affirmed, connected by the verb *is*, which forms the affirmation.

The predicate is often included in the verb; as, "The sun shines."

A simple sentence then contains one subject and one personal verb; that is, the *name* and the *verb;* and without these, no proposition can be formed.

A compound sentence consists of two or more simple sentences, joined by connectives. The divisions of a compound sentence may be called members or clauses.

Sentences are *declaratory*, as, I am writing; the wind blows—*imperative*, as, go, retire, be quiet—*interrogative*, as, where am I? who art thou? or *conditional*, as, if he should arrive.

The rules for the due construction of sentences fall under three heads. *First*, concord or agreement—*Second*, government—*Third*, arrangement and punctuation.

Concord is the agreement of words in construction; as, verbs in person and number with their nominatives; adjectives with nouns, in number, case, and gender.

Government is when one word requires another to be in a particular case, mode or position.

In agreement, the *name* or noun is the controlling word, as it carries with it the verb, the substitute and the attribute. In government, the verb is the controlling word; but names and prepositions have their share of influence also.

RULE I.

A verb must agree with its nominative in number and person.

Examples.

In solemn style. "*Thou hast* loved righteousness."—*Heb.* 1. 9.

"*Thou madest* man a little lower than the angels, and *crownedst* him with glory and honor."—*Heb.* 2. 7.

"*Thou shalt* not steal."—*Commandment.*

"*Art thou* called, being a servant?"—1 *Cor.* 7. 21.

"But *ye are* washed; but *ye are* sanctified."—1 *Cor.* 6. 11.

"*Know ye* not that we shall judge angels?"—1 *Cor.* 6. 3.

"*Do ye* not *know* that the saints shall judge the world?" —1 *Cor.* 1. 2.

In familiar language. "*This is* the word of promise."—*Rom.* 9. 9.

I write; John reads; *Newton was* the chief of astronomers; *we are* astonished at his discoveries; *are you* pleased with the new chimistry? *Emilia has* an elegant form.

NOTE 1.—The nominative to a verb is found by young learners, by asking *who* or *what* does what is affirmed. "Eumenes, a young man of great abilities, inherited a large estate from his father. His father, harassed with competitions, and perplexed with a multiplicity of business, recommended the quiet of a private station." Let the question be asked, Who inherited a large estate? The answer is, *Eumenes*, which is the nominative to the verb *inherited.* Who recommended the quiet of a private station? *His father*, which is therefore the nominative to the verb *recommended.*

NOTE 2.—Let the following rules be observed respecting the position of the nominative :—

I. The nominative usually precedes the verb in declaratory phrases; as, "God created the world;" "the law is a rule of right." But the nominative may be separated from its verb, by a member of a period; as, "*Liberty*, say the fanatic favorers of popular power, *can* only be found in a democracy."—*Anach. ch.* 62.

II. The nominative often follows an intransitive verb, for such a verb can have no object after it, and that position of the nominative creates no ambiguity: thus, "Above it stood the *seraphim*."—*Isa.* 6. "Gradual sinks the *breeze*."—*Thomson.*

III. When the verb is preceded by *here, there, hence, thence, then, thus, yet, so, nor, neither, such, the same, herein, therein, wherein*, and perhaps by some other words, the nominative may follow the verb, especially *be;* as, "here are five men;" "there was a man sent from God;" "hence arise wars;" "thence proceed our vicious habits;" "then came the scribes and Pharisees;" "thus saith the Lord." "Yet required not I bread of the governor."—*Neh.* 5. 18. "So panteth my soul after thee, O Lord."—*Psalm* 42. "Neither hath this man sinned nor his parents."—*John* 9. "Such were the facts;" "the same was the fact." "Herein consists the excellency of the English government."—*Blacks. Com. b.* 1.

IV. When an emphatical attribute introduces a sentence, the nominative may follow the verb; as, "Great is the Lord, glorious are his works, and happy is the man who has an interest in his favor."

V. In certain phrases, which are conditional or hypothetical, the sign of the condition may be omitted, and the nominative placed after the auxiliary; as, "Did he but know my anxiety;" for, if he did but know—"Had I known the fact;" for, if I had known—"Would they consent;" for, if they would, &c.

VI. When the words *whose, his, their, her, mine, your,* &c. precede the verb with a governing word, the nominative may follow the verb; as, "*Out of whose* modifications have been made most complex modes."—*Locke*, 2. 22. 10.

VII. In interrogative sentences, the nominative follows the verb when alone, or the first auxiliary; as, Believest thou? Will he consent? Has he been promoted? The nominative also follows the verb in the imperative mode; as, go thou, "be ye warmed and filled." But after a single verb, the nominative is commonly omitted; as, arise, flee.

NOTE 3.—In poetry, the nominative is often omitted in interrogative sentences, in cases where in prose the omission would be improper; as, "Lives there who loves his pain?"—*Milton*. That is, lives there a man or person.

NOTE 4.—In the answer to a question, the whole sentence is usually omitted, except the name which is the principal subject of the interrogation; as, "Who made the chief discoveries concerning vapor?" *Black*. "Whose theory of respiration is generally received?" *Crawford's*.

NOTE 5.—In poetry, the verb in certain phrases is omitted, chiefly such verbs as express an address or answer; as, "To whom the monarch"—that is, said or replied.

NOTE 6.—When a verb is placed between two nominatives in different numbers, it may agree with either; but generally is made to agree with the first, and this may be considered as preferable; as, "His *meat was* locusts and wild honey." "It [piracy] *is* the remains of the manners of ancient Greece."—*Anach. ch.* 36.

NOTE 7.—Verbs follow the connective *than*, without a nominative expressed; as, "Not that any thing occurs in consequence of our late loss, more afflictive than *was* to be expected."—*Life of Cowper, Let.* 62.

"He felt himself addicted to philosophical speculations, with more ardor than *consisted* with the duties of a Roman and a senator."—*Murphey's Tacitus*, 4. 57.

"All words that lead the mind to any other ideas, than *are* supposed really to exist in that thing."—*Locke*, 2. 25.

These forms of expression seem to be elliptical; "more afflictive than *that which* was to be expected." *That which* or *those which* generally supply the ellipsis.

NOTE 8.—We sometimes see a nominative introducing a sentence, the sense suddenly interrupted, and the nominative left without its intended verb; as, "The name of a procession; what a great mixture of independent ideas of persons, habits, tapers, orders, motions, sounds, does it contain!" &c.—*Locke*, 3. 5. 13. This form of expression is often very striking in animated discourse. The first words being the subject of the discourse, and important, are made to usher in the sentence, to invite attention; and the mind of the speaker, in the fervor of animation, quitting the trammels of a formal arrangement, rushes forward to a description of the thing mentioned, and presents the more striking ideas in the form of exclamation.

NOTE 9.—We have one phrase in which the personal pronoun *me* precedes a verb in the third person—*methinks*, *methought*. Anciently, *him* was used in like manner—*him thuhte*, him thought.—*Alf. Orosius*. And names also; as, "tham halgan Gast was gethuht." It thought (or seemed good) to the Holy Ghost. *Lamb. Sax. Laws*. 21. *Him*, *me* and *tham* are here in the Saxon dative case. *Me thinks*, it seems to me, mihi videtur.

RULE II.

A name, a nominative case or a sentence joined with a participle of the present tense, may stand in construction

without a verb, forming the *case absolute*, or *clause independent*; as, "Jesus had conveyed himself away, *a multitude being in that place*."—*John* 5. 13. Here *multitude*, the name, joined with *being*, stands without a verb.

"By memory we conceive heat or light, yellow or sweet, *the object being removed*."—*Locke*, 2. 10.

"I have, *notwithstanding this discouragement*, attempted a dictionary of the English language."—*Johnson's Preface.*

"Whatever substance begins to exist, it must, *during its existence*, necessarily be the same."—*Locke*, 2. 27. 28.*

"The penalty shall be fine and imprisonment, *any law or custom to the contrary notwithstanding*."

The latter phraseology is peculiar to the technical law style. In no other case does *notwithstanding* follow the sentence. But this position makes no difference in the true construction, which is, "any law or custom to the contrary not opposing"—the real clause independent.

It is very common, when this participle agrees with a number of words, or a whole clause, to omit the whole except the participle; and in this use of *notwithstanding*, we have a striking proof of the value of abbreviations in language. For example; "Moses said, Let no man leave of it till the morning. *Notwithstanding*, they hearkened not to Moses."—*Ex.* 16. 20. Here *notwithstanding* stands without the clause to which it belongs; to complete the sense in words, it would be necessary to repeat the whole preceding clause, or the substance of it—"Moses said, Let no man leave of it until the morning. *Notwithstanding this command of Moses*, or *notwithstanding Moses said that which has been recited*, they hearkened not to Moses."

"Folly meets with success in this world; but it is true, *notwithstanding*, that it labors under disadvantages."—*Porteus, Lecture* 13. This passage at length would read thus—

---

* *During* is the participle of an old verb now obsolete; but its derivatives *endure* and *enduring* are in use. *During* is usually called a *preposition;* but no consideration can justify the practice—it retains its true verbal sense. Equally erroneous is the classification of *notwithstanding* with conjunctions. The two words *not* and *withstanding* are joined indeed without reason; but the resolution of sentences in which this compound is found, demands a restoration of it to its true place and character.

"Folly meets with success in the world; but it is true, *notwithstanding folly meets with success in the world*, that it labors under disadvantages." By supplying what is really omitted, yet perfectly well understood, we learn the true construction; so that *notwithstanding* is a participle always agreeing with a word or clause, expressed or understood, and forming the independent clause, and by a customary ellipsis, it stands alone in the place of that clause.

Such is its general use in the translation of the Scriptures. In the following passage, the sentence is expressed—"Notwithstanding I have spoken unto you."—*Jer.* 35. That is, "This fact, *I have spoken unto you*, not opposing or preventing." Or, in other words, "In opposition to this fact."

It is also very common to use a substitute, *this*, *that*, *which* or *what*, for the whole sentence; as, "Bodies which have no taste, and no power of affecting the skin, may, *notwithstanding this*, [notwithstanding they have no taste, and no power to affect the skin,] act upon organs which are more delicate."—*Fourcroy. Translation.*

I have included in hooks, the words for which *this* is a substitute.

"To account for the misery that men bring on themselves, *notwithstanding that, they do all in earnest pursue happiness,* we must consider how things come to be represented to our desires under deceitful appearances."—*Locke*, 2. 21. 61.

Here *that*, a substitute, is used, and the sentence also for which it is a substitute. This is correct English; but it is usual to omit the substitute, when the sentence is expressed —"*Notwithstanding they do all in earnest pursue happiness.*"

It is not uncommon to omit the participle of the present tense, when a participle of the perfect tense is employed—"The Son of God, while clothed in flesh, was subject to all the frailties and inconveniences of human nature, *sin excepted.*"—*Locke*, 3. 9. That is, *sin being excepted;* the clause independent.

This omission is more frequent when the participle *provided* is used, than in any other case. "In the one case, *provided the facts on which it is founded be sufficiently numerous*, the conclusion is said to be morally certain."—*Campbell on Rhet.* 1. 114. Here *being* is omitted, and the whole clause in italics is independent—"*The facts on which it is founded are sufficiently numerous*, that *being provided*, the conclusion is morally certain." *Provided*, in such cases, is equivalent to *given*, *admitted*, or *supposed*.

"In mathematical reasoning, *provided you are ascertained of the regular procedure of the mind*, to affirm that the conclusion is false, implies a contradiction."—*Ibm*. 134.

In this phrase, *that* may follow *provided*—*provided that*, you are ascertained, &c. as in the case of *notwithstanding*, before mentioned—*that* being a definitive substitute, pointing to the following sentence—*that which follows being provided*.*

It is not uncommon for authors to carry the practice of abridging discourse so far as to obscure the common regular construction. An instance frequently occurs in the omission both of the nominative and the participle in the case independent. For example: "*Conscious of his own weight and importance*, his conduct in parliament would be directed by nothing but the constitutional duty of a peer."—*Junius*, *Let*. 19. Here is no noun expressed to which *conscious* can be referred. We are therefore to supply the necessary words, to complete the construction—"He being conscious"—forming the clause independent.

RULE III.

A sentence, a number of words, or a clause of a sentence, may be the nominative to a verb, in which case the verb is always in the third person of the singular number; as, "*All that is in a man's power in this case*, *is*, only to observe what the ideas are which take their turns in the understanding." *Locke*, 2. 14. Here the whole clause in italics is the nominative to *is*.

"*To attack vices in the abstract, without touching persons*, *may be* safe fighting indeed, but it is fighting with shadows."—*Pope*, *Let*. 48.

"I deny that *men's coming to the use of reason*, *is* the time of their discovery."—*Locke*, 1. 2.

---

* *Provided that*, says Johnson, is an *adverbial expression*, and we sometimes see *provided* numbered among the conjunctions, as its correspondent word is in French. What strange work has been made with grammar!

"*That any thing can exist without existing in space, is* to my mind incomprehensible."—*Darwin, Zoon. sect.* 14. Here the definitive substitute may be transferred to a place next before the verb—"Any thing can exist, without existing in space," that [whole proposition] *is* incomprehensible.

No species of sentences falls under this rule more frequently than those which begin with the infinitive mode. "*To show how the understanding proceeds herein, is* the design of the following discourse."—*Locke*, 1. 4.

This sentence may be inverted without the change of a single word. "The design of the following discourse is to show," &c.

"To fear no eye and to suspect no tongue, *is* the great prerogative of innocence."—*Rambler*. This sentence may be inverted; but according to our idiom, the substitute *it* would precede the verb—"*it* is the great prerogative of innocence to fear," &c. The sentence thus inverted would be good English without the substitute—"The great prerogative of innocence is"—but this alters the sense, and limits the prerogatives of innocence to the one mentioned. By changing *the* to *a*, this inconvenience would be remedied; but in either case the force of the sentiment would be impaired.

"*Our ideas of eternity* can be nothing but an infinite succession of moments of duration."—*Locke*, 2. 17. 16. "*The notion they have of duration*, forces them to conceive," &c.—*Ibm*. In these passages, we observe the nominative or subject of the affirmation consists of several words; for it is not simply *an idea* which is affirmed to be nothing but an infinite succession of moments of duration; but our *idea of eternity*. In like manner, attributes and other words often make an essential part of the nominative. "A wise son maketh a glad father; but a foolish son is the heaviness of his mother." Abstract the name from its attribute, and the propositions cannot always be true—"A son maketh a glad father—a son is the heaviness of his mother."

"He that gathereth in summer is a wise son." Here the predicate belongs to the person described—"He that gathereth in summer." Take away the description, *that gathereth in summer*, and the affirmation ceases to be true or becomes inapplicable.

These sentences or clauses thus constituting the subject of an affirmation, may be termed *nominative sentences*.

RULE IV.

The infinitive mode may be the nominative to a personal verb; as, "*to see* is desirable; *to die* is the inevitable lot of men." Sometimes an attribute is joined with the infinitive; as, "*to be blind* is calamitous." In this case the attribute has no name expressed to which it refers. The proposition is abstract, and applicable to any human being, but not applied to any.

RULE V.

In some cases the imperative verb is used without a definite nominative; as, "I will not take any thing that is thine—*save* only that which the young men have eaten."—*Gen.* 14. 24.

"Israel burned none, *save* Hazor only."—*Josh.* 11. 13.

"I would that all—were such as I am, *except* these bonds." *Acts* 26. 29.

"Our ideas are movements of the nerves of sense, as of the optic nerve in recollecting visible ideas, *suppose* of a triangular piece of ivory."—*Darwin, Zoon. Lect.* 39.

This use of certain verbs in the imperative is very frequent, and there is a peculiar felicity in being thus able to use a verb in its true sense and with its proper object, without specifying a nominative; for the verb is thus left applicable to the first, second or third person. I may save or except, or you may except, or we may suppose. If we examine these sentences, we shall be convinced of the propriety of the idiom; for the ideas require no application to any person whatever.

RULE VI.

When the same thing is affirmed or predicated of two or more subjects, in the singular number, the nominatives are joined by the copulative *and*, with a verb agreeing with them in the plural number; as, "John and Thomas and Peter reside at Oxford." In this sentence, *residence at Oxford* is a predicate common to three persons; and instead of three affirmations—John resides at Oxford, Thomas resides at Oxford, Peter resides at Oxford—the three names are joined by *and*, and one verb in the plural applied to the whole number.

"*Reason* and *truth constitute* intellectual gold, which defies destruction."—*Johnson.* "Why *are whiteness* and *cold-*

ness in snow?"—*Locke*. "Your *lot* and *mine*, in this respect, *have been* very different."—*Cowp. Let.* 38.*

In like manner, names and attributes, representing all the subjects or particulars connected by *and*, must be in the plural number; as, "Plato and Aristotle *were* learned *men; these philosophers* founded the Academic and Peripatetic schools." "The most able *generals* of the last century *were* Frederic of Prussia, the Duke of Marlborough and Prince Eugene." "We look on the *whiteness* and *softness*, produced in the wax, not as *qualities* in the sun, but *effects* produced by its powers."—*Locke*, 2. 8.

When three or more particulars are enumerated, the connective may be omitted, except before the last; as, "The particular bulk, number, figure and motion of the parts of fire or snow are really in them."—*Locke*, 2. 8. The copulative may, however, be inserted where the repetition of it adds to the ideas dignity, force or solemnity.

When terms of number are employed to specify the particulars, the copulative is suppressed; as, "These three then, first the law of God, secondly the law of political societies, thirdly the law of fashion or private censure, are those to which men compare their actions."—*Locke*, 2. 28. 13.

Note 1.—The rule for the use of a plural verb with two or more names in the singular number, connected by *and*, is laid down by critics with too much positiveness and universality. On original principles, all the names, except the first, are in the objective case; for it is probable that *and* contains in it the verb *add*. "John and Thomas and Peter reside at York," on primitive principles, must be thus resolved—"John, add Thomas, add Peter reside at York." But without resorting to first principles, which are now lost or obscured, the use of the singular verb may be justified by considering the verb to be *understood* after each name; and that which is expressed, agreeing only with the last; as, "Nor were the young fellows so wholly lost to a sense of right, as *pride* and *conceit has* since made them affect to be."—*Rambler*, *No.* 97. That is, as pride *has* and as conceit *has*. "Their safety and welfare *is* most concerned."—*Spectator*, *No.* 121. In our best authors the singular verb is frequent in such sentences.†

---

* Is the last example an evidence that *mine* is in the possessive case!!

† This was also a very common practice with the best Greek and Roman writers—"*Mens* enim, et *ratio*, et *consilium* in senibus *est*.—*Cicero. de Senec. ca.* 19.

"Sed etiam ipsius terræ *vis* et *natura delectat*."—*Ibm.* 15.

See *Homer*, *Il.* 1. 61.

See also examples in the Greek Testament.—*Matt.* 12. 31.—13. 42. 50.—16. 17.—28. 1.

What will the hypercritic say to this sentence, "Either sex and every age *was* engaged in the pursuits of industry."—*Gib. Rom. Emp.* ch. 10. Is not the distributive effect of *either* and *every*, such as to demand a singular verb? So in the following: "The judicial and every other power *is* accountable to the legislative."—*Paley. Phil.* 6. 8.

NOTE 2.—When names and pronouns belonging to different persons, are thus joined, the plural pronoun must be of the first person in preference to the second and third, and of the second in preference to the third—*I*, *you* and *he* are represented by *we*; *you* and *he*, by *you*. Pope in one of his letters makes *you* or *I* to be represented by *we* or *you*. "Either you or I *are* not in love with the other." The sentence is an awkward one, and not to be imitated.

RULE VII.

When an affirmation or predicate refers to one subject only among a number, which are separately named in the singular number, the subjects are joined by the alternative *or* or *nor*, with a verb, substitute and name in the singular number; as, "Either John or Peter *was* at the Exchange yesterday; but neither John nor Peter *is* there to-day."

Errors.—"A circle *or* square *are* the same in idea."
Locke, 2. 8.

"But whiteness or redness *are* not in the porphyry."
Ibm.

"Neither of them [Tillotson and Temple] *are* remarkable for precision."—*Blair*.

Substitutes for sentences, whether they represent a single clause, or the parts of a compound sentence, are always in the singular number; as, "*It* is true indeed *that* many have neglected opportunities of raising themselves to honor and to wealth, and rejected the kindest offers of fortune."—*Rambler*, No. 58. Here *it* and *that* refer to the clauses which follow—"*It* is true *that*, many have rejected the kindest offers," &c.

"*It* being unavoidable in discourses, differing from the ordinary received notions, either *to make new words, or to use old words in a new signification*."—*Locke*, 2. 12. 14. Here *it* refers to the two alternative clauses which succeed.

RULE VIII.

Collective or aggregate names, comprehending two or more individuals under a term in the singular number, have a verb or pronoun to agree with them in the singular or plural; as, The council *is* or *are* unanimous; the company *was* or *were* collected; *this* people, or *these* people.

No precise rule can be given to direct, in every case, which number is to be used. Much regard is to be had to usage, and to the unity or plurality of idea. In general, modern practice inclines to the use of the plural verb and pronoun; as may be seen in the daily use of clergy, nobility, court, council, commonalty, audience, enemy, and the like.

"The *clergy* began to withdraw *themselves* from the temporal courts."—*Blackstone's Com. Introduction.*

"Let us take a view of the principal incidents attending the nobility, exclusive of *their* capacity as hereditary counselors of the crown."—*Bl. Com.* 1. 12.

"The commonalty *are* divided into several degrees."

Ibm.

"The enemy *were* driven from their works."

Portuguese Asia, Mickle, 163.

"The chorus *prepare* resistance at his first approach—the chorus *sings* of the battle—the chorus *entertains* the stage."

Johnson's Life of Milton.

"The nobility *are* the pillars to support the throne."

Bl. Com. 1. 2.

Party and *army*, in customary language, are joined with a verb in the singular number. *Constitution* cannot be plural. *Church* may be singular or plural. *Mankind* is almost always plural.

The most common and palpable mistakes in the application of this rule, occur in the use of *sort* and *kind*, with a plural pronoun—*these sort, those kind.* This fault infects the works of our best writers; but these words are strictly singular, and ought so to be used.

When a collective name is preceded by a definitive which clearly limits the sense of the word to an aggregate with an idea of unity, it requires a verb and pronoun to agree with it in the singular number; as, *a* company of troops *was* detached; *a* troop of cavalry *was* raised; *this* people *is* become a great nation; *that* assembly *was* numerous; a "government established by *that* people."—*Bl. Com.* 1. 2.

Yet our language seems to be averse to the use of *it*, as the substitute for names even thus limited by *a*, *this* or *that*. "How long will *that people* provoke me, and how long will it be ere *they* will believe me for all the signs that I have shewed among *them*?"—*Num.* 14. 11. "Liberty should reach every individual of *a people;* as *they* all share one common nature."—*Spectator, No.* 287. In these passages, *it*, in the place of *they*, would not be relished by an English ear; nor is it ever used in similar cases.*

RULE IX.

When the nominative consists of several words, and the last of the names is in the plural number, the verb is commonly in the plural also: "A *part of the exports* consist of raw silk." "The *number of oysters increase*."—*Golds. Anim. Nat.* Vol. 4. ch. 3. "Of which seeming equality we have no other measure, but such as the *train of our ideas have* lodged in our memories."—*Locke*, 2. 14. 21. "The greater *part of philosophers have* acknowledged the excellence of this government."—*Anach.* Vol. 5. p. 272.

NOTE 1.—The practice of using a plural verb after these and similar nominatives, is a proof of the propriety of considering the whole of the words, or the name and its adjuncts, as the actual nominative. Separate the words *part* and *exports* in the first example, and the affirmation of the verb cannot with truth be applied to either; and as the whole must be considered as the nominative, the verb is very naturally connected in number with the last name.

NOTE 2.—When an aggregate amount is expressed by the plural names of the particulars composing that amount, the verb is often in the singular number; as, "There *was* more than a hundred and fifty thousand pounds sterling."—*Mavor's Voyages*, 1.

However repugnant to the principles of grammar, this may seem at first view, the practice is correct; for the affirmation is not made of the individual parts or divisions named, the *pounds*, but of the entire sum or amount. (See this subject more fully explained under Rule XIV.)

The correctness of these rules as universal, is questioned; and in some cases, it may not be vindicable. A *part* of the exports *consists*, seems to be the most correct; yet, a *part* of philosophers *have*, seems to be more agreeable to usage than a *part* of philosophers *has*.

---

* The Romans used a greater latitude in joining plurals with collective names than we can—" Magna *pars* in villis *repleti* cibo vinoque."—*Liv.* 2. 26. Here is a pronoun plural of the masculine gender, agreeing with a noun in the singular, of the feminine gender.

RULE X.

Pronouns or substitutes must agree with the names they represent, in number, gender and person; as,

"Mine *answer* to them that do examine me is *this*."
1 *Cor*. 9. 3.

"*These* are not the *children* of God."—*Rom*. 9. 8.

"Speak to the *children* of Israel, and say to *them*, when *ye* come into the land whither I bring *you*."—*Num*. 15. 18.

"This is the heir; come, let us kill *him*, and let us seize on *his* inheritance."—*Matt*. 21. 38.

"*Esther* put on *her* royal apparel—*she* obtained favor in his sight—then the king said unto *her*."—*Esth*. 5.

"A river went out of Eden to water the garden, and *it* was parted."—*Gen*. 2. 10.

"The *woman whom* thou gavest to be with me."
Gen. 3. 12.

"*Ignatius, who* was bishop of Antioch, conversed with the apostles."—*Paley's Evid*. Sect. 3.

"A *letter, which* is just received, gives us the news."

"O *thou who rulest* in the heavens."

Who and *whom* are exclusively the substitutes for persons; *whose* is of all genders, and as correctly applied to things as to persons.

"The question *whose solution* I require."—*Dryden*.

"That forbidden *fruit whose* mortal taste."—*Milton*.

"A *system whose* imagined suns."—*Goldsmith*.

"These are the charming agonies of *love*
Whose miseries delight."—*Thom*.

It, though neuter, is used as the substitute for *infant* or *child;* the distinction of sex in the first period of life being disregarded.

Formerly *which* was used as a substitute for *persons;* as appears from old authors, and especially in the vulgar version of the scriptures—"mighty *men which* were of old." But this use of the word is entirely discarded. *Which* however represents persons, when a question is asked or discrimination intended; as, *which* of the men was it; I know not *which* person it was.

Who is sometimes used as the substitute for things, but most unwarrantably: "The countries who."—*Davenant on Rev.* 2. 13. "The towns who."—*Hume, Contin.* 11. ch. 10. "The faction or party who."—Equally faulty is the use of *who* and *whom* for brutes: "The birds who—"

The use of *it* for a sentence, seems to have given rise to a very vague application of the word in phrases like this: How shall I contrive *it* to attend court? How fares *it* with you? But such phrases, whatever may have given rise to them, are used chiefly in familiar colloquial language, and are deemed inelegant in any other style.

A more justifiable use of *it* is seen in this sentence: "But it is not this real essence that distinguishes them into species; *it* is men who range them into sorts," &c.—*Locke*, 3. 6. 36.

Here *it* is in the singular, though referring to *men* in the plural. The cause or origin of this, in our language as in others, may perhaps be found in the disposition of the mind to combine the particular agents employed in performing an act, into a single agent. The *unity* of the *act* or *effect* seems to predominate in idea, and control the grammatical construction of the substitute.

RULE XI.

In compound sentences, a single substitute, *who, which* or *that*, employed to introduce a new clause, is the nominative to the verb or verbs belonging to that clause, and to others connected with it; as, "The thirst after curiosities, *which* often draws contempt."—*Rambler, No.* 83. "He *who suffers* not his faculties to lie torpid has a chance of doing good."—*Ibm.* "They *that are* after the flesh, do mind the things of the flesh."—*Rom.* 8. 5. "Among those *who are* the most richly *endowed* by nature, and [are] *accomplished* by their own industry, how few are there whose virtues are not obscured by the ignorance, prejudice or envy of their beholders!"—*Spec. No.* 255.

In a few instances, the substitute for a sentence or a clause, is introduced as the nominative to a verb *before* the sentence or clause, which it represents; as, "There was therefore, *which is* all that we assert, a course of life pursued by them, different from that which they before led."—*Paley, Evid. ch.* 1. Here *which* is the representative of the whole of the last part of the sentence, and its natural position is *after* that clause.

The substitute *what* combines in itself the offices of two substitutes, which, if expressed, would be the nominatives to two verbs, each in distinct subsequent clauses; as, "Add to this, *what*, from its antiquity *is* but little known, *has* the recommendation of novelty."—*Hermes, pref.* 19. Here *what* stands for *that, which*—and the two following verbs have no other nominative.

This use of *what* is not very common. But *what* is very frequently used as the representative of two cases—one, the objective after a verb or preposition, and the other, the nominative to a subsequent verb. Examples:

"I heard *what* was said." "He related *what* was seen."

"We do not so constantly love *what* has done us good."
Locke, 2. 20. 14.

"Agreeable to *what* was afterwards directed."
Bl. Com. b. 2. *ch.* 3.

"Agreeable to *what* hath been mentioned."
Prideaux, p. 2, 6, 3.

"There is something so overruling in *whatever* inspires us with awe."—*Burke on the Sublime*, 304. In these sentences *what* includes an object after a verb or preposition, and a nominative to the following verb. "I have heard *that, which* was said."

RULE XII.

When a new clause is introduced into a sentence with two pronouns, or with one pronoun and a name, one of them is the nominative to the verb, and the other is governed by the verb or a preposition in the objective case, or by a noun in the possessive; as, "Locke, *whom* there is no *reason* to *suspect* of favoring idleness, has advanced."—*Ramb.* 89. Here *reason* is the nominative to *is*, and *whom* is governed by *suspect*.

"Take thy only son Isaac, *whom thou* lovest."—*Gen.* 22. Here are two substitutes, one the nominative to the verb, and the other governed by it in the objective.

"God is the Sovereign of the universe, whose majesty ought to fill us with awe, *to whom* we owe all possible reverence, and *whom* we are bound to obey."

It is not unusual to see in periods, a third clause introduced within a second, as a second is within the first, each with a distinct substitute for a nominative; as, "Those modifications of any simple idea, *which, as* has been said, I call simple modes, are distinct ideas."—*Locke*, 2. 13.

Involution to this extent may be used with caution, without embarrassing a period; but beyond this, if ever used, it can hardly fail to occasion obscurity. Indeed the third member included in a second, must be very short, or it will perplex the reader.

Substitutes are sometimes made to precede their principals; thus, "When a man declares in autumn, when he is eating *them*, or in spring, when there are *none*, that he loves *grapes*."—*Locke*, 2. 20. But this arrangement is usually awkward and seldom allowable.

RULE XIII.

When there are antecedents in different persons, to which a nominative pronoun refers, the pronoun and verb following may agree with either, though usage may sometimes offer a preference; as, "I am the Lord that make all things; that stretch forth the heavens alone; that spread abroad the earth," &c.—*Isa.* 44. Here *I* and *Lord* are of different persons, and *that* may agree with either. If it agrees with *I*, the verbs must be in the first person; "I am the Lord *that make*." If *that* agrees with *Lord* in the third person, the verb must be in the third person; "I am the Lord that *maketh*." But in all cases the following verbs should all be of the same person.

RULE XIV.

The definitive adjectives, *this* and *that*, the only attributes which are varied to express number, must agree in number with the names to which they refer; as, this city, that church; these cities, those churches.

This and *that* are often used as substitutes for a name in the singular number, which is omitted; but the same name in the plural immediately follows after a connective; as in this example, "The mortality produced by *this* and other *diseases*."—*Life of Washington*, 3, 6. That is, by this disease and other diseases. The sentence may be varied thus—by this disease and others—but the first form is the most common, and it occasions no obscurity.

Other adjectives and participles, used as adjectives, are joined to the names which they qualify without inflection; as, a wise man, wise men; an amiable child, or amiable children; a received truth, or received truths; a shining character, or shining characters.

Adjectives are often used as substitutes for the names of men and things which they describe by their qualities; as, *few* were present; the *wise* are respected; the *bravest* are not always victorious.

In this character, attributes take a plural form, and are qualified by other attributes; as, the *goods* of fortune, two *finites* or *infinites*, *universals*, *generals*—the *chief good*, a *happy few;* "the *extraordinary great*."—*Burke on the Sublime*, 304. "The *blue profound*."—*Akenside.*

When nouns are joined by a copulative, an adjective preceding the first, is applied to the others without being repeated; as, "From *great* luxury and licentiousness"—here *great* belongs to licentiousness as well as to luxury. "Converted to *strict* sobriety and frugality of manners."—*Enfield.*

When a period of time is described by its component parts or portions, specified by plural names, an attribute in the singular number, or denoting unity, is often joined to the plural names of the parts; as, "I have not been to London *this five years;*" "an election regularly takes place *every seven years;*" that is, in every *single period* or *term* of seven years.

This idiom is explainable on very natural principles. The whole portion of time has no name, and we are therefore obliged to express our idea of it by something equivalent, which, in this instance, are the parts *five* and *seven years.* The mind is fixed upon the entire period, and while the lips utter the name of the parts, the mind naturally considers the whole as a *unity*, and overlooking the several portions, attaches the attribute to that *unity* or whole period. Hence originated the customary abbreviation of *twelve months*, into a *twelvemonth; seven nights* into *se'night; fourteen nights* into a *fortnight;* and hence dozen, hundred, &c. admit the definitive *a.*

To the same cause probably may be ascribed the common phrases, *twenty pound*, *thirty foot*, and others similar; in which a whole quantity or space, for which we have no appropriate name, is described by smaller portions equivalent. The idea of *unity*, in all such cases, being predominant, and the only one which the speaker wishes to communicate, is very apt to control the language, and occasion the omission of the sign of the plural even when it is necessary to the very purpose intended.

Hence we learn the cause why enumeration and addition of numbers are usually expressed in the singular number; two and two *is* four; seven and nine *is* sixteen; that is, the *sum* of seven and nine *is* sixteen. But modern usage inclines to reject the use of the verb in the singular number, in these and similar phrases.

RULE XV.

Adjectives are usually placed before the nouns to which they belong; as, a *wise* prince; an *obedient* subject; a *pious* clergyman, a *brave* soldier.

Exception 1. When some word or words are dependent on an attribute, it follows the name; as, knowledge *requisite* for a statesman; furniture *convenient* for a family.

Exception 2. When an attribute becomes a title, or is emphatically applied to a name, it follows it; as, Charles, the Great; Henry, the First; Lewis, the Gross; Wisdom incomprehensible.

Exception 3. Several attributes belonging to the same name, may precede or follow the name to which they belong; as, a learned, wise and martial prince, or a prince learned, wise and martial.

Exception 4. The verb *be* often separates the name from its attribute; as, war *is* expensive; gaming *is* ruinous.

Exception 5. An emphatical attribute is often used to introduce a sentence, in which case it precedes the name which it qualifies, and sometimes at a considerable distance; as, "*Great* is the Lord;" *auspicious* will be that event; *fortunate* is that young man who escapes the snares of vice.

Exception 6. The attribute *all* may be separated from its noun by *the*, which never precedes it in construction; as, "all the nations of Europe." *Such* and *many* are separated from names by *a;* as, "such a character is rare;" "many a time."

All adjectives are separated from names by *a* when preceded by *so* and *as*—*so* rich a dress—*as* splendid a retinue; and they are separated by *a* or *the*, when preceded by *how* and *however;* as, "how distinguished *an* act of bravery,"—"how brilliant the prize." "However just the complaint;" and by *too;* as, *too* costly *a* sacrifice.

The word *soever* may be interposed between the attribute and the name; "how clear soever this idea of infinity"—"how remote soever it may seem."—*Locke.*

Double is separated from its noun by *the;* as "double the distance,"—*the,* in such cases, never preceding *double.* But *a* precedes *double,* as well as other attributes.

All and *singular* or *every* precede *the* before the name in these phrases. "All and singular the articles, clauses and conditions." "All and every of the articles"—phrases of the law style.

RULE XVI.

Adjectives belong to verbs in the infinitive mode; as, "to see is pleasant,"—"to ride is more agreeable than to walk;" "to calumniate is detestable."

Sometimes the attribute belongs to the infinitive in union with another attribute or a name; as, "to be blind is unfortunate;" "to be a coward is disgraceful." Here the attribute *unfortunate* is the attribute of the first clause, *to be blind,* &c.

RULE XVII.

Adjectives belong to sentences, or whole propositions: Examples:

"*Agreeable* to this, *we read of names being blotted out of God's book.*"—*Burder's Oriental Customs,* 375.

What is agreeable to this! The answer is found in the whole of the last clause of the sentence.

"Antiochus—to verify the character prophetically given of him by Daniel—*acted the part of a vile and most detestable person, agreeable* to what hath been aforementioned of him."—*Prideaux, part* 2, *b.* 3.

"Her majesty signified her pleasure to the admiral that as soon as *he had left a squadron for Dunkirk, agreeable* to what he had proposed, he should proceed with the fleet."—*Burchet, Nav. Hist.* 439.

"*Independent* of his person, *his nobility, his dignity, his relations and friends may be urged,*" &c.—*Guthrie's Quinctilian.*

"No body can doubt but that *these ideas of mixed modes are made by a voluntary collection of ideas put together in the mind, independent* from any original patterns in nature."—*Locke*, 3, 5.

"Whereupon God was provoked to anger, and put them in mind how, *contrary* to his directions, *they had spared the Canaanites*."—*Whiston's Josephus, b.* 5, *ch.* 2.

"Greece, which had submitted to the arms, in her turn, subdued the understandings of the Romans, and *contrary* to that which in these cases commonly happens, *the conquerors adopted the opinions and manners of the conquered*."—*Enfield, Hist. Phil. b.* 3, 1.

"This letter of Pope Innocent enjoined the *payment of tithes to the parsons of the respective parishes, where any man inhabited, agreeable* to what was afterwards directed by the same Pope in other countries."—*Blacks. Comment. b.* 2, *ch.* 3.

"*Agreeable* to this, we find *some of the Anglo-Saxon ladies were admitted into their most august assemblies*."—*Henry, Hist. Brit. b.* 2, *ch.* 7, and *b.* 4, *ch.* 1, *sec.* 4.

"As all language is composed of significant words variously combined, *a knowledge of them is necessary, previous* to our acquiring an adequate idea of language."—*Encyclop. art. Grammar.*

"*His empire could not be established, previous* to the institution of pretty numerous societies."—*Smellie, Ph. Nat. Hist.* 339.

"*Suitable* to this, we find that *men, speaking of mixed modes, seldom imagine*," &c.—*Locke*, 3, 5, 11.

"*No such original convention of the people was ever actually held, antecedent* to the existence of civil government in that country."—*Pal. Phil. b.* 6, *ch.* 3.

NOTE.—Writers and critics, misapprehending the true construction of these and similar sentences, have supposed the attribute to belong to the verb, denoting the *manner of action*. But a little attention to the sense of such passages will be sufficient to detect the mistake. For instance, in the example from Enfield, the attribute *contrary* cannot qualify the verb *adopted;* for the conquerors did not adopt the opinions of the conquered in a *manner contrary* to what usually happens—the *manner of the act* is not the thing affirmed, nor does it come into consideration. The sense is this, the fact, that *the conquerors adopted the opinions and manners of the conquered*, was *contrary* to what commonly happens in like cases. The attribute belongs to the whole sentence or proposition. The same explanation is applicable to every similar sentence.

In consequence of not attending to this construction, our hypercritics, who are very apt to distrust popular practice, and substitute their own rules for customary idioms, founded on common sense, have condemned this use of the attribute, and authors, suffering themselves to be led astray by these rules, often use an adverb in the place of an adjective.

"The greater part of philosophers have acknowledged the excellence of this government, which they have considered, some *relatively* to society, and others as it has relation to the general system of nature." *Anach. ch.* 62.

"The perceptions are exalted into a source of exquisite pleasure *independently* of every particular relation of interest."
Studies of Nature, 12.

In the first of these examples, *relatively* is used very awkwardly for *as relative*, or *as relating*, or *as it relates*, or *in relation;* for the word has a direct reference to *government*.

In the second example, *independently* is used as if it had been intended to modify the verb *exalt*—the perceptions are *independently exalted*. But the *manner of exalting* is not the thing described. It is not that the perceptions are exalted in an independent manner, nor in a manner independent of a relation to interest: but the fact, that the *perceptions are exalted into a source of exquisite pleasure*, is independent of every relation of interest. Equally faulty is the following sentence:

"*Agreeably* to this law, children are bound to support their parents."
Paley, Phil.

Johnson, in his life of Thomson, has this sentence—"Why the dedications are to winter and the other seasons, *contrarily* to custom, left out in the collected works, the reader may imagine." It is strange that a man of this author's discernment should not perceive that it was not the *manner* of leaving out, which he was stating, but the *fact*—The dedications to winter and other seasons are left out, which fact or thing is *contrary* to custom.* I do not recollect this use of *contrary* in any other passage; though it is certainly as vindicable as the use of any other modifier under like circumstances; for in every case it entirely perverts the sense of the passage. In this instance, the use of the adverb instead of the attribute, may have been an oversight.

In this kind of phrase, I have even seen an instance of the participle *according* converted into *accordingly*. See this word explained in the sequel. I have not seen *priorly* used for *prior*, in like sentences—"Priorly to his arrival in England"—Nor *anteriorly*, *posteriorly*, *exteriorly*, *inferiorly*, nor *adjacently* or *contiguously* to the river; and the like barbarisms; but *subsequently*, *antecedently*, *consistently*, *conformably*, are frequent in our best authors. "To do what we will, *consistently* with the interests of the community, is civil liberty." *Paley, Phil.* 6. 5. This is not English; for it is not the *manner of doing*, but the *thing done*, which must be *consistent* with the public interest. A misapprehension of the true import and construction of such passages, has done immense mischief to the language.

---

* The idiom in question has resulted from that disposition to abridge the number of words used in communicating ideas, which I have repeatedly mentioned; the effects of which are among the prime excellencies of every language.

In the place of this awkward phrase, in which an adverb is made to precede *to*, I would use a noun with a preposition. Instead of "In considering sound *relatively to* its external cause"—I would use *in relation*—"In considering sound *in relation* to its external cause." "This was one in *conformity with*," not *conformably to*. He could not *in consistency with*, not *consistently with*. *In agreement or accordance with*; not *agreeably to*.

These forms of expressions are genuine and more elegant and correct English; but in most instances, the adjectives, *relative*, *conformable*, *consistent*, *agreeable*, referring to a clause in the sentence, would be equally correct.

RULE XVIII.

Adjectives are used to modify the action of verbs, and to express the qualities of things in connection with the action by which they are produced. Examples:

"*Open* thine hand *wide*.—*Deut*. 15. 17.

We observe in this passage, that *wide*, the attribute of hand, has a connection with the verb *open*; for it is not "open thy *wide hand*;" but the attribute is supposed to be the *effect* of the act of opening. Nor can the modifier, *widely*, be used; for it is not simply the *manner* of the act which is intended; but the *effect*.

"Let us write *slow* and *exact*."—*Guthrie, Quinct*. 2. 375.

We might perhaps substitute *slowly* for slow, as describing only the manner of writing; but *exactly* cannot be substituted for *exact*; for this word is intended to denote the *effect* of writing, in the correctness of what is written. The attribute expresses the idea with a happy precision and brevity.

As this is one of the most common, as well as most beautiful idioms of our language, which has hitherto escaped due observation, the following authorities are subjoined to illustrate and justify the rule.

"We could hear distinctly the bells—which sounded sweetly *soft* and *pensive*."—*Chandler's Travels, ch*. 2.

"A southerly wind succeeded blowing *fresh*."—*Ib. v*. 2. 3.

"His provisions were grown very *short*."

Burchet's Nav. Hist. 357.

"When the caloric exists *ready* combined with the water of solution."—*Lavoisier. Trans. ch*. 5.

"The purest clay is that which burns *white*."

Encyc. art Chimistry.

"*Bray*, to pound or grind *small*."—*Johnson's Dict*.

"When death lays *waste* thy house."—*Beattie's Mins.*

"All which looks *very little like* the steady hand of nature."—*Pal. Phil. ch.* 5.

"Magnesia feels *smooth;* calcarious earths feel *dry;* lithomarga feels very *greasy*, or at least *smooth;* yet some feel *dry* and *dusty*."—*Kirwan. vol.* 1, 12. 189.

"By this substance, crystals and glasses are colored *blue*."—*Chaptal, Trans.* 299.

"There is an apple described in Bradley's work, which is said to have one side of it a sweet fruit, which boils *soft;* and the other side, a *sour* fruit, which boils *hard*."

Darwin, Phytol. 105.

"Drink *deep* or taste not the Pierian spring."—*Pope.*

"Heaven opened *wide* her ever during gates."

Milton, P. L. 7.

"The victory of the ministry cost them *dear*."

Hume, Contin. 11.9.

"And *just* as *short* of reason he must fall."—*Pope.*

"*Thick* and more *thick* the steely circle grows."

Hoole's Tasso, b. 8.

"Ancus marched *strait* to fidenæ."—*Hook. Rom. Hist.* 1. 6.

"The cakes eat *short* and *crisp*."—*Vicar of Wakefield.*

"A steep ascent of steps which were cut *close* and *deep* into the rocks."—*Hampton's Polybius*, 2, 65.

"It makes the plow go *deep* or *shallow*."—*Enc. art. Agri.*

"The king's ships were getting *ready*."—*Lusiad*, 1. 91.

"After growing *old* in attendance."—*Spect. No.* 282.

"The sun shineth *watery*."—*Bacon, Apoph.*

"*Soft* sighed the flute."—*Thomson, Spring.*

"I made him *just* and *right*."—*Milton*, 3. 98.

"He drew not *nigh* unheard."—*Ibm.* 645.

"When the vowel of the preceding syllable is pronounced *short*."—*Murray's Grammar.*

"Here grass is cut *close* and gravel rolled *smooth*. Is not that trim?"—*Boswell, Johnson*, 3.

"*Slow* tolls the village clock—*deep* mourns the turtle."

Beattie's Minstrel.

"If you would try to live *independent*."—*Pope, Let.*

"He obliged the Nile to run *bloody* for your sakes."*—*Whiston's Josephus*, 3. 5.

"Correct the heart and all will go *right*."—*Porteus, Lect.* 3.

The poets sometimes use adjectives in this manner, when modifiers would express the idea. Sometimes they are induced to it by the measure; and not unfrequently by the obvious superiority of the attribute in expressing the idea with force and precision.

When two qualifying words are wanted, the latter may be an adjective, though applied to a verb; as, "He beat time *tolerably exact*."—*Golds. An. Nat. ch.* 12.

"The air will be found diminished in weight *exactly equal* to what the iron has gained."—*Lavoisier, ch.* 3.

"Horses are sold *extremely dear*."—*Golds.*

"And *greatly independent* lived."—*Thom. Spring.*

"This was applying a just principle *very ill*."—*Vattel. Trans.* 2. 7.

It will be remarked that we have no adverbial form of the attribute in the comparative and superlative degrees, except that of *more* and *most*, *less* and *least*, prefixed. But we use the adjectives with the regular terminations, in these degrees, to qualify verbs. Examples :—

"To hands that *longer* shall the weapon wield."
Hoole, Tas. 7.

——"Then the pleasing force
Of nature and her kind parental care,
Worthier I'd sing." *Akenside, Pl. of Im.* 1. 323.

"So while we taste the fragrance of the rose,
Glows not her blush the *fairer?*" *Ibm.* 2. 77.

"When we know our strength, we shall the *better* know what to undertake with hopes of success."—*Locke*, 1. 6.

"And he that can *most* inform or *best* understand him, will certainly be welcomed."—*Rambler, No.* 99.

"How much *nearer* he approaches to his end."

"I have dwelt the *longer* on the discussion of this point."
Junius, Let. 17.

---

* "*Cruentam* etiam fluxisse aquam Albanam, quidam auctores erant." —*Liv. lib.* 27. 11. Some authors related that the Alban river ran *bloody*.

"The next contains a spirited command, and should be pronounced much *higher*."—*Murray's Grammar*.*

"Leviathan, which God of all his works
Created *hugest* that swim th' ocean's stream."
Milton, 1. 201.

"But mercy first and last shall *brightest* shine."—*Ib*. 3. 134.

"Such opinions as seemed to approach *nearest* [to] the truth."—*Enfield. Hist. Phil.* 2. 59.

"Her smiles, amid the blushes, *lovelier* show;
Amid her smiles, her blushes *lovelier* glow."
Hoole. Tasso. b. 15.

Authors, misguided by Latin rules, and conceiving that every word which is used to qualify a verb, must be an *adverb*, have pronounced many of the passages here recited and similar ones to be incorrect—and in such as are too well established to bear censure, they call the adjective an *adverb*. Were it not for this influence in early education, which impresses a notion that all languages must be formed with the like idioms, we should never have received an idea that the same word may not modify a noun, an adjective and a verb.

So far are the words here used from being adverbs, that they cannot be changed into adverbs, without impairing the beauty, weakening the force or destroying the meaning of the passages. Let the sentences be put to the test—Magnesia feels smoothly—the cakes eat shortly and crisply—the apples boil softly or hardly—glows not her blush the more fairly. Every English ear rejects this alteration at once—the sentences become nonsense. Nor can the attribute be separated from the verb—"Amid her smiles, her blushes, being lovelier, glow"—this is not the sense—nor will it answer to say, "her lovelier blushes glow"—this is not the idea. The sense is, that the attribute expressed by *lovelier*, is not only a quality of *blushes*, but a quality derived, in a degree, from the action of the verb, *glow*.

Thus, clay burns *white*—objects may be seen *double*—may rise *high*—fall *low*—grow *strait*, or *thick*, or *thin*, or

* In remarking upon such phrases as "The vices which enter *deeper* or *deepest* into the soul," Murray says, *deeper* and *deepest* should be *more deeply*, *most deeply*. It is recommended to change the adjective in the two passages I have cited—"The vowel of the preceding syllable is pronounced *shortly*"—"The next should be pronounced much *more highly!*" This alteration will put his rule to the test

fat, or *lean*—one may speak *loud*—the sun shines *clear*—the *finer* a substance is pulverized—to grow *wiser*, to plunge *deeper*, spread *wider*—and similar expressions without number, constitute a well established idiom, as common as it is elegant.*

The attributes thus connected with verbs may easily be distinguished from those which merely qualify names, the latter being separable from the verb. Thus,

"Our great enemy
All uncorruptible, would, on his throne,
Sit *unpolluted*." *Milton, P. L.* 2

Here *unpolluted* has no effect at all upon the verb; but may be separated from it, and carried into the first line without altering the sense.

"And the birds sing *concealed*." *Thomson.*

"He roved *uncertain* through the dusky shade."—*Hoole.*

RULE XIX.

Some adjectives are used to modify the sense of others and of participles; as a *very clear* day, *red hot* iron, a *more* or *most* excellent character. "Without coming *any* nearer."—*Locke; more* pressing necessity, *most* grating sound, "a *closer* grained wood."—*Lavoisier. Trans.*

"*Full* many a gem with purest ray serene."—*Gray.*

"Some deemed him *wondrous* wise."—*Beattie's Minstrel.*

---

* The Roman writers availed themselves of the same idiom.—"Ob multitudinem familiarum, quæ gliscebat *immensum*."
Tacitus. An. lib. 4. 27.

"Fabius—Arpos primum institit oppugnare—quæ maxime neglectam custodiam vidit, ea *potissimum* adgredi statuit."—*Liv. lib.* 24. 46.

How much more impressive is the description which Tacitus here gives of an alarming insurrection of slaves, than if he had used the adverb! "A multitude of slaves which was increasing and growing immense!" this is giving to prose the rhetorical sublimity of verse. It is giving the verb its full effect, and at the same time, attaching the attribute to that effect.

In the word *potissimum*, in Livy, as in many others, we see the effect of not understanding this elegant use of attributes. Such words are marked in dictionaries as adverbs! How would Tully, Livy and Tacitus smile to see their native tongue, disfigured with accents to distinguish adverbs from adjectives, in a modern dictionary of the language! It is a just remark of Mr. Tooke, that all words which critics have not understood, they have thrown into the *common sink of adverbs.*

In these expressions the last attribute belongs more immediately to the noun expressing its quality—and the *first* attribute qualifies the *second*.

Not unfrequently two attributes are used to modify a third, or the principal one; as, "The manner in which external force acts upon the body is *very little* subject to the will."—*Rambler, No.* 78.

RULE XX.

Adjectives are used to qualify the sense of adverbs; as, a city was *very* bravely defended; the soldiers were *most* amply rewarded; a donation *more* beneficially bestowed; a house *less* elegantly furnished; a man the *least* peaceably disposed.

In these phrases, the modifier attends the verb or participle to mark the *manner* or *character* of the act or affirmation; and the attribute attends the modifier to mark the degree or extent of that manner of character.

For a like purpose of defining the *degrees* of quality and modification, we make great use of *much* before attributes of the comparative and superlative degrees; as, a prince *much* more humanely disposed; or much less martially inclined.

We have a few other words which are often used to modify attributes as well as verbs—as, a *little*, a *great deal*, a *trifle*. "Many letters from persons of the best sense—do not a *little* encourage me."—*Spectator*, 124. "It is a great deal better;" "a *trifle* stronger;" the last of which expressions is colloquial.

RULE XXI.

The adjectives *each*, *every*, *either* and *neither*, have verbs and substitutes agreeing with them in the singular number; as,

"*Each one was* a head of the house of *his* fathers."
Josh. 22. 14.

"*Every one* that *findeth* me, shall slay me."—*Gen.* 4. 14.

"And take every man *his* censer."—*Num.* 16. 17.

"Nadab and Abihu took *either* of them his censer."
Lev. 10. 1.

"*Neither* of the ways of separation, real or mental, *is* compatible to pure space."—*Locke*, 2. 13.

Errors.—"Let each esteem others better than *themselves.*" It ought to be *himself.*

"There are bodies, *each* of which *are* so small." It ought to be *is.*—*Locke*, 2. 8.

NOTE.—A plural verb, which affirms something of a number of particulars, is often followed by a distributive which assigns the affirmation to the particular objects or individuals. Thus, "If metals have, *each* a peculiar earth"—Hence we may consider *each* as the nominative to *has* understood—"If metals have, if each metal has a peculiar earth." There is no other way of resolving the phrase. This manner of expression is common, though quite useless—as the last clause, "if each metal has"—is sufficient. It has not the merit of an abbreviation. This phrase, "Let us love one another," is of a similar construction, but it is not easy to find a substitute of equal brevity.

RULE XXII.

Names of measure or dimension stand without a governing word, followed by an adjective; as, "a wall seven feet high and two feet thick"—"a carpet six yards wide"—"a line sixty fathoms long"—"a kingdom five hundred miles square"—"water ten feet deep."

"An army forty thousand strong," is a similar phrase.

NOTE.—Double comparatives and superlatives, *most straitest, most highest,* being improper and useless, are not to be used. The few which were formerly used are obsolete. *Worser,* a mistake in spelling *wyrsa,* is obsolete; but *lesser,* a mistake for *lessa,* is still used, as well as its abbreviation, *less.* We never say, the less Asia, but lesser.

The superlative form of certain adjectives, which, in the positive degree, contain the utmost degree of the quality, as *extremest, chiefest,* is improper and obsolete. But authors indulge in a most unwarrantabe license of annexing comparison to attributes whose negative sense precludes increase or diminution; as in these sentences, "These are more formidable and *more impassable* than the mountains."—*Golds. An. Nat. ch.* 2. "This difficulty was rendered still *more insurmountable* by the licentious spirit of our young men."—*Murphy, Tacit. Orat.* 35. "The contradictions of impiety are still *more incomprehensible.*"—*Massillon, Serm. to the Great.*

Similar to these are numerous expressions found in good authors—*more impossible, more indispensable, less universal, more uncontrollable;* and others, in which the sign of comparison is not only improper, but it rather enfeebles the epithet; for the word itself expressing the full extent of the idea, ought to bear some emphasis, which, if a qualifying word is prefixed, will naturally be transferred to that word.*

* This effect may proceed also from another consideration. If the attribute alone is used, its sense precludes the idea of increase or diminu-

In a few instances, this usage seems to be too well established to be altered, and particularly in the use of *more* and *most*, *less* and *least perfect*. In general, it would indicate more precision of thought to apply a term of *diminution* to the *affirmative* attribute—*less possible*, *less surmountable*, *less controllable*; rather than a term of *increase* to a *negative* attriоute.

Note 2.—In English, two names are frequently united to form a new name; as, *earth-worm*, *drill-plow*, *ink-stand*, *book-case*. In some cases, these compounds are by custom effectually blended into one term; in other cases, they are separated into their component parts by a hyphen; in other cases, words are united, and the first term forms a sort of occasional attribute to the second; as, *family-use* or *family-consumption*.

Note 3.—From a disposition to abridge the number of words in discourse, we find many expressions which are not reducible to any precise rule, formed at first by accident or ellipsis; such are *at first*, *at last*, *at best*, *at worst*, *at most*, *at least*, *at farthest*, *at the utmost*. In these expressions there may have been an ellipsis of some name; but they are well established, brief and significant.

Note 4.—We have certain attributes which follow a verb, and a name to which they belong, but never precede the noun. Such are *adry*, *afeared*, *afraid*, *alone*, *alike*, *aware*, *akin*, *alive*, *asleep*, *awake*, *athirst*, *aloft*, *aghast*, *afloat*, *askew*, *ashamed*, *pursuant*, *plenty*, *worth*; to which may be added *amiss*, *aground*, *ashore*, *aside*, and a few others which may be used as attributes or modifiers. We say, one is *adry*, *ashamed*, *alive* or *awake*. But never an *adry* person, an *ashamed* child, &c. We say, "A proclamation was issued *pursuant* to advice of council." But we can in no case place *pursuant* before the noun.

Plenty, as an attribute, has not yet been recognized by critics; but critics do not make language, nor can they reject what a nation has made. *Plenty* is constantly used as an adjective after a name in colloquial language, and is found in our best writers; to cavil at this usage, therefore, is as idle as it is impertinent.

"The sea muscle is perhaps the most *plenty*."—*Golds. An. Nature.*

"Where shrubs are *plenty* and water scarce."—*Ibm.* 2. 21.

"In those provinces where wood was *plenty*."

Rycaut Garcillaso, 923.

"This species is more *plenty* in France."—*Encyc.*, *Art. Loxia.*

"Provisions are *plenty* and living cheap."—*Ibm.*, *Art. Adrianople.*

Worth not only follows the name which it qualifies, but is followed by a name denoting price or value; as, a book *worth* a *dollar* or a *guinea*—it is well *worth* the money—"It is *worth observation*."—*Beloe's Herodotus*, *Erato*, 98. If a substitute is used after *worth*, it must be in the objective case. *It is worth them* or *it*.

But *worthy*, the derivative of *worth*, follows the usual construction of attributes, and may precede the name it qualifies; as, a worthy man.

---

tion; it expresses all that can be expressed. But admit comparison, and it ceases to express the utmost extent of the quality.

RULE XXIII.

One name signifying the same thing with another, or descriptive of it, may be in apposition to it; that is, may stand in a like character or case, without an intervening verb; as, Paul, the apostle; John, the baptist; Newton, the philosopher; Chatham, the orator and statesman.

NOTE 1.—In the following sentence, a name in the plural stands in apposition to two names in the singular, joined by an alternative. "The terms of our law will hardly find words that answer them in the *Spanish* or *Italian*, no scanty *languages*."—*Locke*, 3. 5. 8.

NOTE 2.—Names are not unfrequently set in apposition to sentences; as, "Whereby if a man had a positive idea of infinite, either duration or space, he could add two infinites together; nay, make one infinite infinitely bigger than another; *absurdities* too gross to be confuted."—*Locke*, 2. 17. 20. Here the *absurdities* are the whole preceding propositions.

"You are too *humane* and *considerate; things* few people can be charged with."—*Pope, Let.* Here *things* are in apposition to *humane* and *considerate*. Such a construction may be justified, when the ideas are correct, but it is not very uncommon.

"The Dutch were formerly in possession of the coasting trade and freight of almost all other trading nations; they were also the bankers for all Europe; *advantages* by which they have gained immense sums." *Zimmerman's Survey*, 170. Here *advantages* is put in apposition to the two first members of the sentence.

RULE XXIV.

When two names are used, one denoting the possessor, the other the thing possessed, the name of the possessor precedes the other in the possessive case; as, "In my *Father's house* are many mansions." Men's bravery; England's fleet; a Christian's hope; Washington's prudence.

NOTE 1.—When the thing possessed is obvious, it is usual to omit the name; as, "Let us go to St. Paul's," that is, church; "He is at the President's," that is, house.

"Nor think a lover's are but fancied woes."—*Cowper*.

That is, a lover's woes. "Whose book is this? William's."

NOTE 2.—When the possessor is described by two or more names, the sign of the possessive is generally annexed to the last; as, "Edward, the Second of England's Queen."—*Bacon on Empire*.

"In Edward the Third's time."—*Black. Com.* b. 1. ch. 2.

"John the Baptist's head."—*Matt.*

"*A member of parliament's paying* court to his constituents."
Burke.

But if the thing possessed is represented as belonging to a number severally specified, the sign of the possessive is repeated with each; as, "He has the surgeon's and the physician's advice." "It was my father's, mother's, and uncle's opinion."*

Note 3.—When *of* is used before the possessive case of nouns, there is a double possessive, the thing possessed not being repeated; as, "Vital air was a discovery *of Priestley's*." "Combustion, as now understood, was a discovery of Lavoisier's." The sense of which is, that vital air was one of the discoveries of Priestley. This idiom prevents the repetition of the same word.

Note 4.—The possessive may be supplied by *of*, before the name of the possessor; as, "the hope of a christian." But *of* does not always denote possession; it denotes also *consisting of*, or *in*, *concerning*, &c.; and in these cases, its place cannot be supplied by the possessive case. Thus *cloth of wool*, cannot be converted into *wool's cloth;* nor a *cup of water*, into *water's cup;* nor an *idea of an angel*, into an *angel's idea;* nor the *house of Lords*, into the *Lord's house*.

RULE XXV.

Participles are often used for nouns, and have the like effect in governing them in the possessive case; as, "A courier arrived from Madrid, with an account of his Catholic *majesty's having agreed* to the neutrality." "In case of his Catholic *majesty's dying* without issue." "Averse to the *nation's involving* itself in another war."—*Hume, Cont.* vol. 7, b. 2, ch. 1. "Who can have no notion of the same *person's possessing* different accomplishments."—*Spect. No.* 150.

This is the true idiom of the language; yet the omission of the sign of the possessive is a common fault among modern writers, who learn the language by grammar, and neglect usages which are much better authority, and the basis of correct grammar. "Pieces of iron arranged in such a way as seemed most favorable for the *combustion being* communicated to every part."—*Lavoisier, Trans.*

* The contrary rule in Murray is egregiously wrong; as exemplified in this phrase—"This was my father, mother and uncle's advice:"—this is not English. When we say, "The king of England's throne," the three words *king of England*, are one name in effect, and can have but one sign of the possessive. But when two or three distinct names are used, the article possessed is described as belonging to each: "It was my father's advice, my mother's advice, and my uncle's advice." We can omit *advice* after the two first, but by no means, the sign of the possessive.

"There is no reason for *hydrogen being* an exception." —*Ibm.* These expressions are not English.

RULE XXVI.

Transitive verbs and their participles require the objective case or the object of action to follow them; as, "In the beginning, God *created* the *heaven* and the *earth.*"

"If ye love *me*, keep my commandments." "O righteous Father, the world hath not known *thee.*"

.Sometimes the object and often the objective case of substitutes precedes the governing verb; as, "The spirit of truth, *whom* the world cannot *receive.*" "*Whom* ye ignorantly worship, *him* declare I unto you."

Whom and *which*, when in the objective case, always precede the verb.

In verse, a greater license of transposition is used, than in prose, and names are often placed before the governing verb.

"But through the heart
Should jealousy its *venom* once *diffuse.*"—*Thomson.*

"She with extended arms his *aid implores.*"—*Ibm.*

A name with *whatever, whatsoever* or *whichever*, preceding, is placed before the governing verb; as, "*whatsoever* positive *ideas* we *have.*"—*Locke*, 2. 17.

The object is often omitted after a transitive verb; as, he *reads.*

NOTE 1.—We have some verbs which govern two words in the objective case; as,

"Did I request thee, Maker, from my clay
To mold *me man ?*"—*Milton*, 10, 744.

"God seems to have made *him what* he was."—*Life of Cowper.*

"Ask *him* his *opinion ;*" "You have asked *me the news.*"

Will it be said that the latter phrases are elliptical, for "ask *of* him his opinion ?" I apprehend this to be a mistake. According to the true idea of the government of a transitive verb, *him* must be the *object* in the phrase under consideration, as much as in this, "Ask *him* for a guinea ;" or in this, "Ask him to go."

This idiom is very ancient, as we often see in the Latin—"Interrogatus sententiam." *Liv.* 26. 33. "Se id Scipionem orare."—*Ibm.* 27. 17. "Auxilia regem orabant."—*Ibm. lib.* 28. 5. The idiom in both languages had a common origin.

NOTE 2.—Some verbs were formerly used as transitive, which are no longer considered as such; as, "he repented *him*,"—"flee *thee* away," —"he *was* swerved"—"the sum *was* amounted," &c. which are held improper.

Cease, however, is used as a transitive verb by our best writers— "Cease this impious rage."—*Milton*. "Her lips their music cease."— *Tasso by Hoole*.

RULE XXVII.

Intransitive verbs are followed by the name of the *act* or *effect*, which the verb expresses in *action;* as, "To *live* a *life* of virtue;" "to *die* the *death* of the righteous;" "to *dream dreams;*" "to run a race;" "to *sleep* the *sleep* of death."

We observe, in these examples, *life* is the *name of living* supposed to be complete; as *race* is the name of the *act of running*, when accomplished.

NOTE.—Nearly allied to this idiom is that of using, after verbs transitive or intransitive, certain nouns which are not the objects of the verb, nor of precisely the same sense; but which are either the names of the result of the verb's action, or closely connected with it. Examples: "A guinea weighs five penny weight, six grains;" "a crown weighs nineteen penny weight;"* "a piece of cloth measures ten yards."

"And on their hinges grate harsh thunder." "And rivers run potable gold." "The crispid brook ran nectar." "Groves whose rich trees wept odorous gums and balm." "Grin a ghastly smile."—*Milton*.

"Her lips blush deeper sweets."—*Thomson*.

"To ascend or descend a flight of stairs, a ladder, or a mountain"— "To cost a guinea."

Under this rule or the following may be arranged these expressions— "Let them go their way"—"When matters have been brought *this length*." *Lavois. Translation*. "We turn our eyes *this way* or *that way*." "Reckoning *any way* from ourselves, a yard, a mile," &c.
Locke, 2, 17.

Similar to this idiom are the phrases to *go west* or *east—pointing north* or *south—north-west* or *south-east* and the like, which I find to be Saxon phrases and very ancient.

In some instances verbs of this sort are followed by two objects; as, "a ring cost the *purchaser* an eagle."

---

* The radical idea of *weight* is *carry*, *bear* or *sustain*, from the Saxon *wæg*, a balance. The idiom in question has its original in that idea—a guinea *weighs* five penny weights six grains—that is, *carries* or *sustains* that weight in the scales. How much of the propriety, and even of the beauty of language is lost, by neglecting to study its primitive state and principles!

RULE XXVIII.

Names of certain portions of time and space, and especially words denoting continuance of time or progression, are used without a governing word; as, "Jacob said, I will serve thee *seven years* for Rachel." "And dust shalt thou eat *all the days of thy life.*" "And he abode with him the *space of a month.*" "The tree of life yielded her fruit *every mouth.*" "In those days I Daniel was mourning *three full weeks.*" "Whosoever shall urge thee to go a *mile*, go with him *twain.*" "To walk a *mile*, or a *league.*"

"Effects occurring *every moment* to ourselves."

"You have asked me news *a hundred times.*"—*Pope.**

Words expressing particular or precise points of time are usually preceded by a preposition; as, "at that hour;" "on that day." But to both these rules there are exceptions.

RULE XXIX.

The verb *be* has the same case after it as before it; or two substitutes connected with *be* in construction are in the same case. "*It* is *I*, be not afraid." "*Thou* art *she,*" "*it* is *he.*" "*Who* was *he?*" "*Who* do men say that *I* am?" "*Whom* do they represent *me* to be?" But "*Whom* do men say that I am," is incorrect.

RULE XXX.

Transitive verbs and their participles admit of a sentence, a clause or a number of words as their object; as, "He is not alarmed so far, as to consider *how much nearer he approaches to his end.*"—*Rambler, No.* 78.

Consider what? The whole following clause, which is the object of the verb.

---

* Lowth, followed by the whole tribe of writers on this subject, alledges some prepositions to be understood before these expressions of time. But this is a palpable error, arising from preconceived notions of the necessity of such words. The fact is otherwise. All these peculiar phrases are idiomatic; and the remains of the early state of our language.

The same idiom is found in the Greek and Latin languages, which were built on a Teutonic foundation—it is found in the Saxon, from which it is derived to modern English; and is therefore to be considered as original, or coeval with the language.

"For to say, *a man has a positive clear idea of any quantity, without knowing how great it is*, is as unreasonable as to say, *he has a positive clear idea of the number of sands on the sea shore.*"—*Locke*, 2, 17. 15. Here the parts of this period in italics are the *things said*, the objects of the verb *say*. The first clause, being the object after *say*, forms, with the preceding words, the nominative to *is*—and the same clause of the period is qualified by the attribute *unreasonable*—*For to say all which follows is as unreasonable*, &c.

"If he escapes *being banished* by others, I fear he will banish himself." *Pope, Let. to Swift.*

Here *being banished* stands in the place of a noun, as the object after *escapes.*

"*Whether that which we call ecstasy be not dreaming with the eyes open*, I leave to be examined." *Locke*, 2, 19.

"We cannot avoid observing *their sensible qualities, nay the very substances to be in a continual flux.*"—*Locke*, 2, 19.

This rule comprehends the construction of the verbs *save, except, add, admit, allow, suppose*, and many others when used to govern sentences; and in strictness, the old verbs *if, though, unless.* Examples:—

"Add to this, *what, from its antiquity, is but little known, has from that very circumstance, the recommendation of novelty*"—*Hermes, Preface.* In this sentence the whole of the clauses in italics, is what is to be added—and is the actual object governed by the verb *add.*

"Suppose then *the world we live in to have had a Creator.*" —"Suppose *the disposition which dictated this council to continue.*" *Paley, Evid.* 1.

"Not forgetting therefore *what credit is due to the evangelical history*, supposing even *any one of the four gospels to be genuine.*" *Ibm. ch.* 9.

"It is good also not to try experiments in states, except *the necessity be urgent, or the utility evident.*"
Bacon on Innovation.

"They are in effect no more than standing commissions, save *that they have greater authority.*"—*Ibm. of Council.*

"For that mortal dint,
Save *he who reigns above*, none can resist."
Milton, 2, 815.

"I wish I could give you any good reasons for your coming hither, except *that, I earnestly invite you.*"—*Pope, Let.*

"Lord Bathurst is too great a husbandman to like barren hills, except *they are his own to improve.*"
Pope, Let. Sept. 3, 1726.

"The ships of either party may freely traffick with the enemies of the other, excepting *with contraband merchandise.*" *Anderson, Commerce,* 3, 71.

"Suppose I was to say, *light is a body.*"—*Hermes,* 78.

"Except *ye repent,* ye shall all likewise perish."
Luke 13.

"Ye cannot bear fruit, except *ye abide in me.*"—*John* 15.

"He that sacrificeth to any god, save *to the Lord only,* shall be put to death." *Ex.* 22, 20.

"And he could there do no mighty works, save *that he laid his hand on a few sick and healed them.*"—*Matt.* 6, 5.

"He that is washed, needeth not, save *to wash his feet.*"
John 13.

"Add to this *their custom of plantation of colonies.*"
Bacon.

In these and similar passages, the object of the verb is a whole proposition or statement, in a sentence or clause of a sentence. In this passage, "Except *ye repent,* ye shall all likewise perish," the fact excepted is affirmed in a single verb. *Take away this fact "that you shall repent"*—and the consequence must be, you will perish. This is one of the modes of abbreviation in language which I have so frequently mentioned, and which constitutes a principal excellence of the English.

We observe in some of the passages here cited, the pronoun *that,* after the verb. This is probably the true original construction; the substitute *that,* pointing to the whole following clause. "He could do no mighty works there, save *that,* [except that single fact which follows] he laid his hand on a few sick and healed them."

NOTE.—It may be here observed that in some of the passages cited the verb has no definitive nominative—the verbs *save, except, suppose, add,* &c. are in the imperative mode; but the address is not made to any particular person or persons. And this probably has led authors to class *save* and *except* among conjunctions, prepositions or adverbs, or to consider them as used adverbially; for it has been already observed that the class of adverbs has been a sort of common sink to receive all words which authors have not been able to comprehend.

Is it not strange that *suppose*, *add*, *admit*, *allow*, and other verbs, which are constantly used in the same manner, should have hitherto escaped the same doom? In the passages above cited from Paley, *suppose* is used precisely in the same manner as *except* and *save* in others. Indeed nothing but the most inexcusable negligence could have led critics to this classification of *save* and *except*—for in many passages of scripture, these very words, in the sense in which they are called conjunctions or adverbs, have an object following them, like other transitive verbs; as, "Israel burned none of them *save Hazor only*."—*Josh.* 11. 13. "Ye shall not come into the land, *save Caleb and Joshua*."—*Num.* 14. 30. "I would that all were as I am, *except these bonds*."—*Acts*.

This use of verbs without a definite nominative occasions no inconvenience; for the address is not made to any particular person, but is equally applicable to any one who will apply it. See the subject further explained under rule 38. The following passage in Locke, 2, 27, 2, contains another verb used in the same manner; "Could two bodies be in the same place at the same time, then those two parcels of matter must be one and the same, *take* them great or little."

The error of considering *save* as an adverb or conjunction, has however produced a multitude of mistakes in construction, as in these passages: "Save *he* who reigns above."—*Milton*. "Which no man knoweth, saving *he* that receiveth it."—*Rev.* 2. 17. The nominative *he* cannot be reconciled to any principle of true construction. *He* ought to be *him*, the object after the verb. *Except* might have been used, and this word being *called* a preposition, would have required after it the objective case. But both words are verbs, and ought to have the same construction.

RULE XXXI.

The infinitive mode follows, first, another verb or participle; as, "He loves *to cherish* the social affections"—"be persuaded *to abandon* a vicious life"—"he is willing *to encounter* danger"—"he was proceeding *to relate* his adventures."

2dly. The infinitive follows a noun; as, "The next thing natural for the mind *to do*."—*Locke*. "He has a desire to improve."

3dly. It follows an adjective or verbal attribute; as, "a question difficult *to be solved*." "It is delightful *to contemplate* the goodness of Providence." "God is worthy *to be loved and trusted*." "Be prepared *to receive* your friend."

4thly. It follows *as*; thus, "an object so high *as to be* invisible;" "a question so obscure *as to perplex* the understanding."

5thly. It follows *than* after a comparison; as, "Nothir makes a man suspect much, more *than to know* little."—*B con on Suspicion.*

6thly. It follows the preposition *for*, noting cause or m tive; as, "What went ye out *for to see*."—*Matth.* 11.

This is the true original idiom; but it is usual now omit *for;* as, "he went to see a reed shaken with the wind In every phrase of this sort, *for* is implied in the sens but the use of the word is vulgar.

The infinitive mode is independent, standing as a substitu for a whole phrase; as, "It is not once in ten attempts th you can find the case you seek, in any law book; *to s* nothing of those numerous points of conduct concerni which the law professes not to prescribe."—*Paley, Philos.*

RULE XXXII.

The verbs *bid*, *make*, *see*, *hear*, *feel*, *let*, with the auxil ries, *may*, *can*, *must*, *shall* and *will*, and *dare* and *need*, wh used as auxiliaries, are followed by the infinitive without t prefix *to;* as, "He bids me *come*"—"We cannot make the *understand*"—"Let me see you *write*"—"We heard h *relate* the story"—"We felt the earth *tremble*"—"Whi they *let* pass."—*Locke.* "He may go, can go, must g shall go, will go." "I dare engage; I dare say"—"I need not be anxious."

Note 1.—In the uses of *dare* and *need*, there are some peculiarit which deserve remark.

When *dare* signifies to *defy* or *challenge*, it is regular in the ten and persons, is a transitive verb, and followed by the infinitive with t usual prefix; as, "he dares me to enter the list." But when it is transitive, denoting *to have courage*, it more generally drops the p sonal terminations, has an anomalous past tense, and is followed by infinitive without *to;* in short it has the form of an auxiliary; and the German, it is classed with the auxiliaries. Examples: "I dare gage."—*Pope's Works, Letter to Gay.* "I dare not confess."—*Swif Gay.* "I dare say."—*Locke.* "But, my Lord, you dare not do ther."—*Junius, Let.* 23. "Durst I *venture* to deliver my own se ment."—*Hume, Es.* 7.

The past tense, when regular, is followed by the infinitive with usual prefix:—"You have *dared to throw* more than a suspicion u mine."—*Junius, Let.* 20. The same remark may be extended to future tense; "He will not *dare to attack* his adversary."

In like manner, *need*, when a transitive verb, is regular in its infl tions; as, "A man needs more prudence"—"The army needed prov ions."—But when intransitive, it drops the personal terminations in present tense; is formed like an auxiliary, and followed by a verb, without the prefix *to;* as, "Nobody *need be* afraid he shall not have scope enough."—*Locke*, 2, 22, 9. "I need not *go* any farther."—*Ibm.* "Nor need we *wonder.*"—*Ibm.* "The lender need *be* under no fear."—*Anach. ch.* 69. "There need be no difficulty."—*Beddoes, Hygeia*, 1. 27. "She need *dig* no more."—*Spectator, No.* 121. "A man *need* not be uneasy on these grounds."—*Boswell*, 3, 41. "He *need* not urge to this honorable court."—*Judge Chase.*

In the use of this verb, there is another irregularity, which is peculiar, the verb being without a nominative, expressed or implied. "Whereof here *needs* no account."—*Milt. P. L.* 4. 235. There is no evidence of the fact, and there *needs* none. This is an established use of *need.*

Note 2.—The infinitive mode has, in its sense and use, a near affinity to a noun, and often has the construction of one. It is much employed to introduce sentences which are the nominative to verbs, as well as the objects following them; as, "*To will* is present with me, but *to perform* that which is good I find not." Here the first infinitive is the nominative to *is*, and the second begins the sentence which is the object after *find.*

Note 3.—A common mistake in the use of the infinitive is, to use the perfect tense after another verb in the past time; when in fact one of the verbs in the past time would correctly express the sense, thus, "It *would have been* no difficult matter to *have compiled* a volume of such amusing precedents."—*Cowp. to Hill, Let.* 29. Here the first verb states the time past when it was not difficult to compile a volume; at that time the compilation could not be past; the verb therefore should have been *to compile*, which is present and always indefinite.

In the following passage, we have a like use of verbs which is correct. "A free pardon was granted to the son, who *was known* to *have offered* indignities to the body of Varus."—*Murphy, Tacitus*, 6. 1. Here the *offering of indignities* was a fact precedent to the time stated in the verb *was known;* and therefore the verb, to *have offered*, is well employed.

RULE XXXIII.

The infinitive signifying motive or purpose, often introduces a clause or sentence which is not the nominative or objective to any verb; as, "*To see how* far this reaches, and what are the causes of wrong judgment, we must remember that things are judged good or bad in a double sense."—*Locke*, 2, 21, 61. "To prevent property from being too unequally distributed, no person should be allowed to dispose of his possessions to the prejudice of his lawful heirs." —*Anach. ch.* 62.

Note.—This form of sentence seems to be derived from the use of *for* before the verb, *for to see.* The modern practice is to prefix some noun; as in *order to see*, or "With a view to prevent."

RULE XXXIV.

In the use of the passive form of the verb, there is often an inversion of the order of the subject and object; thus, "The bishops and abbots were allowed their seats in the house of lords."—*Blacks. Com. b.* 1, *ch.* 2.

Here the true construction would be, "Seats in the house of lords were allowed to the bishops and abbots."

"Theresa was forbid the presence of the emperor."—*Murphy's Tacitus*, 2, 540. Note.—This is a common phrase. It may be resolved thus: the presence of the emperor was forbid to Theresa—or, Theresa was forbid to approach the presence of the emperor.

"I was this day shown a new potato."—*Darwin, Phytol. Sect.* 18.

"He was shown that very story in one of his own books."
Guth. Quinc. 1. 32.

This idiom is outrageously anomalous; but perhaps incorrigible.

RULE XXXV.

The participle of the present tense without a definitive *a* or *the*, or with any possessive attribute, usually retains the sense of its verb, and has the objective case after it; as, "The clerk is *engrossing* the bill." "The love we bear our friends is generally caused by *our finding the same dispositions* in them, which we feel in ourselves."
Pope's Letters.

"In return to *your inviting me* to your forest."—*Ibm.*

But when the participle is preceded by *a* or *the*, it takes the character and government of a noun, and in most cases, must be followed by *of;* as "The middle station of life seems to be most advantageously situated for *the gaining of* wisdom. Poverty turns our thoughts too much upon *the supplying of* our wants, and riches, upon *enjoying* our superfluities." *Spectator, No.* 464.

In many cases this participle becomes a noun, without *a* or *the;* as, "It is more properly *talking* upon paper, than *writing*."—*Pope, Let.*

Note.—The foregoing rule is often violated by our best writers, and to make it universal is to assume an authority much too dictatorial.

"Some were employed in blowing of glass; others in weaving of linen."
Gibbon, Rom. Emp. ch. 10.

"When the hindering any action."—*Locke*, 2, 21.

In these two examples the rule is disregarded to the prejudice of the language. But let us attend to the following—"*The attributing to faculties* that which belonged not to them."—*Locke*, 2, 21. Here the participle preceded by *the* cannot be followed by *of*, nor does it perform the office of a noun, but it retains the nature and government of a verb. "*The not making a will* is a culpable omission."—*Paley, Phil. ch.* 23. These expressions are perfectly good English.

RULE XXXVI.

Participles of the present tense, either single or in union with the participle of the perfect tense, often perform, at once, the office of a verb and a noun; as, "*The taking* from another what is his, without his knowledge or allowance, is called stealing."—*Locke*, 2. 28. 16.

"By the *mind's changing the object* to which it compares any thing." *Locke*, 2. 25.

"To save them from other *people's damning them*."
Wycherly to Pope.

"Such a plan is not capable of *being carried into execution*."—*Anach. ch.* 62.

"They could not avoid *submitting* to this influence."
Boling. on Hist. Let. 8.

"Suppose a Christian, Platonist or Pythagorean, should, upon God's *having ended* all his works, think his soul has existed ever since."—*Locke*, 2. 27. 14.

"Taking a madman's sword to prevent *his doing* mischief."—*Ibm.* 1. 2. 20.

"He was displeased with the *king's having disposed* of the office, or with *his having bestowed it* upon a worthless man."—*Henry, Hist. Brit. b.* 3.

"Its excesses may be restrained, without *destroying* its existence."—*Blacks. Com. b.* 1. *ch.* 2.

"Supposing it had a right to meet, without *being called together*."—*Ibm.*

"He was near *losing* his life."
Dobson's Life of Petrarch, 1. 29.

"*The advising* or *attempting* to procure any insurrection."—*Judge Chase.*

NOTE 1.—The participle in *ing*, though strictly active in its signification, is not unfrequently used by modern authors in a passive sense; as, "More living particles are produced—than are necessary for nutrition or for the restoration of *decomposing* organs;" that is, organs suffering decomposition.—*Darwin, Zoon. sect.* 39. 9. "From which caloric is *disengaging*"—that is, undergoing the process of separation.—*Lavoisier, Translation.* "The number is *augmenting* daily."—*Ibm.* "They seemed to think Cesar was *slaying* before their eyes rather than that he was slain."—*Guth. Quin.* 2. 18. "The nation had cried out loudly against the crime while it was *committing*."—*Boling. on Hist. Let.* 8. "My lives are *re-printing*."—*Johns. to Boswell*, 1782.

Many of this kind of participles have become mere attributes; as, "Writing paper; looking glass; spelling or pronouncing dictionary." *Wanting* and *owing* have long had the character of passive participles—with the sense of *wanted, owed.*

NOTE 2.—The use of two participles in the place of a noun is one of the most frequent practices of our best writers; as, "This did not prevent John's *being acknowledged* and *solemnly inaugurated* Duke of Normandy."—*Henry, Hist. Brit. b.* 3. The participle *being* with an attribute, supplies the place of a noun also. "As to the difference of *being more general*, that makes this maxim more remote from *being innate*."—*Locke*, 1. 2. 20.

RULE XXXVII.

Participles, like attributes, agree with a sentence, a part of a sentence or a substitute for a sentence; as, "*Concerning* relation in general, *these things may be considered.*"

Locke, 2. 25.

Here *concerning* relates to the whole of the last clause of the sentence—"These things may be considered"—all which is *concerning* relation in general.

"*This criterion will be different, according* to the nature of the object which the mind contemplates."

Enfield, Hist. Ph. 2. 15.

That is, the difference of criterion will *accord* with the nature of the object.

"*According* to Hierocles, Ammonius was induced to execute the plan of a distinct eclectic school," &c.

Ibm. p. 63,

Here the whole statement of facts in the last clause was *according to Hierocles;* that is, it accorded with his testimony.

"I have accepted thee, *concerning* this thing also."

Gen. 19.

"I speak *concerning* Christ and the church."
Eph. 5. 32.

"Thus shalt thou do unto the Levites, *touching* their charge."—*Num.* 8. 26.

"And *touching* the house of the king of Judah, say, Hear ye the word of the Lord."—*Jer.* 21. 10.

"Now as *touching* things offered unto idols, we know that we all have knowledge."—1 *Cor.* 8. 1.

In general, *as* is used in scripture before *touching*, and the construction is, "Now, *as*, or *that* which follows is *touching* things offered to idols." Since the translation of the Bible, this word *touching*, in this sense, has been obsolescent, and *respecting* has taken its place.

"He finds the ideas he has in his mind to agree or disagree, *according as* the words standing for them are affirmed or denied one of another in the proposition."
Locke, 1. 2. 23.

Note.—The use of participles explained under this rule, coincides with that of attributes as explained under rule 17.

RULE XXXVIII.

Participles often stand without a name, sentence or substitute on which they immediately depend, being referable to either of the persons indefinitely; as, "It is not possible to act otherwise, *considering* the weakness of our nature." —*Spectator*.

Note 1.—Johnson, in his Dictionary, calls this a *kind of conjunction*, and adds—"It had been more grammatically written *considered*, vu French, but *considering* is always used."

This criticism indicates an incorrect view of the subject. *Considered* cannot be used without a change in the structure of the sentence—"The weakness of our nature being considered." But to make this form of expression correspondent to the other clause, that ought also to be varied, and a definite person introduced, thus—"It does not appear (to us) possible to act otherwise, the weakness of our nature being considered." But this amendment would be of no advantage.

To comprehend the use of such expressions, we should consider that men find it useful to deal in abstract propositions and lay down truths without reference to persons. This manner of discoursing is often less invidious than to apply propositions or opinions to persons. To accomplish this purpose, men have devised words and modes of speech which enable them thus to communicate their ideas. In the passage cited, the first clause contains a general abstract proposition, equally applicable to any person—"It is not possible to act otherwise." That is, it is not possible for me, for you, for him, or for her—but it might be invidious t. specify persons. It is not possible for John or Thomas to act otherwise, he considering the weakness of his nature. Hence the proposition is left without application—and it follows naturally that the persons who are to consider the cause, the *weakness of our nature*, should be left indefinite, or unascertained. Hence *considering* is left without a direct application to any person.

Whatever foundation there may be for this explanation, the idiom is common and well authorized.

"Generally *speaking*, the heir at law is not bound by the intention of the testator."—*Paley, Phil.* 23.

"*Supposing* that electricity is actually a substance, and *taking* it for granted that it is different from caloric, does it not in all probability contain caloric, as well as all other bodies?"

Thompson, Chim. art. Caloric.

Here is no noun expressed or implied, to which *supposing* and *taking* can be referred; *we* would be most naturally understood—

"*Supposing* the first stratum of particles to remain in their place, after their union with caloric, *we* can conceive an affinity," &c.—*Ibm.* Here *supposing* may be referred to *we*, but is this the real construction?

"For *supposing* parliament had a right to meet spontaneously, without being called together, it would be impossible to conceive that all the members would agree," &c.—*Blacks. Com. b.* 1. 2.

"The articles of this charge, *considering* by whom it was brought, were not of so high a nature as might have been expected."

Henry. Brit. b. 4. *ch.* 1.

"It is most reasonable to conclude that, *excepting* the assistance he may be supposed to have derived from his countrymen, his plan of civilization was the product of his own abilities."—*Enfield. H. Ph.* 1. *ch.* 9.

"None of us put off our clothes, *saving* that every one put them off for washing."—*Neh.* 4. 23.

"And he said unto them, Hinder me not, *seeing* the Lord hath prospered my way."—*Gen.* 24. 56.

"Lie not one to another, *seeing* that ye have put off the old man with his deeds."—*Col.* 3. 9.

"*Comparing* two men, in reference to a common parent, it is easy to frame the ideas of brothers."—*Locke*, 2. 25.

"*Granting* this to be true, it would help us in the species of things no farther than the tribes of animals and vegetables."—*Locke*, 3. 6. 23.

Bating for *abating*, in a like construction, is found in old authors, but now obsolete. *Admitting*, *allowing*, and some others are frequent in a like construction.

The substitute, which, in most of these phrases, might be most conveniently supplied, is *we*, as the writer may be considered as addressing himself to his readers, and including them with himself.

It will be readily observed how nearly this idiom is allied to the independent clause; for, by a trifling change, these sentences may be resolved into that case. "Two men being compared in reference to a common parent, it is easy [for us, you or him] to frame the ideas of brothers."—"Hinder me not, since (seeing) the Lord hath prospered my way."

RULE XXXIX.

Adverbs or modifiers are usually placed near the words whose signification they are intended to affect.

First. They are placed before adjectives; as, *truly* wise; *sincerely* upright; *unaffectedly* polite.

Secondly. They usually follow a verb when single; as, he spoke *eloquently;* and if a verb is transitive with an object following, the modifier follows the object; as, "John received the present *gratefully*."

To this rule, the exceptions are very numerous, and not to be classed under general heads. "So it *frequently* happens;" "men *often* deceive themselves."—Indeed, in many cases, the position of the modifier makes no difference in the sense, and may be regulated entirely by the preference of sound, in the general structure of the period, provided it is not such as to mislead the reader, in the application of the word.

Thirdly. When one auxiliary and a participle are used, the modifier is usually placed between them, or it follows the participle; as, "he was *graciously* received," or "he was received *graciously*." The first is the most elegant.

Fourthly. When two auxiliaries are used, the adverb is usually placed after the second; as, "We have been *kindly* treated"—But it may follow the participle, "We have been treated kindly;" and in some cases it may precede the auxiliaries; as, "And *certainly* you must have known."—*Junius, Letter* 8.

Fifthly. When adverbs are emphatical, they may introduce a sentence, and be separated from the word to which they belong; as, "*How completely* this most amiable of human virtues *had taken possession* of his soul!"—*Port. Lect.* 8. This position of the modifier is most frequent in interrogative and exclamatory phrases.

The adverb *always* is usually placed before a verb.

Never commonly precedes a single verb, except *be,* which it follows; as, "We are *never absent* from church on Sunday." It is sometimes placed before an auxiliary; as, "He *never* has been at court;" but it is more correctly and elegantly placed after the first auxiliary; as, "He has never been at court"—"He has never been intoxicated."

This word has a peculiar use in the phrase, "ask me *never* so much dowry."—*Gen.* 34. "The voice of charmers, charming *never* so wisely."—*Psalm* 58. The sense is, "Ask me so much dowry as *never was asked before*"—an abbreviation singularly expressive of the idea of asking to any amount or extent. Authors not understanding it, have substituted *ever* for *never*, which impairs the force, if it does not destroy the sense, of the phrase. The use of both is now common, but *never* is preferable—"Some agreements indeed, though *never* so expressly made, are deemed of so important a nature, that they ought not to rest in verbal promise only."—*Black. Com. B.* 3. *ch.* 9.

The use of *here* and *there*, in the introduction of sentences before verbs, forms an authorized idiom of the language; though the words may be considered as redundant. The practice may have originated in the use of the hand in pointing, in the early stage of society.

Here, there, and *where*, originally denoting *place*, are now used in reference to words, subjects and various ideas of which place is not predicable. "It is not so with respect to volitions and actions; *here* the coalescence is intimate."—*Hermes, ch.* 8. "We feel pain, in the sensations, *where* we expected pleasure."—*Locke*, 2. 7. 4.

Hence, whence, and *thence*, denoting the place from which a departure is stated, are used either *with* or *without* the preposition *from*. In strictness, the idea of *from* is included in the words, and it ought not to be used. These words also are used not only in reference to place, but to any argument, subject, or idea, in a discourse.

Hither, thither, and *whither*, denoting *to* a place, are nearly obsolete in popular practice; and obsolescent in writing; being superseded by *here, there, where*. This change is evidently the effect of the all-controlling disposition of men to abridge speech by dismissing useless syllables, or by substituting short words of easy pronunciation for those which are more difficult. Against this disposition and its effects, the critic remonstrates in vain; and we may rest assured that common convenience and utility are better guides in whatever respects the use of words, than the opinion of men in their closets. No word or syllable in a language, which is essential, or very useful, is ever lost.

While is a noun denoting *time*, and not a modifier. In this phrase, "I will go *while* you stay," the word is used in its primitive manner, without government, like many other names of portions of time—*a month, a week*.

We are accustomed to use, as modifiers, *a little* and *a great deal*. "The many letters I receive, do not *a little* encourage me."—*Spect.* No. 124. Many names are used in like manner, as modifiers of the sense of verbs. "You don't care *six-pence*, whether he was wet or dry."—*Johnson.*

RULE XL.

In polite and classical language, two negatives destroy the negation and express an affirmative; as, "*Nor* did he *not* perceive them,"—that is, he did not perceive them. This phraseology is not common nor agreeable to the genius of our tongue.

The following is a common and well authorized use of negatives: "His manners are not inelegant," that is, are elegant. This manner of expression, however, when not accompanied with particular emphasis, denotes a moderate degree of the quality.

Note.—In popular language, two negatives are used for a negation, according to the practice of the ancient Greeks and the modern French. This idiom was primitive, and was retained in the Saxon; as, "Oc se kinning Peada *ne* rixade *nane* while."—*Sax. Chron.* p. 33. And the king Peada did *not* reign *none* while—that is, not a long time. The learned, with a view to philosophical correctness, have rejected the use of *two* negatives for *one* negation. The consequence is, we have two modes of speaking directly opposite to each other, but expressing the same thing. "He did not owe nothing," in vulgar language, and "he owed nothing," in the style of the learned, mean precisely the same thing.

RULE XLI.

Prepositions are followed by the names of objects and the objective case; as, *from* New York *to* Philadelphia; *across* the Delaware; *over* land; *by* water; *through* the air; *with* us; *for* me; *to* them; *in* you; *among* the people; *toward* us.

The preposition *to* is supposed to be omitted after verbs of *giving*, *yielding*, *affording*, and the like; as, "give them bread," instead of "give bread *to* them." "Afford him protection;" "furnish her with books." But this idiom seems to be primitive, and not elliptical.

From is sometimes suppressed, as in this phrase: "He was banished the kingdom."

Home, after a verb denoting motion *to*, is always used without *to*; as, "We are going home."

After the attribute *near*, *to* is often omitted; as, "To bring them nearer the truth."—*Massillon.* Also, after *adjoining*; as, "a garden adjoining a river."

The preposition is sometimes separated from the word which it governs; as, "With a longing for that state *which* he is charmed *with*," instead of "*with which* he is charmed."

In many cases, the relative pronoun may be suppressed; as, "I did not see the person he came *with*," that is, *with whom* he came—and in other cases, *what* is employed for the word governed; as, "I know not what person he gave the present *to*."

This separation of the preposition from the word governed by it, and the suppression of the substitute, are most common and most allowable in colloquial and epistolary language. In the grave and elevated style, they are seldom elegant; and never to be admitted to the prejudice of perspicuity; as in the following passage—"Of a space or number, *which*, in a constant and endless enlarging progression, it can in thought never attain *to*."—*Locke*, 2. 17. 8.

A separation of the preposition to such a distance from the word with which it is connected in construction, is perplexing and inelegant.

Note.—In the use of *who* as an interrogative, there is an apparent deviation from regular construction—it being used without distinction of case; as, "Who do you speak to?" "Who is she married to?" "Who is this reserved for?" "Who was it made by?" This idiom is not merely colloquial; it is found in the writings of our best authors. It is the Latin *cui* and *quo*.

RULE XLII.

Prepositions govern sentences and clauses, or members of sentences; as, "The marine acid—dissolves all metals, *without* excepting gold, silver or mercury."—*Encyc. Art. Mineralogy.*

"*Without* seeking any more justifiable reasons of hostility."—*Hume*, 1. 5.

"*Besides* making an expedition into Kent."

Hume, 1. 36.

"*From* what has been said."—*Blair's Serm.*

"*To* the general history of these periods will be added," &c.—*Enfield, Prelim.*

"*About* the beginning of the eleventh century."—*Ibm.*

"*By* observing these rules and precautions."—*Ibm.*

"*In* comparing the proofs of questionable facts."—*Ibm.*

"*For* want of carefully attending to the preceding distinction."—*Enfield, H. Ph.* b. 2.

"*After* men became christians."—*Paley's Evid.* ch. 1.

"*Before* you were placed at the head of affairs."
Junius, Let. 8.

"Personal bravery is not enough to constitute the general, *without* he animates the whole army with courage."
Fielding's Socrates, p. 188.

"Pray get these verses by heart *against* I see you."
Chesterfield, Let.

"*After* having made me believe that I possessed a share in your affection."—*Pope, Let.* 7.

"Ambition, envy,—will take up our minds, *without* we can possess ourselves with sobriety."—*Spect. No.* 143.

Note.—We observe, in the foregoing passages, the preposition has two uses—one is to precede a word to which other words are annexed as necessary to complete the sense—"about the beginning." Here the sense is not complete—the time is not designated. To define the time which is the object of the preposition *about*, it is necessary to add the words "of the eleventh century"—*about that time.* So that the whole clause is really the object after the preposition.

The other use of the preposition is to precede nouns, verbs or other words, which are not the object of the preposition, but which have a construction independent of it; as, "*after* men became christians." Here *men* is the nominative to *became;* yet the whole proposition is as really the object governed by *after*, as the word *hour*, in the phrase, *after that hour.* "Against I see you," is a phrase of like construction. No single word is an object or in the objective case after *against;* but the whole affirmation is the object. "*Without* we can possess ourselves," has a like construction, and though superseded, in a degree, by *unless*, a word of similar import, is a true English phrase: After [this fact] men became christians—Against [that time when] I see you—Without [this fact] we can possess ourselves.

Let us examine the following sentence: "After thus considering what was likely to happen, we are next to inquire," &c.—*Paley, Evid.* ch. 2. Here *considering* refers to *we;* but is it not, with the whole clause, governed by *after* as the object?

"When we would consider eternity *a parte ante*, what do we *but* repeat in our minds the idea of years and ages?"—*Locke*, 2. 17, 10. Here *but* has the force of a preposition, or of a verb in the imperative mode—equivalent to *except:* What do we—*except this—we repeat*, &c.

"Man, *but* for this, no action could attend,
And, *but* for that, were active to no end."—*Pope.*

"What with more decency were in silence kept,
And *but for this unjust reproach*, had slept."—*Dryd. Virg.* 10. 96.
"The law never speaks *but* to command."—*Paley, Ph.* 3.

RULE XLIII.

The words *if*, *though*, *unless*, and *lest*, may be followed by verbs in the future tense, without the usual auxiliaries *shall*, *will* or *should;* as, "If his son *ask* bread, will he give him a stone?" "If he *ask* a fish, will he give him a serpent?" "Though he *slay* me, yet will I trust in him." "He shall not eat of the holy things, unless he *wash* his flesh with water." "Lest thou *say*, I have made Abram rich."

Except has a like effect upon the following verb; as, "I will not let thee go, except thou *bless* me." *Whether* has been numbered also among the conjunctions, which require the conditional mode, but by an egregious mistake. It is not a connective, nor does it imply a condition or hypothesis, but an alternative.

NOTE.—The arrangement of the foregoing form of the verb, in the present tense of the subjunctive mode, is one of the most palpable mistakes that the compilers of English grammars have committed. It seems to have originated in the Saxon and ancient English practice of omitting the personal termination, to express *future* time—*shall* and *will* not being much used, in ancient times, for this purpose. In consequence of this practice, the translators of the Bible, who wrote the style of the age of Elizabeth,* rarely made any difference between a *present uncertainty* and a *future contingency;* so that the present and future tenses of the original are confounded, and the form of the verb in English which comprehends both, has been placed by grammarians in the present tense of the conditional mode.

Deut. 9. 28. Lest the land say—In the original, lest the land *shall* say—in the future.

Deut. 30. 17. If thine heart *turn* away, so that thou wilt not hear—original—if thine heart *shall* turn—in the future.

1 *Kings* 8. 31. If any man trespass against his neighbor—original—*shall* trespass.

As a general fact, the original Hebrew verb, which the translators have rendered by a verb without *shall* or *will* or a personal termination, is in the future tense; and the English verb, having the sense of the future, ought to be arranged in grammars under that tense.

---

* The present translation of the Bible is commonly considered as made in the reign of James I. but on comparing it with the translations published in the beginning of Elizabeth's reign, it is evident that the last translators merely revised the former copies, altering a few phrases and words; but leaving the body of the style unaltered.

This remark is confirmed by the Greek translation of the seventy—who render the Hebrew by a verb in the future or by an aorist, the sense of which after a sign of condition, is future.

Job 13. 15. Though he *should* slay me.

Levit. 22. 6. Unless he *shall* wash his body.

Gen. 14. 23. Lest thou *shouldst* say—or that thou shouldst not say.

Gen. 32. 26. Except thou *shalt* bless me.

See also *Gen.* 19. 15, *Ex.* 20. 19, and indeed examples in almost every chapter in the Old Testament.

In the New Testament, the aorist, with the sense of a future, is generally rendered by a like form of the English verb. "Take heed lest any man *deceive* you"—that is, *shall* or *should* deceive you. See 1 *Cor.* 10. 12, *Heb.* 3. 12, a future tense,—*Luke* 8. 12, and numerous other examples.

The translation may be considered as correct; but to make it correct, the verbs should in grammars be arranged under the future tense, or an aorist.

For want of attention to the distinction between present uncertainty and future contingency, the translators have confounded two tenses of the original, into one in English. Thus *Matt.* 4. 3. ought to be translated—if thou *art* the son of God; so also *Luke* 23. 35. The original is in the indicative—if he *is* the son of God. So also in *John* 10. 24—1. 25—15. 18. If the world *hates* you; in the indicative. *Acts* 3. 39—if it *is* of God. See also *John* 7. 17—1 *John* 4. 1. and 8. 13.

In these and numerous other passages, the original Greek tense is correctly placed in the present tense of the *indicative*—expressing a condition or uncertainty respecting a *present* fact or event. And our common people who learn the language by tradition, preserve this use of the Indicative, which was its primitive use; for the Greeks and English derive it from the same source.

"And shall not God avenge his own elect, who cry to him day and night, though he *bear* long with them?"—*Luke* 18. 7. In the original, though he *bears* long with them. The fact is not mentioned as a future contingency—though he *should bear;* but as a fact admitted—though he bears long with them, still he will be avenged.

"But though our outward man *perish*, yet the inward man is renewed day by day."—2. *Cor.* 4. 16. The original, *diaphtheiretai*, is in the present tense of the indicative—though our outward man *perishes*, or rather is *perishing* or *decaying*. The translation, which indicates a future casual event, though our outward man *perish*, [that is, *should perish*,] seems not to convey the Apostle's meaning, for he evidently speaks of a fact conceded, as present.

I might extend these criticisms to almost every passage in the Bible, in which this pretended present tense of the subjunctive mode is used in our version, and show that the translators have confounded two tenses, which, in the original, are uniformly kept distinct.

To demonstrate the impropriety of that practice, let us attend to the principles of our own tongue.

It has been before remarked that *if*, *though* and *unless*, are old Saxon verbs in the imperative mode, and that the ingenious invention of our ancestors to express a condition or supposition was, to employ a verb, with the sense of *give*, *grant*, *put*, *be*, *if*, that is, *give* the fact. We retain the idiom, and the words employed; but as these have lost their inflections, critics have ignorantly classed them with conjunctions—a part of speech to which they have no more alliance than they have to nouns or adjectives.* We have also certain words of Latin original, employed for precisely the same purpose—*suppose, allow* and *admit*, which indeed are not yet misnamed and classed with conjunctions.

The Saxon method therefore of expressing condition, doubt or hypothesis, was to declare the fact which was to be supposed, by a verb in the indicative mode, and prefix to this fact or statement, a verb in the imperative mode, denoting *give, grant* or *suppose*. Thus, "Give his son shall ask bread, will he give him a stone?" *Give*, in the imperative, and *his son shall ask bread*, a sentence following *give* as its object. This is precisely the construction of such sentences of a conditional kind. Now to omit the personal termination of the verb in the hypothetical sentence, "Give, he ask bread," is to convert the sentence into false English, unless we suppose the tense future, and the auxiliary *will* or *shall* suppressed. In the present tense, it is just as bad English, as to omit the termination after the Latin equivalent words *suppose* or *admit*. "Suppose his son ask bread"—"Suppose he be the son of God."

Unless is a verb, *onlysan*, to unloose, release, dismiss, put away, remove. Unless he wash his flesh, he will be unclean. That is, dismiss (or suppose not to exist) this fact—*he wash his flesh*, and he will be unclean. This shows that the sentence is not English, except we consider *wash* as in the future, and the auxiliary *shall* suppressed. That the tense is future, is not only obvious, from the sense of the verb itself, but from the following clause—If his son (shall) ask bread, *will* he give him a stone?—Unless he (shall) wash his flesh, he *will be* unclean—the last clauses are in the future, corresponding in time with the contingent events expressed in the first clause.

The use of the present tense of the subjunctive, without the personal terminations, was formerly very general. It was reserved for the classical writers of the eighteenth century to lay aside the pedantic forms, *if he go, if it proceed, though he come*, &c., and restore the native idiom of the language, by writing it as men spoke it, and as they still speak it, unless perverted by grammars.

"If they *are* notions imprinted."—*Locke on Und. p.* 15. *Lon.* 1796.

"If principles *are* innate."—*p.* 28.

"If any person *hath* put such a notion into his head."—*p.* 73.

"Whether that substance *thinks* or no."—*p.* 82.

---

* "*If* his son ask bread, will he give him a stone?" In the name of reason, what single property of a conjunction has *if?* "*Though* he slay me, yet will I trust in him." What connecting powers has *though?* Not the least; and this is equally true of *si* and *nisi* in Latin.

"Whether the soul *doth* think—whether it *has* pleasure or pain—or *be* [is] capable of happiness or misery."—*p.* 83.

"Though a shadow *consists* in nothing but the absence of light."—*p.* 110.

"Whether these his observations *are* justly grounded, I cannot tell."—*Spect. No.* 265.

"If I *am* rightly informed."—*Ibm.*

"If he *has* not the pomp of a numerous train."—*No.* 264.

"Though mutual esteem *produces* mutual desire to please." *Rasselas*, 29.

"If he *was* but feared."—*Rambler, No.* 4.

"If his health *was* impaired."—*No.* 5.

"If he *is* born to think."—*No.* 7.

"If he *is* dwelling with delight."—*No.* 8.

"If he *pretends* to hold him to syllogism."—*No.* 9.

"Of which the writer, if he *was* to live now, would be ashamed."—*No.* 29.

"If it *was* not for you."—*Pope's Letters.*

"If there *was* no other way."—*Hume continued*, 7. *ch.* 2.

"If the revolution *was* not lawful—if the doctor *was* guilty."—*Ibm. ch.* 5.

"If this *was* the decision of man only."—*Porteus, Lect.* 3.

"If he *has* declared."—*Ibm.*

"If the reality *is* proved."—*Ibm. Lect.* 6.

"Though this institution *is* calculated."—*Coxe, Trav. Russia.*

"Unless some powerful motive *animates* this regularity and decency of appearance."—*Anacharsis, Trans. ch.* 47.

"If a soldier *has* quitted his rank—if he *is* married—if the person *admits* the augmentation—if he *does* not."—*Ibm. ch.* 56.

"If the physician *does* not enjoin a proper regimen—if the patient *deviates* from his injunctions."—*Beddoes, Hygeia, Es.* 8.

"If newspapers *are* scurrilous."—*Junius, Let.* 16.

"If no circumstances *are* alledged in his favor—if no allegation *be* [is] made to lessen the force of evidence."—*Ibm.* 62.

"If he *means* Antigonus—if he *means* Demetrius."—*Prideaux*, 1. 2.

"Unless he *thinks* it proper or prudent so to do."—*Blacks. Comment.* 1. 3.

It is needless to multiply authorities—they may be cited without end—and such is THE LANGUAGE.

The poets omit the auxiliary of the future tense, without the sign of contingency—a license not admissible in prose.

"To-morrow, ere fresh morning *streak* the east."—*Milt.*

That is, *shall streak*.

The auxiliary is omitted also after a command.

"Gabriel—hath given
Charge and strict watch, that to this happy place,
No evil thing *approach* or enter in."—*Milton.*

To the false rules of Grammars, we may ascribe the omission of the personal terminations of verbs after *till* and *before*—"At the end of which a new shaft is sunk, and this is done repeatedly, till the shaft *penetrate* to the bottom of the mine."—*Heron's Fourcroy*, 2, 248. "The resounding of the rock when it is struck, warns the workmen before this event *take* place."—*Ibm.* 249.

It has been remarked under the head of *tenses*, that the present tense is properly used for the future, after words which carry the mind forward to the time. *Till* is a word of this sort—its meaning is, *to the time*, which has such an effect upon future time, that we conceive and speak of it in the present tense.

In the first passage just cited, *shall* may perhaps be supplied—*shall* penetrate—which will render the sentence tolerable; but it cannot be prefixed to *take* in the second passage, and the sentence appears not only incorrect, but ludicrous. The same fault in Pinkerton's Geography, renders many passages incorrect, and some ridiculous.

"Though the Mersey *present* a grand estuary, its course is not of great extent."—*Pinkerton's Geography, v.* 1. *Phil.* 82.

"This is not English even upon Lowth's principles, for he lays it down as a rule, that when a fact is certain, admitted, or taken for granted, the indicative mode is the most proper—and he condemns this translation—"Though he *were* a son, yet learned he obedience." "Though the Mersey *presents*," is the true English idiom.

"A large river, which there divides itself into three branches before it *join* the sea."—*Vol.* 2. 135.

"In Neged, a young Arab cannot marry till he *have* proved his valor."—*Ibm.* 316.

Pinkerton's works abound with similar mistakes; he carries the false rules of Lowth to an extent never intended by the learned author. The like errors abound in the works of Paley.*

"Those who hold such doctrine must require that a man so attacked, must, *before he strike* the assailant, stop and ascertain how the pistol is loaded."—*Trial of Selfridge, p.* 160.

I know not whether this inaccuracy is the fault of the judge or of the reporter; but *strike* cannot be considered here as either future or conditional: it expresses time in that indeterminate manner, which constitutes a principal office of a present tense of the indicative—it ought to be *strikes*.

RULE XLIV.

Connectives join two or more clauses or members in a compound sentence; as, "Keep thy tongue from evil, *and* thy lips from speaking guile."

Here are two clauses united by *and*, which continues the sense and prevents the repetition of the verb *keep*.

"I sought the Lord, *and* he heard me, *and* delivered me from all my fears." Here are three clauses combined into a sentence or period by the help of *and;* but a new verb is introduced in each, and the second connective prevents the repetition of the substitute *he* only.

"A wise son heareth his father's instruction; *but* a scorner heareth not rebuke." Here *but* joins the two clauses, but a new character is the nominative to a distinct verb, in the second clause, which exhibits a contrast to the first, and no word is omitted.

---

* From a careful survey of the history of our language, I have ascertained beyond any reasonable doubt, that the English Grammars which have been published within the last forty years, have introduced more errors than they have corrected.

RULE XLV.

Connectives join single words, which are the nominatives to the same verb, expressed or understood—or words which follow a transitive verb or a preposition in the same case. Connectives also join verbs, attributes, and modifiers. Examples:

"*Peter* and *John* went up into the temple."

Here *Peter* and *John* are the nominatives to the verb, and the connective *and* prevents the repetition of the verb and following part of the sentence—Peter went up into the temple. John went up into the temple. I *and* you will go to Boston—William *and* Thomas must go to Washington. Neither I *nor* John was present—Peter *or* Henry will attend. "I am the way *and* the truth *and* the life."

In the following, the connective joins words which are the object of a verb or preposition. "The torch of truth discovers malevolence *and* envy." "I have dispatched my correspondents with fair words *and* general civility."—*Rambler.*

I esteem him *and* her *and* them—He loves us *and* you. It is for you *and* me.

In the following, two verbs in the same tense or mode are joined by a connective. "Their fondness of allegory dazzled *and* confounded their understanding."—*Enfield.* "Plutarch *taught* philosophy *and was* a voluminous writer." —*Ibm.* "All *are* of the dust and *turn* to dust." "The idea is likely to *sink* deeper and *spread* the farther."

Connectives join attributes and modifiers; as, "He is wise *and* virtuous." "An orator pleads eloquently *and* plausibly."

The connectives perform a very important office in abridging language, by enabling us to omit words which must otherwise be repeated. Thus, when I say, "I esteem religion and virtue," two affirmations, "I esteem religion, I esteem virtue," are actually included in the sentence.

When several words or clauses succeed each other, it is not uncommon to omit the connective; as, "We hear nothing of causing the blind to see, the lame to walk, the deaf to hear, the lepers to be cleansed."—*Paley, Evid.*

After the connective *than*, there may be and usually is an ellipsis of a verb, name or other words; as, "There is none greater in this house than I."—*Gen.* 39. 9, that is, than I am.

"In the throne only will I be greater than thou."—*Gen.* 61, that is, than thou shalt be.

"He loves his money more than his honor," that is, more than he loves his honor.

"The king of the north shall return and set forth a multitude greater than the former."—*Dan.* 11. 13, that is, than the former multitude.

"I will pull down my barns and build greater."—*Luke* 12, that is, greater barns.

Sometimes other words may be suppressed without obscuring the sense, as, "It is better for me to die than to live." —*Jonah* 4. That is, better than *for me* to live.

Precise rules for the ellipsis of words, in all cases, cannot be given. In general, a writer will be governed by a regard to perspicuity, and omit no word, when the want of it leaves the sense obscure or ambiguous, nor when it weakens the strength of expression. But the following remarks and examples may be of use to the student.

1. When a number of words are joined in construction, the definitive may be omitted, except before the first; as, *the* sun, moon and stars—a house and garden.—So also when two or more attributes agree with the same name; as, a great, wise, and good prince. But when attributes or names are particularly emphatical, the definitive should be expressed before each—the sun, the moon and the stars.

2. The repetition of names adds emphasis to ideas; as, "Christ the power of God and the wisdom of God," is more emphatical than "Christ the power and the wisdom of God."

3 An adjective belonging to two or more nouns joined by a connective, may be omitted except before the first; as, *my* house and garden—*good* qualities and actions—"*their* interest and solicitation"—*Rambler*, 56. Nor does it make any difference that the names are in different numbers; as our attributes have no distinction of number, the same word may be applied to the singular number and the plural; as, a *magnificent* house and gardens—his house and lands. But when *a* precedes the first attribute, this construction is not elegant.

4. In compound sentences, a nominative pronoun or name may be omitted before all the verbs except the first; as, I love, fear and respect the magistrate—instead of I love, I fear and I respect. The substitute may sometimes be suppressed; as, the man I saw, for the man *whom* I saw.

NOTE.—In this particular of the substitute, authors often indulge an unwarrantable license. The use of *that* for *that which* is obsolete and not justifiable. "We speak *that* we do know," is an original English phrase, but has ceased to be used by good writers.

The omission of the substitute in phrases like this—"There was an instance occurred"—for *which* occurred—is found in all our good authors—but it is so gross a violation of syntax, without utility or pretext of any kind, that every writer should avoid it.

The verb may often be omitted; as, he is wise and virtuous—that is, he is wise, he is virtuous. They go to see and be seen—that is, they go to see, they go to be seen.

After *hence, thence* and *whence* a verb is often omitted without occasioning obscurity; as, "Hence the flood of vice which overspreads the land."

The auxiliaries often supply the place of a principal verb; as, John loves money better than you do; John has read more books than Peter has [read ;] John shall go, but Peter shall not [go.]

5. An adverb need not be repeated with every word which it qualifies, the connective *and* rendering it unnecessary; as, he spoke and acted *gracefully*. Here *gracefully* belongs to *speaking* as well as to *acting*.

A preposition may be omitted after a connective; as, he walked *over* the hills and the valleys—that is, *over* the valleys.

After *like* and *near*, *to* is usually omitted; as, "Like three distinct powers in mechanics."—*Blacks. Com.* 1. 2. That is, like *to* three—"Such opinions as seemed to approach nearest the truth."—*Enfield*, 2. 59—that is, nearest *to* the truth.

Likewise after *join* and *adjoin*, *to* is sometimes omitted; as, "a garden adjoining the river."

For is omitted by the poets after *mourn*.

"He mourn'd no recreant friend, no mistress coy."

Beattie.

NOTE 1.—The common rule respecting connectives is, that they join like *modes* and *tenses*, as well as like cases; or if the tense or mode is changed, the nominative to the additional verb must be repeated. But this is often false. "*He lives* temperately and *he has long lived* temperately," is an instance in which the repetition of the nominative is alledged to be indispensable. This I apprehend to be a great mistake—the sentence is more correct, as well as more easy and familiar, without the last nominative. So when we pass from the affirmative to the negative or from the negative to the affirmative, the subject or nominative is said to be *always* resumed. This is doubtless an egregious error.—"He is rich, but *he is* not respectable," is not so common a sentence, as, "He is rich, but not respectable." The general rule respecting the ellipsis, is, that a word may always be suppressed, when the omission occasions no obscurity or ambiguity. "He is indolent, and therefore will be poor," is perfectly good English. But let the rule be put to the test of authorities.

"Not that *he is* or *ever was*, obliged by these statutes to call a new parliament every year."—*Blacks. Com. b.* 1. 2.

Is this incorrect? No man will pretend that this is not an authorized idiom and perfectly correct. And how shall we supply the ellipsis? Not that *he* is or *he* ever was! What sort of language is this?

"For when a man says gold is malleable, he *means* and *would* insinuate something more than this."—*Locke, b.* 3. *ch.* 10. 17.

What necessity is there of repeating the nominative before *would?* Not the least. It is impossible to improve the perspicuity of the sentence.

"That *they have* contributed and *will* probably yet contribute in a considerable degree to the abridgment of the labor."—*Miller's Retrospect, Vol.* 1. 390.

"But whatever *they were* or *are*."—*Burke. Reflections on the Fr. Rev.* 72.

"The whole *has* been done under the auspices, and *is* confirmed by the sanction, of religion and piety."—*Ibm.*

"It *has* opened and *will* more and more open their eyes."—*Ibm.*

"If I *have been* born, or *dwell* or *have served* an apprenticeship in one town."—*Paley. Phil. b.* 6. 7.

"He neither *receives* nor *can give* delight."—*Johnson.*

"Cowper's exhortation—is not inferior to similar exhortations—in the accomplished translator of Tansillo's poem, the Nurse, by which these enchanting writers *have induced* and *will continue* to induce, so many mothers,"&c.—*Life of Cowper*. Will any person say, this latter sentence is not correct? How will the grammarian supply the nominative? It cannot be done without repeating a part of the preceding clause—by which these enchanting writers have induced, and *by which they* will continue to induce—And of what use is this repetition? Does it add any thing to the perspicuity or elegance? Not the least. Nothing can show, in a stronger light, the falsity of the rule.

"The philosopher who *hath busied* himself in considering their natures, and *thinks* he knows how far," &c.—*Locke, b.* 2. *ch.* 8. 3.

Here a repetition of the nominative *who* before *thinks*, would improve the structure of the sentence, but is by no means indispensable.

"These are the fountains of knowledge, from whence all the ideas we *have* or *can have*, do spring.—*Locke*, 2. 1.

"I neither *do* nor *can* comprehend all I would."—*Ibm.* 2. 17.

In the two last examples, the repetition of the nominative, instead of improving, would impair the structure of the sentences.

The mischiefs resulting from a vague manner of instituting Grammar rules, will be fully seen in the perpetual confusion of tenses which occur in almost every author. We are told that conjunctions connect like tenses and modes—and *whether* is a conjunction. Let us see the consequence, "If I *should* ask any one, whether ice and water *were* two distinct species of things."—*Locke*, 3. 6. 18.

To resolve this sentence by common grammars, we are to say, that *should ask* is a verb in the imperfect tense of the subjunctive mode, *whether* is a conjunction, and *were*, a verb connected with *ask* by that conjunction. And what sort of language is this—"If I should ask"—a contingent event or hypothesis—of course the time future—"Whether ice and water *were*, two distinct things," that is, *were*, in time past, and perfectly past; for *were* by itself never denotes time imperfectly past?

In this way, the author is led to write what he never intended—sheer nonsense. The verb was intended to express a fact of general existence—one which is always true or false—that is, the identity or diversity of *ice* and *water*—a fact existing in nature, and therefore to be mentioned in the present tense indefinite—"Whether ice and water *are* two distinct substances."

"It *would seem* that inquietude *was* as natural to it as its fluidity."—*Golds. An. Nat. ch.* 17. Here is a similar mistake—the use of the first verb in what is called *past* time, leading the author to use a second verb in the same tense—But *that* is no connective, any more than every substitute in the language—The inquietude of the ocean is a natural property, existing at all times—and the author meant the verb to express that idea. "It would seem that inquietude *is* as natural to the sea as its fluidity." To show this to be the real construction, let the order of the words be changed. "Inquietude *was* as natural to the sea as its fluidity—*that* would seem." This arrangement exhibits the mistake in its true light. Let the reader attend to the following passages.

"If my readers will turn their thoughts back on their old friends, they will find it difficult to call a single man to remembrance, who *appeared* to know *that* life *was* short, [is short] till he *was* about to lose it."—*Rambler, No.* 71.

"Upon this supposition the alchimists *went*, who, supposing *that*—all bodies *were* [are] composed of salt, sulphur and mercury."—*Encyclop. art. Chimistry*, 23.

"They considered the body as a hydraulic machine, and the fluids as passing through a series of chimical changes; forgetting *that* animation *was* [is] its essential characteristic."—*Darwin, Zoon. pref.*

"A stranger to the poem would not easily discover *that* this *was* [is] verse."—*Murray's Grammar.*

"From the figure and movements of the feathered tribes, we should be led to imagine that the structure of their organs *was* [is] extremely different from that of quadrupeds—their economy and way of living *required* [require] some variations of their frame."—*Smellie, Phil. of Nat. Hist. p.* 71.

"Supposing Parliament had a right to meet spontaneously—and if half of the members met [should meet] and half *absented* [should absent] themselves, who shall determine which is the legislative body?"—*Blacks. Com.* 1. 2.

"Two more were stationed in Dalmatia, in a situation, if a war *broke* [should break] out at their back, to support the other legions; and if a sudden emergence *required* [should require] their presence, ready to advance by rapid marches into Italy."—*Murphy's Tacitus*, 1. 264.

The employment of these verbs by the translator is the less excusable, as he had the original to guide him to the true sense—" Quæ—si repentinum auxilium Italia posceret, haud procul accirentur." If Italy *should require* sudden aid—the legions *might be called* from a small distance.

Examples of this mistake may be cited without end—but those which I have collected are amply sufficient to show the miserable state of grammatical knowledge. How easy would it have been to detect these blunders, had the parts of speech been understood, and properly classed! Take for example, the passage from Murray—and resolve it according to the explanation of that which is given in the preceding pages—" This *was* verse—a stranger to the poem would not easily discover *that*." What nonsense! But correct the verb. " This *is* verse—a stranger would not easily discover *that*." The whole error has arisen probably from considering *that* as a conjunction—when in fact it is a representative of the following member of the period—and the sentence is found to consist of two clauses—one hypothetical, the other declaratory—" A stranger to the poem, (if he should attempt) would not easily discover *that—this is verse*."

From the practice of connecting like tenses, probably has arisen a similar misapplication of tenses, where no connective is used; as, " In this way we *might indicate* which of their elements *existed* [exists] in excess."—*Lavoisier by Kerr.*

" It would be true gold to him and belong to that species, who *include* malleableness in his nominal essence."—*Locke*, 3. 6. 35.

It ought to be who *should include*. A similar mistake in the following passage is really ludicrous—" I said to him that he should rebuild the Greek cities and give them wise laws, until a proper time *arrived* to restore them to liberty."—*Anacharsis*, 3. 231. It ought to be *should arrive*.

A few authors, led by their own sense of right and wrong, [for surely they have had no Grammar to guide them,] have occasionally avoided these errors and written the language with correctness. And among these is the translator of Anacharsis, notwithstanding the mistake just cited.

" They *said* that man *is* an animal."—*Anach. vol.* 4, *note.*

" He *told* us these birds *are* natives of Samos."—*Ibm. ch.* 74.

" Sabellius, who openly *taught* that there *is* but one person in the Godhead."—*Encyc. art. Sabellius.*

" His master had *taught* him that happiness *consists* in virtue."
Anach. ch. 7.

" D. Laertius says, the Egyptians *taught* that matter *is* the first principle."—*Enfield, Hist. Phil.* 1, *ch.* 8.

" Anaxagoras *affirmed* that a pure mind *governs* the universe."
Ibm. ch. 3. *b.* 2.

If we examine these sentences, we shall find the time correctly affirmed in each member—The first declares a fact *past*—the last, a fact *now existing*, as well as when the affirmation was made.

" He *told* us that these birds *are* natives of Samos"—or according to the idea before explained—these birds *are* natives of Samos—he *told* us *that*—

Man *is* an animal—they *said* that—happiness *consists* in virtue—his master *taught* him *that.*

I told my brother that, if he *went* [should go] to-morrow, I would accompany him.

How far is it to England? three thousand miles? Indeed, I thought it *was* [to be] four thousand.

What day of the week is it? Monday. Then I mistake; I thought it *was* [to be] Tuesday.

It rains. Is it best to begin work in the rain? I should think it *was* not, [I should think it not to be best, or I should think it not best.] *To be*, may be omitted.

What is the color of the cloth? I should think it *was* [to be] blue.

I told the man that if he *came* [should come] to-morrow, I would converse with him.

It was agreed that if the contract *was* fulfilled [should be fulfilled] by the tenth of next month, the interest should be deducted.

Let him who is not guilty of such mistakes, cast the first stone!!

I have been the more particular in illustrating this part of my subject, to show the necessity of tracing the idioms to their true source, of understanding the principles of construction, and of calling the parts of speech by their true names.

Punctuation.

Punctuation is the marking of the several pauses which are to be observed, in reading or speaking a sentence or continued discourse. By means of pauses, a discourse is divided into periods or complete sentences, and these, into phrases.

A period is a sentence complete, making perfect sense, and not connected in construction with what follows. The pause after the period is marked by a point [.] and in speaking, is distinguished by a cadence or fall of the voice.

The members of a period, or clauses and phrases, are all more or less connected in sense, and according to the nearness of the connection, are marked by a comma, [,] a semicolon [;] or a colon [:]

The comma is the shortest pause, and is often used to mark the construction, where very little interruption of voice is allowable.

A simple sentence or clause contains an affirmation, a command or a question, that is, one personal verb, with its nominative and adjuncts. By *adjunct*, is meant any phrase or number of words added by way of modifying or qualifying the primary words. Thus when it is said, "Cicero was an orator *of a diffuse style*," the latter words, *of a diffuse style*, are the *adjunct* of *orator*, and the whole forms a complete simple sentence, with one *verb* or affirmation.

A phrase contains no assertion, or does not amount to a proposition.

COMMA.

RULE I. In general, the parts of a simple sentence or clause are not to be separated by any point whatever; as "Hope is necessary in every condition of life." But when a simple sentence is long, or contains a distinct phrase or phrases, modifying the affirmation, it may be divided by a comma; as, "To be very active in laudable pursuits, is the distinguishing characteristic of a man of merit." "By revenging an injury, a man is but even with his enemy." In most cases, where a short pause will give distinctness to ideas, a comma is well placed after an important word; "To mourn without measure, is folly; not to mourn at all, insensibility."

The pause after *measure*, in this sentence, is essential to the strength of the expression. "The idea of beauty is vague and undefined, different in different minds, and diversified by time or place."—*Rambler*.

RULE II. When a connective is omitted between two or more words, whether names, adjectives, pronouns, verbs or modifiers, the place is supplied by a comma; as, "Love, joy, peace and blessedness are reserved for the good." "The miseries of poverty, of sickness, of captivity, would, without hope, be insupportable."—*Rambler*. "We hear nothing of causing the blind to see, the lame to walk, the deaf to hear, the lepers to be cleansed."—*Paley*. "He who loves, serves and obeys his Maker, is a pious man." "Industry steadily, prudently and vigorously pursued, leads to wealth." "David was a brave, martial, enterprising prince." "The most innocent pleasures are the most rational, the most delightful and the most durable."

RULE III. Two or more simple sentences closely connected in sense, or dependent on each other, are separated by a comma only; as, "When our vices leave us, we flatter ourselves we leave them." "The temperate man's pleasures are durable, because they are regular." "That all the duties of morality ought to be practised, is without difficulty discoverable, because ignorance or uncertainty would immediately involve the world in confusion and distress."—*Rambler*, 81.

RULE IV. The sentence independent or case absolute, detached affirmations or phrases involved in sentences, and other important clauses, must be separated from the other parts of a sentence, by a comma; as, "The envoy has returned, his business being accomplished." "The envoy, having accomplished his business, has returned." "Providence has, I think, displayed a tenderness for mankind."—*Rambler.* "The decision of patronage, who was but half a goddess, has been sometimes erroneous."—*Rambler.* "The sciences, after a thousand indignities, retired from the palace of patronage."—*Ibm.* "It is, in many cases, apparent." *Ibm.*

RULE V. A comma is often required to mark contrast, antithesis, or remarkable points in a sentence, and sometimes very properly separates, words closely dependent in construction; as, "a good man will love himself too well to *lose,* and his neighbor too well to *win,* an estate by gaming." "Prosperity *gains* friends, and adversity *tries* them." "It is harder to avoid censure, than to gain applause."

"Though deep, yet clear; though gentle, yet not dull."

RULE VI. A single name in apposition is not separated by a comma; as, "the Apostle Peter"—but when such name is accompanied with an adjunct, it should be separated; as, "Parmenio, a friend of Alexander's, hearing the great offers that Darius had made, said, 'Were I Alexander, I would accept them.'" "So would I, (replied Alexander,) were I Parmenio."

RULE VII. Terms of address, and words of others repeated, but not introduced as a quotation, are separated by a comma; as, "Wherefore, sirs, be of good cheer." "My son, hear the counsel of thy father." "Thus shalt thou say to the children of Israel, I AM hath sent me unto you." *Exodus.*

RULE VIII. Modifying words and phrases, as, however, nay, hence, besides, in short, finally, formerly, &c. are usually separated by a comma; as, "It is, however, the task of criticism to establish principles."—*Rambler.*

SEMICOLON.

The semicolon is placed between the clauses of a period, which are less closely connected than such as are separated by a comma.

First. When the first division of a sentence completes a proposition, so as to have no dependence on what follows, but the following clause has a dependence on the preceding, the two parts are separated generally by a semicolon; as, "It may be laid down as a maxim, that it is more easy to take away superfluities than to supply defects; and therefore he that is culpable, because he has passed the middle point of virtue, is always accounted a fairer object of hope, than he who fails by falling short."—*Rambler.* In this sentence, the part of the sentence preceding the semicolon, is a perfect period in itself, and might have been closed with a full point; but the author has added another division, by way of inference, and this is dependent on the first division. The author proceeds—"The one has all that perfection requires, and more, but the excess may be easily retrenched; the other wants the qualities requisite to excellence." Here the first division makes a complete proposition; but the antithesis, begun by the numeral *one,* is not complete, without the last division.

"Economy is no disgrace; for it is better to live on a little, than to outlive a great deal."

"Be in peace with many; nevertheless, have but one counselor of a thousand."

"A friend cannot be known in prosperity; an enemy cannot be hid in adversity."

In general then, the semicolon separates the divisions of a sentence, when the latter division has a dependence on the former, whether the former has a dependence on the latter or not.

Secondly. When several members of a sentence have a dependence on each other, by means of a substitute for the same principal word, and the clauses, in other respects, constitute distinct propositions, the semicolon may be used; as, "Wisdom hath builded her house; *she* hath hewn out her seven pillars; *she* hath killed her beasts; *she* hath mingled her wine; *she* hath also furnished her table."—*Prov.* 9.

COLON.

The colon is used when the sense of the division of a period is complete, so as to admit of a full point, but something is added by way of illustration; as, "A brute arrives at a point of perfection that he can never pass: in a few years he has all the endowments he is capable of; and were he to live ten thousand more, would be the same thing he is at present."—*Spect. No.* 111.

NOTE.—This point is of little use; the difference between the colon and semicolon is so small, that the two pauses are frequently confounded, as may be seen in our present version of the Proverbs. It is said that a colon should be placed before a quotation; but I consider the use of the semicolon as preferable. I conceive the colon might be rejected without injury to the perspicuity of sentences; and punctuation very much simplified by substituting the semicolon and the full point. That slight dependence of a subsequent sentence upon a preceding one, which is marked by a colon, is also marked by the full point; for we are not to suppose a full point precludes a connection between sentences. Let the following sentences from the Rambler, No. 31, be cited as an example.

"With the great and ambitious, I would discourse of honors and advancements. To the rich I would tell of inexhaustible treasures and the sure method to attain them. I would teach them to put out their money on the best interest, and instruct the lovers of pleasure how to secure and improve it to the highest degree. The beauty should learn of me how to preserve an everlasting bloom. To the afflicted I would administer comfort, and relaxation to the busy."

All the parts of a continued discourse are connected; and often by such nice grades of dependence, that it is not easy to discern, much less to mark the minute distinctions. I have never examined any author, whose use of the points is either accurate or uniform; and in particular the colon is every where confounded with the semicolon or the period.

PERIOD.

The period or full point marks a completion of the sense, a cadence of the voice, and the longest pause used between sentences. It closes a discourse also, or marks the completion of a subject, chapter or section.

The full point is used also after initials when used alone; as, after N. S. for New Style; and after abbreviations; as, *Croc. Anglic.* for Crocus Anglicanus.

To these may be added,

The dash — which marks a break in the sentence, or an abrupt turn; as, "If thou art he—but O how fallen!"

The interrogation point ? that closes a sentence which asks a question; as, "How long, ye simple ones, will ye love simplicity?"

The exclamation point ! which is used after sudden expressions of surprise, or other emotion; as, "O happiness! our being's end and aim!"

The parenthesis ( ) and hooks [ ] include a remark or clause, not essential to the sentence in construction, but use ful in explaining it or introducing an important idea. They mark a moderate pause, and the clause included is read with a depressed tone of voice; as,

"Know then this truth (enough for man to know)
Virtue alone is happiness below."—*Pope.*

It will be readily seen that the sentence is not at all dependent on the parenthetical clause; but the converse is not true, for that clause has a dependence more or less remote, on the sentence. Thus, *enough for man to know*, is not intelligible without connecting it with the parts of the sentence preceding and following. So in this passage; "If any one pretends to be so sceptical, as to deny his own existence, (for really to doubt of *it*, is manifestly impossible,) let him enjoy his beloved happiness."—*Locke*, 4, 10, 2. The included clause here is connected with the preceding part of the sentence, and *it* is a substitute for *existence.*

With regard to the duration of the pauses, it may be observed that the comma, semicolon, colon, and full point, may bear to each other the proportion of one, two, three, four, and the interrogation point and exclamation point may be considered each as equal in time to the colon or period. But no precise rule can be given, which shall extend to every case; the length of the pauses must depend much on the nature of the discourse, and their respective proportions may be often varied to advantage by a judicious speaker.

*Prosody.**

Prosody is that part of Grammar which treats of the pronunciation of words, and the laws of versification.

Pronunciation is regulated principally by *accent* and *quantity*.

Accent is a particular stress of voice with which a certain syllable of a word is uttered, and by which it is distinguished from the others. Thus, in pronouncing *probability*, we lay a greater stress of voice upon the third syllable, than

* The substance of the remarks under this head was published more than forty years ago. For some of the observations I am indebted to Sheridan's Art of Reading; but for more of them, to the Honorable John Trumbull, Esq. one of the judges of the Supreme Court of Connecticut. His rules of metrical composition, originally published in my Grammar, and afterwards in my Dissertations on the English Language, are probably the best that have been written.

upon the others—the voice naturally resting upon that, and passing over the others with rapidity and a slight enunciation. This stress of voice on a particular part of a word, is equally necessary to the ease of utterance and the melody of speaking.

In addition to the accent, which may be called primary, there is, in pronouncing words of many syllables, a secondary accent, less distinct than the principal accent, but evidently distinguishing some one syllable, from those which are unaccented. Thus in the word *indiscriminate*, the principal accent is on the third syllable; but the first syllable is evidently uttered with more force of voice, than the second and last two syllables. The final cause of both accents is the *ease of pronunciation*, and by this should both be regulated; for that manner of pronouncing words which is most easy for the speaker, enables him to utter the several syllables with the most distinctness, which is consistent with a rapid communication of thoughts; and this is necessary to render his enunciation agreeable to his hearers. Hence no rules of pronunciation drawn from the termination of words, from their etymologies, or from the practice of popular speakers, should be suffered to interfere with this fundamental principle, *the ease of utterance*—for a forced, unnatural accent is not only painful to the speaker, but utterly destructive of melody.

The accent may fall on a vowel or on a consonant. When it falls on a vowel, the vowel is long; as in glōry, tāble, lāwful. When it falls on a consonant, the consonant closes the syllable, and the preceding vowel is short; as in hab′it, grat′itude, deliv′erance.*

---

* It may be thought that I am captious in criticising the works of English authors, or of others who have written on this subject, but the propriety of detecting error, wherever found, supersedes the necessity of apology.

It has been the practice of most English authors to place the marks of accent, in all cases, over the vowel of the accented syllable—a practice probably borrowed from the Greek language. Thus in Johnson's Dictionary, the vowel *a* in *hábit*, as well as *o* in *hóly*, has the mark of accent, for which reason the mark is no guide to the true sound of the letter, and a learner would be led to give to *a* its long sound thus, hābit—as well as to *o* its long sound in holy.

But this is not the worst evil. The usual rules for dividing syllables, are not only *arbitrary*, but false and absurd. They contradict the very definition of a syllable given by the authors themselves. Thus Lowth defines a syllable to be " a sound, either simple or compound, *pronounced*

The *quantity* of a syllable is the time in which it is pronounced. In English this time is *long* or *short*—long, as in frāme, denōte, compensātion—short, as in thăt, nŏt, mĕlon.

The accent hȧs no small influence in determining the length of a syllable, by prolonging the sound of the vowel; but, in many words, vowels have their long sound, though not under the accent; as, nosegāy, agitāte.

There are some general rules for accenting syllables, which may be discovered by attending to the analogy of formation. Thus words ending in *tion* and *sion* have the accent on the last syllable save one; as *protection*, *adhesion:* words ending in *ty* usually have the accent on the last syllable except two; as, *vanity*, *hostility*.

Few of these rules however are so general, that the exceptions to them are not almost as numerous as the words which fall within the rule; and therefore the accent of words is best learnt from a dictionary and general usage. The rules laid down for this purpose in several works of distinction, are so numerous, and subject to so many exceptions, that they tend rather to embarrass, than to assist the student.

Most prosodians who have treated particularly of this subject, have been guilty of a fundamental error, in considering the movement of English verse as depending on long and short syllables, formed by long and short vowels. This hypothesis has led them into capital mistakes. The truth is, many of those syllables which are considered as *long* in verse, are formed by the shortest vowels in the language; as, *strength*, *health*, *grand*. The doctrine, that long vowels are necessary to form long syllables in poetry, is at length

---

by a single impulse of the voice, and constituting a word or part of a word." But in dividing syllables, no regard is had to the definition—for *manifest* Lowth divides thus, ma-ni-fest. Here, the first syllable *man* is pronounced with a *single impulse of the voice*—according to the definition; yet in writing, the syllable is split—the *constituent part* of a word is divided into *two parts*—that which is to be pronounced with a *single impulse of the voice*, is so separated, as to require *two impulses*. A syllable in pronunciation is an *indivisible* thing; and strange as it may appear, what is *indivisible* in utterance, is *divided* in writing; when the very purpose of dividing words into syllables in writing, is to lead the learner to a just pronunciation. Thus Murray, though he admits that "a syllable is short when the accent is on the consonant," yet separates that consonant from the syllable—as in me-lon—ci-vil—ti-mid. Most of the English elementary books which I have seen are liable to the same objection.

exploded, and the principles which regulate the movement of our verse, are explained; viz. *accent* and *emphasis*. Every emphatical word, and every accented syllable, will form what is called in prose a long syllable. The unaccented syllables, and unemphatical monosyllabic words, are considered as short syllables.

But there are two kinds of emphasis; a natural emphasis, which arises from the importance of the idea conveyed by a word; and an accidental emphasis, which arises from the importance of a word in a particular situation.

The first or natural emphasis belongs to all nouns, verbs, participles and adjectives, and requires no elevation of the voice; as,

"Not *half* so *swift* the *trem*bling *doves* can *fly*."

The last or accidental emphasis is laid on a word when it has some particular meaning, and when the force of a sentence depends upon it; this therefore requires an elevation of the voice; as,

"Perdition catch my soul—but I *do* love thee."

So far the prosody of the English language seems to be settled; but the rules laid down for the construction of verse, seem to have been imperfect and disputed.

Writers have generally supposed that our heroic verse consists of five feet, all pure Iambics, except the first foot, which they allow may be a Trochee. In consequence of this opinion, they have expunged letters from words which were necessary; and curtailed feet in such a manner as to disfigure the beauty of printing, and in many instances, destroyed the harmony of our best poetry.

The truth is, so far is our heroic verse from being confined to the Iambic measure, that it admits of eight feet, and in some instances of nine. I will not perplex my readers with a number of hard names, but proceed to explain the several feet, and show in what places of the line they are admissible.

An Iambic foot, which is the ground of English numbers, consists of two syllables, the first *short* and the second *long*. This foot is admitted into every place of the line. Example, all Iambics;

"Whĕre slāves ŏnce mōre thĕir nātĭve lānd bĕhōld,
Nŏ fiēnds tŏrmēnt, nŏ Chrīstiăns thīrst fŏr gōld."

Pope.

The Trochee is a foot consisting of two syllables, the first *long* and the second *short*. Example;

"*Wārms ĭn* the sun, refreshes in the breeze,
Glōws ĭn the stars, and blossoms in the trees.' *Pope.*

The Trochee is not admissible into the second place of the line; but in the third and fourth it may have beauty, when it creates a correspondence between the sound and sense.

"Eve rightly call'd *mōthĕr* of all mankind."

"And staggered by the stroke, *drōps thĕ* large ox."

The Spondee is a foot consisting of two long syllables. This may be used in any place of the line.

1. "*Gōod līfe* be now my task, my doubts are done." *Dryden.*

2. "As some *lōne moūn*tain's monstrous growth he stood." *Pope.*

But it has a greater beauty when preceded by a Trochee.

"Lōad the *tāll bārk* and lanch into the main."

3. "The mountain goats *cāme bōund*ing o'er the lawn."

4. "He spoke, and speaking in *prōud trī*umph spread
The long contended honors of her head." *Pope.*

5. "Singed are his brows, the scorching lids *grōw blăck*." *Pope.*

The Pyrrhic is a foot of two short syllables; it is graceful in the first and fourth places, and is admissible into the second and third.

1. "*Nŏr ĭn* the helpless orphan dread a foe." *Pope.*

2. ———————"On they move,
Indiss*ŏlŭ*bly firm."——————*Milton.*

3. "The two extremes appear like man and wife,
Coupled togeth*ĕr fŏr* the sake of strife." *Churchill.*

But this foot is most graceful in the fourth place.

"The dying gales that pant *ŭpŏn* the trees."

"To farthest shores the ambrosial spirit flies,
Sweet to the world and grate*fŭl tŏ* the skies."

The Amphibrach is a foot of three syllables, the first and third short, and the second long. It is used in heroic verse only when we take the liberty to add a short syllable to a line.

"The piece you say is incorrect, *why tāke ĭt*,
I'm all submission, what you'd have *ĭt*, *māke ĭt*."

This foot is hardly admissible in the solemn or sublime style. Pope has indeed admitted it into his Essay on Man.

"What can ennoble sots or slaves ŏr cōwărds?
Alas! not all the blood of all thĕ Hōwărds."

Again;

"To sigh for ribands, if thou art sŏ sīlly;
Mark how they grace Lord Umbra or Sĭr Bīlly."

But these lines are of the high burlesque kind, and in this style the Amphibrach closes lines with great beauty.

The Tribrach is a foot of three syllables, all short; and it may be used in the third and fourth places.

"And rolls impet*ŭoŭs tŏ* the plain."

Or thus;

"And thunders down impet*ŭoŭs tŏ* the plain."

The Dactyl, a foot of three syllables, the first long and the two last short, is used principally in the first place in the line.

"*Fūrĭoŭs* he spoke, the angry chief replied."
"*Mūrmŭrĭng*, and with him fled the shades of night."

The Anapest, a foot consisting of three syllables, the two first short and the last long, is admissible into every place of the line.

"Căn ă bōsŏm sŏ gēntlĕ rĕmāin
Unmoved when her Corydon sighs?
Will a nymph that is fond of the plains,
These plains and these valleys despise!
Dear regions of silence and shade,
Soft scenes of contentment and ease,
Where I could have pleasantly stay'd,
If aught in her absence could please."

The trisyllabic feet have suffered most by the general ignorance of critics; most of them have been mutilated by apostrophies, in order to reduce them to the Iambic measure. Thus in the line before repeated,

"*Murmuring*, and with him fled the shades of night,"

we find the word in the copy reduced to two syllables, *murm'ring*, and the beauty of the Dactyl is destroyed. Thus in the following,

"On every side with shadowy squadrons deep,"

by apostrophizing *every* and *shadowy*, the line loses its harmony. The same remark applies to the following.

"And hosts infuriate shake the shudd'ring plain."
"But fashion so directs, and moderns raise
On fashion's *mould'ring* base, their transient praise."
Churchill.

Poetic lines which abound with these trisyllabic feet, are the most flowing and melodious of any in the language; and yet the poets themselves, or their printers, murder them with numberless unnecessary contractions.

It requires but little judgment and an ear indifferently accurate, to distinguish the contractions which are necessary, from those which are needless and injurious to the versification. In the following passage we find examples of both.

"She went from op'ra, park, assembly, play,
To morning walks and prayers, three times a day;
To pass her time 'twixt reading and bohea,
To muse and spill her solitary tea;
Or o'er cold coffee trifle with the spoon,
Count the slow clock, and dine exact at noon;
Divert her eyes with pictures in the fire,
Hum half a tune, tell stories to the 'squire;
Up to her godly garret after sev'n,
There starve and pray, for that's the way to heav'n."
Pope's Epistles.

Here *e* in *opera* ought not to be apostrophized, for such a contraction reduces an Amphibrachic foot to an Iambic. The words *prayers, seven* and *heaven* need not the apostrophe of *e;* for it makes no difference in the pronunciation. But the contraction of *over* and *betwixt* is necessary; for without it the measure would be imperfect.

PAUSES.

Having explained the several kinds of feet, and shown in what places of a verse they may be used, I proceed to another important article, the pauses. Of these there are two kinds—the *cesural* pause, which divides the line into two equal or unequal parts; and the *final* pause, which closes the verse. These pauses are called *musical*, because their sole end is melody of verse.

The pauses which mark the sense, and for this reason are denominated *sentential*, are the same in verse as in prose. They are marked by the usual stops, a comma, a semicolon, a colon or a period, as the sense requires, and need no particular explanation.

The cesural pause is not essential to verse, for the shorter kinds of measure are without it; but it improves both the melody and the harmony.

Melody in music is derived from a succession of sounds; harmony from different sounds in concord. A single voice can produce melody; a union of voices is necessary to form harmony. In this sense harmony cannot be applied to verse, because poetry is recited by a single voice. But harmony may be used in a figurative sense, to express the effect produced by observing the proportion which the members of verse bear to each other.*

The cesural pause may be placed in any part of the verse; but has the finest effect upon the melody, when placed after the second or third foot, or in the middle of the third. After the second;

"In what retreat, inglorious and unknown,
Did genius sleep, when dullness seiz'd the throne?"

After the third;

"O say what stranger cause, yet unexplored,
Could make a gentle belle reject a lord?"

In the middle of the third;

"Great are his perils, in this stormy time,
Who rashly ventures, on a sea of rhyme."

In these examples we find a great degree of melody, but not in all the same degree. In comparing the divisions of verse, we experience the most pleasure in viewing those which are equal; hence those verses which have the pause in the middle of the third foot, which is the middle of the verse, are the most melodious. Such is the third example above.

In lines where the pause is placed after the second foot, we perceive a smaller degree of melody, for the divisions are not equal; one containing four syllables, the other six, as in the first example.

---

* Sheridan's Art of Reading.

But the melody in this example, is much superior to that of the verses which have the cesural pause after the third foot; for this obvious reason: When the pause bounds the second foot, the latter part of the verse is the greatest, and leaves the most forcible impression upon the mind; but when the pause is at the end of the third foot, the order is reversed. We are fond of proceeding from small to great, and a climax in sound pleases the ear, in the same manner as a climax in sense delights the mind. Such is the first example.

It must be observed further, that when the cesural pause falls after the second and third feet, both the final and cesural pauses are on accented syllables; whereas, when the cesural pause falls in the middle of the third foot, this is on a weak syllable, and the final pause on an accented syllable. This variety in the latter, is another cause of the superior pleasure we derive from verses divided into equal portions.

The pause may fall in the middle of the fourth foot; as,

"Let favor speak for others, worth for me:"

but the melody, in this case, is almost lost. At the close of the first foot, the pause has a more agreeable effect.

"That's vile; should we a parent's fault adore,
And err, because our fathers err'd before?"

In the middle of the second foot, the pause may be used, but produces little melody.

"And who but wishes to invert the laws
Of order, sins against the eternal cause."

Harmony is produced by a proportion between the members of the same verse, or between the members of different verses. Example;

"Thy forests, Windsor, and thy green retreats,
At once the monarch's and the muse's seats,
Invite my lays. Be present, sylvan maids,
Unlock your springs, and open all your shades."

Here we observe, the pause in the first couplet is in the middle of the third foot; both verses are in this respect similar. In the last couplet, the pause falls after the second foot. In each couplet, separately considered, there is a uniformity; but when one is compared with the other, there is a diversity. This variety produces a pleasing effect.* The variety is further increased, when the first lines of several succeeding couplets are uniform as to themselves, and different from the last lines, which are also uniform as to themselves. Churchill, speaking of reason, lord chief justice in the court of man, has the following lines;

"Equally form'd to rule, in age or youth,
The friend of virtue, and the guide to truth;
To *her* I bow, whose sacred power I feel,
To *her* decision make my last appeal;
Condemn'd by *her*, applauding words in vain
Should tempt me to take up my pen again;
By *her* absolv'd, the course I'll still pursue;
'If *Reason's* for me, *God* is for me too.'"

The first line of three of these couplets, has the pause after the second foot; in this consists their similarity. The last line in three of them, has the pause in the middle of the third foot; they are uniform as to themselves, but different from the foregoing lines. This passage, which on the whole is very beautiful, suffers much by the sixth line, which is not verse, but rather hobbling prose.†

The foregoing remarks are sufficient to illustrate the use and advantages of the cesural pause.

The final pause marks the close of a line or verse, whether there is a pause in the sense or not. Sentential pauses should be marked by a variation of tone; but the final pause, when the close of one line is intimately connected with the beginning of the next, should be merely a suspension of the voice without elevation or depression. Thus;

"Of man's first disobedience, and the fruit
Of that forbidden tree, whose mortal taste
Brought death into the world, and all our woe," &c.

---

* Sheridan.

† Churchill has improved English versification, but is sometimes too incorrect. It is the remark of some writer, "That the greatest geniuses are seldom correct," and the remark is not without foundation. Homer, Shakspeare and Milton, were among the greatest geniuses that ever lived, and they were certainly guilty of the greatest faults. Virgil and Pope were much inferior in point of genius, but excelled in accuracy. Churchill had genius, but his contempt of rules made him sometimes indulge a too great latitude of expression.

When these lines are read without a pause after the words *fruit* and *taste*, they degenerate into prose. Indeed in many instances, particularly in blank verse, the final pause is the only circumstance which distinguishes verse from prose.

EXPRESSION.

One article more in the construction of verse deserves our observation, which is *Expression*. Expression consists in such a choice and distribution of poetic feet as are best adapted to the subject, and best calculated to impress sentiments upon the mind. Those poetic feet, which end in an accented syllable, are the most forcible. Hence the Iambic measure is best adapted to solemn and sublime subjects. This is the measure of the Epic, of poems on grave moral subjects, of elegies, &c. The Spondee, a foot of two long syllables, when admitted into the Iambic measure, adds much to the solemnity of the movement.

"While the clear sun, rejoicing still to rise,
In pomp *rolls round* immeasurable skies." *Dwight.*

The Dactyl, *rolls round*, expresses beautifully the majesty of the sun in his course.

It is a general rule, that the more important syllables there are in a passage, whether of prose or verse, the more heavy is the style. For example;

"A past, vamp'd, future, old, reviv'd new piece."

"Men bearded, bald, cowl'd, uncowl'd, shod, unshod."

Such lines are destitute of melody, and are admissible only when they suit the sound to the sense. In the high burlesque style, of which kind is Pope's Dunciad, they give the sentiment an ironical air of importance, and from this circumstance derive a beauty. On the other hand, a large proportion of unaccented syllables or particles, deprives language of energy; and it is this circumstance principally which in prose constitutes the difference between the grave historical, and the familiar style. The greatest number of long syllables ever admitted into a heroic verse is seven, as in the foregoing; the smallest number is three

"Or to a sād varĭety of wōe."

The Trochaic measure, in which every foot closes with a weak syllable, is well calculated for lively subjects.

"Softly sweet in Lydian measures
Soon he sooth'd his soul to pleasures;
War he sung is toil and trouble,
Honor but an empty bubble," &c.

The Anapestic measure, in which there are two short syllables to one long, is best adapted to express the impetuosity of passion or action. Shenstone has used it to great advantage in his inimitable pastoral ballad. It describes beautifully the strong and lively emotions which agitate the lover, and his anxiety to please, which continually hurries him from one object and one exertion to another.

"I have found out a gift for my fair,
I have found where the wood pigeons breed;
Yet let me that plunder forbear,
She will say 'twas a barbarous deed.
For he ne'er could prove true, she averr'd,
Who could rob a poor bird of her young:
And I lov'd her the more when I heard
Such tenderness fall from her tongue."

The Amphibrachic measure, in which there is a long syllable between two short ones, is best adapted to lively comic subjects; as, in Addison's Rosamond,

"Since conjugal passion
Has come into fashion,
And marriage so blest on the throne is,
Like Venus I'll shine,
Be fond and be fine,
And Sir Trusty shall be my Adonis."

Such a measure gives to sentiment a ludicrous air, and consequently is ill adapted to serious subjects.

Great art may be used by a poet in choosing words and feet adapted to his subject. Take the following specimen.

"Now here, now there, the warriors fall; amain
Groans murmur, armor sounds, and shouts convulse the plain."

The feet in the last line are happily chosen. The slow Spondee, in the beginning of the verse, fixes the mind upon the dismal scene of woe; the solemnity is heightened by the pauses in the middle of the second and at the end of the third foot: But when the poet comes to shake the plains, he closes the line with three forcible Iambics.

Of a similar beauty take the following example.

"She all night long, her amorous descant sung."

The poet here designs to describe the length of the night, and the music of the nightingale's song. The first he does by two slow spondees, and the last by four very rapid syllables.

The following lines, from Gray's Elegy written in a Country Church-yard, are distinguished by a happy choice of words.

"For who, to dumb forgetfulness a prey,
This pleasing, anxious being e'er resigned,
Left the warm precincts of the cheerful day,
Nor cast one *longing*, *lingering* look behind?"

The words *longing* and *lingering* express most forcibly the reluctance with which mankind quit this state of existence.

Pope has many beauties of this kind.

"And grace and reason, sense and virtue split,
With all the rash dexterity of wit."

The mute articulations with which these lines end, express the idea of *rending asunder*, with great energy and effect. The words *rash* and *dexterity* are also judiciously chosen.

In describing the delicate sensations of the most refined love, he is remarkable for his choice of smooth flowing words. There are some passages in his Eloisa and Abelard, which are extended to a considerable length without a single mute consonant or harsh word.

OF READING VERSE.

With respect to the art of reading verse, we can lay down but a few simple rules; but these may perhaps be useful.

1. Words should be pronounced as in prose and in conversation; for reading is but rehearsing another's conversation.

2. The emphasis should be observed as in prose. The voice should bound from accent to accent, and no stress should be laid on little unimportant words, nor on weak syllables.

3. The sentential pauses should be observed as in prose; these are not affected by the kind of writing, being regulated entirely by the sense. But as the cesural and final pauses are designed to increase the melody of verse, the strictest attention must be paid to them in reading. They mark a suspension of voice without rising or falling.

To read prose well, it is necessary to understand what is read; and to read poetry well, it is further necessary to understand the structure of verse. For want of this knowledge, most people read all verse like the Iambic measure. The following are pure Iambics.

"Above how high progressive life may go!
Around how wide, how deep extend below!"

It is so easy to lay an accent on every second syllable, that any school-boy can read this measure with tolerable propriety. But the misfortune is, that when a habit of reading this kind of meter is once formed, persons do not vary their manner to suit other measures. Thus in reciting the following line,

"Load *the* tall *bark*, and *lanch* *into* the main,"

many people would lay the accent on every second syllable; and thus read, our poetry becomes the most monotonous and ridiculous of all poetry in the world.

Let the following line be repeated without its pauses, and it loses its principal beauty.

"Bold, as a hero, as a virgin mild."

So in the following.

"Reason, the card, but passion, is the gale."

"From storms, a shelter, and from heat, a shade."

The harmony is, in all these instances, improved much by the semi-pauses, and at the same time the sense is more clearly understood.

Considering the difficulty of reading verse, it is not surprising to find but few who are proficients in this art. A knowledge of the structure of verse, of the several kinds of feet, of the nature and use of the final, the cesural and the semi-cesural pauses, is essential to a graceful manner of reading poetry; and even this, without the best examples, will hardly effect the purpose. It is for this reason that children should not be permitted to read poetry of the more difficult kind, without the best examples for them to imitate

They frequently contract, in early life, either a monotony or a sing song cant, which, when grown into a habit, is seldom ever eradicated.

A PRAXIS,

Or Example of Grammatical Resolution.

"If the excellence of Dryden's works was lessened by his indigence, their number was increased; and I know not how it will be proved, that if he had written less, he would have written better; or that indeed he would have undergone the toil of an author, if he had not been solicited by something more pressing than the love of praise."

Johnson's Life of Dryden.

If—the imperative mode of the verb *give,* formerly written *gif,* the imperative of the Saxon *gifan*—used to introduce a supposition of what is expressed in the following words.

the—a definitive, used to limit the sense of *excellence* in its application to "Dryden's works"—*that particular excellence.*

excellence—a name, or noun, the nominative to the verb *was,* or the subject of the passive verb *was lessened.*

of—a preposition, preceding Dryden's works, and showing the relation of those words to *excellence,* which relation is that of property or possession—*of* the works of Dryden.

Dryden's—a proper or appropriate name—that is, a name belonging to an individual, and not to a species—in the possessive case, governed by *works.*

works—a name in the plural number, following *of.*

was lessened—the passive form of the verb *to lessen,* in the past tense, indefinite, subjunctive mode, third person singular, agreeing with *excellence,* its nominative. This form of the verb is composed of the substantive verb *was,* and the participle in *ed.*

by—a preposition.

his—an attribute agreeing with indigence.

indigence—a name in the singular number, following the preposition *by.*

their—an attribute agreeing with *number*.

number—a name, the nominative to *was increased*.

was increased—the passive form of the verb *increase*, in the past tense indefinite of the indicative mode, third person singular, agreeing with *number*.

and—a connective of the two sentences, the preceding and the following. The sense is complete at *increased*, and there the sentence might have been closed; but as other clauses are added by the writer, the pause is marked with a semicolon.

I—a substitute for the writer's name, or a personal pronoun, nominative case to *know*.

know—a transitive irregular verb, affirming a fact, and therefore in the indicative mode—first person singular, in the present tense indefinite, agreeing with *I*.

not—a modifier of the verb *know*, rendering the affirmation negative.

how—a modifier of the verb *will be proved*.

it—a substitute of neuter gender, nominative case—representing the subsequent part of the sentence—the nominative to *will be proved*—inceptive, that is, introducing the verb, before the sentence or clause, which is the real nominative.

will be proved—the passive form of the verb *prove* in the future tense, third person singular, agreeing with the nominative *it*.

that—a substitute representing the same part of the sentence as *it*—how *it* will be proved, viz. *that* which follows.

if—as before an imperative verb, used to introduce a condition.

he—a substitute for Dryden, nominative to *had written*.

had written—a transitive verb, in the prior-past tense, indefinite, subjunctive mode, third person singular, agreeing with *he*.

less—an attribute in the comparative degree, here used as a substitute for a *smaller quantity*, the object after the transitive verb *had written*.

he—a substitute for Dryden, nominative to *would have written*.

would have written—the irregular verb *write*, in the prior-past tense indefinite, third person singular, agreeing with *he*.

better—a modifier qualifying the action of the verb *would have written*—describing the manner of action—in the comparative degree.

or—a connective of the sentences between which it stands, and expressing an alternative.

that—a substitute representing a part of the sentence which follows—the words, *I do not know how it will be proved*, are here understood before *that*.

indeed—an adverb, or rather a compound of *in* and *deed*—a preposition and noun.

he—as before, nominative to *would have undergone*.

would have undergone—the irregular compound verb *undergo*, in the prior-past tense—agreeing with *he*, the third person.

the—a definitive, limiting the sense of *toil* to a particular kind—the toil of an author.

toil—a name or noun, in the singular number—the object after the transitive verb *would have undergone*.

of—a preposition.

an—a definitive, limiting the subsequent word to *one* person.

author—a name in the singular number, following *of*.

if—as before, expressing a condition.

he—a substitute as before, nominative to *had been solicited*.

had been solicited—the passive form of the verb *solicit*, rendered negative by the modifier *not*—in the prior-past tense of the subjunctive mode, third person singular, agreeing with *he*.

by—a preposition.

something—a noun, composed of *some* and *thing*—following *by*.

more—an adverb of the comparative degree, used to modify the sense of *pressing*.

pressing—a participle of the present tense of the verb *press*; but used as an attribute of the preceding word *something*.

than—a connective, uniting the following words in construction with the preceding.

the—a definitive, restraining the sense of *love.*
love—a name, nominative to the verb *is* understood.
of—a preposition.
praise—a name—following *of.*

In parsing the foregoing and all similar combinations of words forming the tenses of verbs, the several auxiliaries may be named separately, if the teacher should prefer that mode. Thus the combination *was lessened* consists of *was*, the substantive verb in the past tense, and *lessened*, the passive participle of the transitive verb *to lessen.* The combination *will be proved* consists of the auxiliary *will*, and the substantive verb *be*, and the participle passive of the transitive verb *to prove;* all together forming the future tense.

Critical Notes.

"I persecuted this way unto *the* death."—*Acts* 22. 4.

As no particular sort of death is here intended, the definitive *the* ought to have been omitted.—*Lowth.*

"When he, the Spirit of truth, is come, he will guide you into *all truth.*"—*John* 16. 13.

As the sense is probably *all evangelical* truth, and not other kinds of truth, Lowth supposes the definitive *the* ought to have been used; *all the truth*, agreeable to the original Greek. This criticism is probably just; but the student must be cautious of following implicitly the use of the Greek article; for nothing is less determinate? and Lowth himself acknowledges that it has puzzled all the grammarians to reduce the use of it to any clear and certain rules. In the New Testament, it is often used in passages where it is not admissible in an English translation. *Matt.* 3. 8, "Bring forth therefore fruits meet *for repentance;*" in the Greek, worthy of *the* repentance. Verse 11, "Whose shoes I am not worthy to bear;" in the original, whose *the* shoes. In the same verse, "He shall baptize you with *the* Holy Spirit;" in the original, with Holy Spirit. *Matt.* 18. 8, "It is better for thee to enter into *life* halt or maimed;" in the original, into *the* life. Same chapter, verse 2, "And Jesus called a little child unto him;" in the original, there is no definitive—And Jesus calling child. Verse 3, "Except ye be converted and become as *little children;*" in the original, as *the* children. *Matt.* 22. 13, "There shall be weeping and gnashing of teeth;" in the original, there shall be *the* [or this] weeping—and *the* gnashing of *the* teeth. Ch. 24. 3, "Upon the mount of the olives." *Rom.* 7. 1, "Know ye not, brethren, [for I speak to them that know *the* law,] how that *the* law;" in the original, I speak to them that know *law.* Verse 2, "For the woman that hath a husband is bound by *the* law;" in the original, bound by *law.* Verse 8, "For without *the* law, sin was dead;" in the original, without *law.* Verse 21, "I find there a law;" in the original, I find there *the* law. A multitude of similar passages might be cited to prove how little is the analogy between the Greek and English languages, in regard to the use of the definitives.

But to place this fact in a stronger light, let it be observed that the Greeks use both the article or definitive in conjunction with the pronoun *this*—that is, two definitives with the same word. *Rom.* 7. 24, "Who shall deliver me from the body of this death?" in the original, from the body of *the this death,* or *the death this.* *Matt.* 4. 3, "If thou art the Son of God, command that these stones be made bread;" in the original, *the these stones.* This is a common idiom of the Greek, and one utterly repugnant to the genius of the English.

Equally singular is the use of the Greek article before proper names. *Matt.* 2. 22, "He turned aside into the parts of Galilee;" in the original, into the parts of *the* Galilee. Chap. 17. 1, "Jesus taketh Peter;" in the original, *the* Peter. Chap. 3. 1,

"Preaching in the wilderness of Judea;" orig. of *the* Judea.

We cannot therefore draw any general inference, respecting the extent of the signification of words in English, from the use of the Greek article. Indeed, there are many cases where this article must be omitted, or utterly pervert the true meaning. *Matt.* 11. 8, "Behold, they that wear soft clothing are *in kings' houses;*" in the original, in the houses of *the* kings. Ver. 11, "Among them that are born of women, there hath not risen a greater than John the Baptist;" in the original, them that are born of *the* women.

In other cases, the English *the* must be used where no article is found in the Greek; as in *Matt.* 11. 5, "*The* blind receive their sight—*the* lame walk—*the* lepers are cleansed

15 *

—and *the* deaf hear." Here is no article in the Greek, but in English it cannot be omitted, except before *lepers*.

Of the arbitrary and uncertain proof of the definite article, the French language furnishes abundant proof.

"L'avarice est de tous les vices, le plus odieux."

The avarice is the most hateful of all vices.

"Le gouvernment doit avant toutes choses protéger les proprietes." *The* government ought before all things to protect *the* properties. "Theophraste loue *l'*hospitalité et il a raison." Theophrast praises *the* hospitality, and he has reason. *Barret. Trans. of Cicer. de Off.*

The use of the *le* before names of general application, is wholly arbitrary and useless, but established by custom.

Some author, I think Blair, boasts of the superiority of the English over the Latin language, in the use of articles. This is a great error. The Latin *unus* is the English *an*—and *is*, *ille*, *hic*, answer all the purposes of *the*, *this* and *that*. The Romans used these definitives when they wanted them, nor is any part of their writings left obscure for want of other articles.

"Truly, this was *the* Son of God." *Matt.* 27, 54. Lowth supposes that *the* should be *a*, as this was spoke by a pagan who probably believed in a plurality of Gods.

So also in *Dan*. 3. 25.

In this passage, "About *an* eight days,"—*Luke* 9. 28,—*an* is redundant or improper.—*Lowth*.

"Nevertheless, Asa *his* heart was perfect with the Lord." 1 *Kings* 15. 14. This mode of expressing possession is obsolete.

"The more shame for *ye*." The use of *ye* in the objective is admissible only in the comic and burlesque style.—*Lowth*.

In popular practice, *that* and *this* are often followed by *there* and *here*—that there house ; this here tree. This idiom is probably as old as language, and is not a corruption. It existed in the Celtic—*an tigh od*, that house there ; and the French has preserved it—*Cet maison la*. It may have had its origin in the poverty of the primitive languages of the world, or it may have proceeded from the practice of pointing to objects described, or from the Saxon genitive of *this, thissere;* but in the improved style of modern language, it is unnecessary, and in English, is confined to the vulgar and colloquial style.

"I had rather," is probably a mistake for "I would rather," but the error, at least in colloquial language, seems incorrigible.

"The rules of our religion, from which we *are* swerved."—*Tillotson.* The passive form of *swerve* is obsolete. "Flee *thee* away"—"*Was entered* into a conspiracy"—"To *vie charities*"—"Take pains to *agree* the sacred and profane chronology"—are incorrect; for intransitive verbs do not admit the passive form, nor an object after them.

Succeed, though numbered among intransitive verbs, has obtained a general use in a transitive sense—"Succeed the means of grace," is the customary language of divines, and well authorized.

"If Jove this arm succeed." *Pope.*

In the words *abed, ashore,* &c. and before the participles *acoming, agoing, ashooting, a* has been supposed a contraction of *on* or *at.* It may be so in some cases; but with the participles, it is sometimes a contraction of the Saxon prefix *ge,* and sometimes perhaps of the Celtic *ag.*

"In him who is, and him who finds, a friend." *Pope.*

Lowth condemns this use of a noun in the nominative and objective at the same time; but without reason, as the cases are not distinguished in English.

In the use of *mistaken,* there is a singularity which deserves notice. When applied to persons, it is equivalent to being wrong or in an error. "I am mistaken—you are mistaken;" mean, I am in an error—you are in an error. But applied to things, it signifies *misunderstood;* his words or opinions are *mistaken,* that is, *misunderstood.*

As used for *that* in the following sentence, and in similar cases, Lowth condemns as improper or obsolete—"the relations are so uncertain *as* they require a great deal of examination."—*Bacon.* This use of *as* is obsolete; but is genuine English.

It is a popular mistake to use *wives* for the possessive *wife's.* It is at my *wife's disposal* is correct; but not, at my *wives disposal.*

On the other hand, printers err in using *proves* for *proofs,* in the plural.

Latter refers both to *time* and *place*—*later* to time only.—*Priestley*.

We sometimes hear the *strongest* of the two, used for the *stronger* of the two. In such cases, the comparative degree is the more correct.

Then and *above* are often used as attributes; the *then* ministry; the *above* remarks; nor would I proscribe this use. It is well authorized and very convenient.

Johnson observes, "*A* has a peculiar signification, denoting the proportion of one thing to another; as, the landlord hath a hundred *a* year." But the only peculiarity of this use is, that no preposition is employed; a hundred *a* year, for a hundred *in* a year or *for* a year—a dollar a day, instead of a dollar *for* a day.

Averse, in Lowth's opinion, should be followed by *from;* but why, any more than *repugnant* or *unwilling?* Practice has established the use of *to*, with propriety.

The verb *lay* is often used for *lie*—I will *lay* down. *Lay* is transitive—I will *lay myself* down. When no object follows, the intransitive verb *lie* should be used; *let him lie down*.

The word *rather* is used to express a small degree of excess; "She is *rather* profuse in her expenses." In like manner is used *full;* "the coffee is *full* strong."—*Priestley*.

The signification of words in construction, sometimes depends on the tone of voice with which they are uttered; thus, "I cannot find one of my books," if uttered without any peculiar force of voice upon *one*, means that *one* of my books is missing. But with an emphasis upon *one*, it means that all are missing. Thus, if I say "No laws are better than the English," the word *no* uttered without emphasis, makes me declare the English to be the best laws—with emphasis, it makes me affirm them to be worse than none.

In the following sentence, an important distinction is made by the definitive *a*—"He behaves with *a* little reverence." This is positive, and rather praises than dispraises; but omitting *a*—"He behaves with *little* reverence," and I rather dispraise the person. Thus, when I say "There were few men present," I speak of the number as inconsiderable by way of diminution—But there were *a* few men present, I intend to represent the number in the most favorable light.—*Priestley*.

When we say "half *a* dollar," we mean in value only—but "*a* half dollar," means a coin or piece of money.

In this mode of expression, "He looks him full in *the* face," *the* is used for *his*, which is rendered unnecessary by the use of *him* preceding.—*Priestley*.

There are many grammatical errors in the writers of the 16th and 17th centuries, which Lowth, Priestley, Blair, and Campbell have enumerated in their respective works, and many of them are copied into Murray's Grammar. But the greatest part of them are now so perfectly obsolete, that students are in no danger of learning them, either from books or common practice; and it seems to be inexpedient to swell the size of a modern grammar, by criticisms upon modes of writing no longer used.

CONCLUSION.

In the preceding pages, I have attempted to unfold the true principles of construction in the English language. It is probably the first correct analysis of many sentences ever attempted. The following observations and examples will show that the same or a similar analysis is necessary to explain the true construction of sentences in other languages.

Οιδα γαρ οτι ουκ οικει εν εμοι, τουτ εστιν εν του σαρκι μου, αγαθον. "For I know *that* in me, that is, in my flesh, dwelleth no good thing."

In this sentence, the Greek οτι, *that*, is called a conjunction, as *that* is in English. This is a mistake; οτι is a pronoun relative or substitute for the following part of the sentence. The sentence is to be thus resolved—"In me, that is, in my flesh, dwelleth no good thing;" *that* I know, or I know *that*. I know the fact stated in the whole of that part of the sentence which in Greek follows οτι. Similar is the use of οτι in most other cases. This pronoun, like *quod* in Latin, and *that* in English, is to be considered as of neuter gender; and never varied for expressing number. The reason is obvious; when such words represent or refer to sentences, no variation is necessary.

Homo autem, quod rationis est particeps, per quam consequentia cernit, facile totius vitæ cursum videt.—*Cicero de Off. ca.* 4. The literal construction of this sentence is, "But man, *that* he is a partaker of reason, readily sees the whole course of life."

We are accustomed to call *quod* a conjunction, and perhaps because it seems to have no word to govern it. But usage constitutes the correctness of the phrase, and no other rule of government is necessary; it is the only rule of correct language in all cases. *Quod* we render by *because*, or *as*, or *since;* but in this use, *quod* expresses *cause, reason*, or *purpose*, in a brief idiomatic form, and is really the relative pointing to the following part of the sentence. It is perhaps elliptically used, for *per quod.*

In unfolding the structure of sentences, it would be useful to the tyro, to resolve compound words into their component parts. Thus *quamobrem*, is *quam ob rem*, or *ob quam rem; quare*, is *qua* and *re*, in the ablative; *interea*, is *inter ea; præterea*, is *præter ea; qualibet*, is *quam* or *quod libet; quamvis*, is *quam* and *vis; quaqua*, a duplication of the relative in the ablative.

The principles explained in this work throw much light on what are called impersonal verbs. As *it is written* in the prophets, "*Behold I send my messenger before thy face, who shall prepare thy way before thee.*"—*Mark* 1. 2. Here the whole passage cited is the nominative to γεγραπται, that *is written* in the prophets. In English *it*—precedes the verb, but, as has been observed, it is the representative of the sentence which follows.

"Sed animadvertendum est diligentius, quæ natura rerum sit."—*Cicero de Off. lib.* 2. 20. Here the last member of the sentence is the real nominative to the verb *est*—what is the nature of things, is to be considered.—It is observable that in this form of construction, where a sentence or member is the nominative, the participle or attribute is of the neuter gender.*

"Quamquam te, Marce fili, annum jam audientem Cratippum, idque Athenis, abundare oportet præceptis institutisque, philosophiæ."—*Ibm.* 1. 1. "Although, Marcus, it behooves you, who have now attended Cratippus a year at Athens, to be well furnished with the precepts and maxims of philosophy."—Here the last part of the sentence is really the nominative to *oportet*. To be well initiated in the principles of philosophy *becomes* you, my son, who enjoy the advantage of the institutions of Cratippus, at Athens, the seat of science and the arts. The same remark is applicable to *licet*,

---

* Yet some verbs appear to be really impersonal, as, "pugnatum est sub muris." It was fought under the walls.

libet, lubet, placet, &c. "Si placet tibi audire"—if to hear pleases you.

But the French exceeds all languages in the number of nouns, verbs and adjectives, which are thrown into the common sink of adverbs, conjunctions and prepositions. Thus *autre fois, aujourd'hui, cependant, autour, autant, pourquoi, peut être*, are denominated adverbs—*autant que, pourvu que, a condition que, de sorte que, pendant que* are called conjunctions—*concernant, suivant, attendu, joignant, pendant, excepté*, all regular verbals or participles, are classed among the prepositions. Yet it would be far better to resolve all words and phrases according to their original principles, as far as it can be done. "Il est, *peut être*, difficile de ranger sous l'ordre de la nature, la divination qui vient de l'art et de l'etude."—*Morabins, Trans. Cic. de Divin. liv.* 1.

It is difficult to rank, in the order of nature, the divination which proceeds from art and study—all this—peut être—may be. In strictness, the whole sentence or proposition which is affirmed to be *possible*, is the nominative to *peut être*. *Ce pendant*—that pending, admitting that to be the fact, is the case absolute or independent. *Pendant que*, that depending, during that—*pourvu que*—that being provided. —"J'ai quelque chose a vous dire *concernant* cette affaire." I have something to say to you, *concerning* that affair. Here *concerning* retains its verbal signification, as in English, and relates to or agrees with the preceding part of the sentence. "J'obeis *suivant* vos ordres." I obey, *following* your orders. "Il travaille toute la semaine *excepté* le dimanche." He labors the whole week, *Sunday excepted*—that is, Sunday being excepted—the case independent.—*Parce que*—because—that is, *for that which* follows—*Parce que* il pretend qu il y a dans la nature des signes des choses —*Par* the preposition, *ce* the pronoun or definitive, and *que* the substitute representing the following part of the sentence. "*Soit qu'* il parte ou qu' il demeure." *Whether* he goes or stays—that is, *Be it, soit que*—be that fact which is expressed by *il parte*—*que* is a substitute or relative referring to the following affirmation—*il parte*—and the nominative to *soit*. In the second member of the sentence *soit* is understood before *que*.

The sentence fully expressed would stand thus; soit que —il parte; ou soit que, il demeure. Be that, he goes; or, be that, he remains.

"Qui a fait *que* j'ai trouvé grace devant le roi." Literally, who hath made *that* I have found favor before the king. But let the clauses of the sentence be transposed. "I have found favor before the king; who hath made or caused *that*."

Mais *pendant que* les hommes dormoient. But while men slept; literally, but *pending that* men slept. Here *que* relates to the last words, *les hommes dormoient.*—*Matt.* 13.

Pourvu que j'acheve avec joie ma course. *Provided that*, I may [or might] finish my course with joy. Here *pourvu* is a participle, which with *que*, constitutes the case absolute, or independent sentence; and *que*, the relative, refers to the following part of the sentence.—*Acts* 20.

These criticisms, already extended to an inconvenient length, considering the limited nature of this work, may serve to show the reader how artificial and arbitrary are the distribution and denominations of the several species of words, in our grammars, and how ill calculated are the common rules to illustrate the origin or the true principles of language. Before a language can be correctly understood, words must be traced to their source, their radical significations explained, their mutations, contractions, and combinations, developed. It is not the English language only whose history and principles are yet to be illustrated; but the grammars and dictionaries of all other languages, with which I have any acquaintance, must be revised and corrected, before their elements and true construction can be fully understood.

APPENDIX.

The following Examples of the Declension of Nouns may be added under the article Case, *page* 24.

	Sing.	*Plu.*		
Nom.	book	books	Richard	William
Poss.	book's	books'	Richard's	William's
Obj.	book	books	Richard	William

In the following, the possessive case singular is pronounced with an additional syllable.

Nom.	face	faces	Thomas	flesh
Poss.	face's	faces'	Thomas's	flesh's
Obj.	face	faces	Thomas	flesh
Nom.	horse	horses	tress	miss
Poss.	horse's	horses'	tress's	miss's
Obj.	horse	horses	tress	miss
Nom.	church	churches	highness	peeress
Poss.	church's	churches'	highness's	peeress's
Obj.	church	churches	highness	peeress.

Singular Number.

Nom.	flax	plexus	Syrius	Venus
Poss.	flax's	plexus's	Syrius's	Venus's
Obj.	flax	plexus	Syrius	Venus

Let it be observed that after *ce* and *se* in *face, horse;* after *ch* in *church;* after *s, sh* and *ss* in *Thomas, flesh, tress,* and *Venus,* and after *x* in *flax,* the possessive case must be pronounced with an additional syllable, as if the word ended in *es.*

FALSE SYNTAX.

EXAMPLES TO BE CORRECTED BY RULE I.

Present Tense.

I goeth ; I goes ; I loveth ; I walketh ; I is ; I art.
Thou loves ; thou write ; thou hate ; thou trembles.
He, she or it, desire ; he commend ; she dress ; it rain.
We finds ; we sees the clouds ; we dreadeth the cold.
Ye or you studies ; you ploweth the field ; you runs fast.
They playeth ; they strikes the ball ; they sells corn.
The teacher smileth ; the woman spinneth ; the children cries.

EXAMPLE 2 BY RULE II.

It was declared to me, *him* being present.
It was said of him, *them* being in the company.
This was done, *her* not knowing it—or *thee* not knowing it.

BY RULE III AND IV.

To publish slanderous words *are* wrong and wicked.
To rise early *contribute* to health.
To be kind *art* a duty, and *are* a pleasure.
To be just, *are* a divine command.
To be unjust, *are* mean as well as wicked.

EXAMPLE 3 BY RULE VI.

America and Europe *is* three thousand miles distant from each other.
Gold and tin *is* both useful metals.
Instruction and wisdom *leads* to honor.
Strong drink and laziness soon *wasteth* an estate.
Labor and economy seldom *fails* to produce wealth.
Anger and envy *destroys* happiness.
Love and kindness *insures* domestic peace.
Your lot and mine *has* been very different.
I and you *am* very intimately acquainted.
You and he *resembles* each other.

EXAMPLE 4 BY RULE VII.

John or Thomas *have* done the mischief.

Envy or jealousy *were* the cause of his misery.

Extreme cold or heat *are* painful.

It is difficult to determine whether the poor man or the miser most *deserve* pity.

EXAMPLE 5 BY RULE VIII.

That sort of goods *are* not fashionable. What *sort* then *are* to be preferred?

These sort of clothes *are* not durable.

This kind of lands *are* not fertile. *These* kind *are* less valuable.

A troop of horse *were* raised. This assembly *were* numerous.

That company *were* very noisy and rude.

A council *were* called to deliberate.

EXAMPLE 6 BY RULE X.

This are not my children.

Speak to the men and say to *him*.

There are twelves states *who* are adjacent to the Atlantic.

I see several horses *who* were brought from Arabia.

The men *which* I saw were tall and robust.

He has four daughters *which* are young and handsome.

Piety is the ornament *who* most adorns the female sex.

EXAMPLE 7 BY RULE XII.

Take thy only son *who* thou lovest.

John is the man *who* we admire for his integrity.

Washington was the man *who* the electors chose first President.

EXAMPLE 8 BY RULE XVII.

Congress assembled *agreeably* to adjournment.

Accordingly to order, the house proceeded to business.

The sun rose, *previously* to his arrival.

Antecedently to the introduction of christianity, there was no public provision for the poor.

Antecedently to the gospel, bravery was considered one of the first of virtues.

Subsequently to the promulgation of the gospel, humility was held to be the first of virtues.

We cannot indulge in intemperance, *consistently* with the principles of religion. [In consistency.]

He voted in the negative, *conformably* to his former opinions. [In conformity.]

The subject was considered, *relatively* to the condition of the society. [In relation.]

Isaac was called the seed of Abraham, *preferably* to Ishmael. [In preference.]

EXAMPLE 9 BY RULE XXI.

Each of the men *are* furnished with the Bible.
Every one of them *were* able-bodied men.
Neither of the roads *were* the shortest.
Either of the houses *are* sufficiently large.

EXAMPLE 10 BY RULE XXV.

We seldom hear that a man holding fire in his hand produces no pain.

A person selling cheap and buying dear will probably end in ruin.

A man agreeing to a covenant binds him to a performance.

EXAMPLE 11 BY RULE XXVI.

Do you love *he?* Does he love *thou?*
Who do you seek?

EXAMPLE 12 BY RULE XXIX.

It is *me.* It was *him.* It was *them:* it was *her.*

Who do men say that I am? *Who* do men alledge me to be?

EXAMPLE 13 BY RULE XXXII.

Bid my son *to* go. Make the man *to* work. See the student *to* read. Hear him *to* recite. Feel the chair *to* move. Let him *to* see the place. He may not *to* go. He might not *to* learn. We must *to* be industrious. Shall we *to* be compelled. Will they *to* fulfill their obligations?

"Nothing *could have* engaged him to *have undertaken* this voyage."

"It would *have been* easy to *have swelled* this portion of my volume with correspondence."—

"I *did not* mean to *have been* so troublesome."

"They are intended to be such explanations as I conceived the author would have made, *had he have had* in view the purpose to which the book is now applied."

EXAMPLE 14 BY RULE XXXV.

By not favoring *of* his proposal—By engaging *of* his men in service.

By *the* wasting his estate—by *the* employing his resources to bad purposes.

FORMATION OF VERBS IN THE SEVERAL TENSES AND PERSONS.

To turn, a regular verb.

Indicative. Present. Indefinite. Singular. I turn, thou, he, she or it. *Plural.* We, ye or you, they.

Definite. I am turning, &c. Grammar, p. 66.

Past, indefinite. I turned, thou, &c.

Definite. I was turning, &c.

Perfect, indefinite. I have turned, &c.

Definite. I have been turning, &c.

Prior-Past, indefinite. I had turned, &c.

Definite. I had been turning, &c.

Future indefinite. I shall or will turn, &c.

Definite. I shall be turning, &c.

Prior-Future, indefinite. I shall have turned, &c.

Definite. I shall have been turning, &c.

The pupil is to form the tenses; repeating all the combinations, and the inflections of the verbs in the several persons.

To Go, an irregular verb.

Indicative. Present time. Indefinite. I go, thou, he, she, it. We, ye or you, they.

Definite. I am going, &c.

Past Tense, indefinite. I went, &c.

Definite. I was going, &c.

Perfect Tense, indefinite. I have gone, &c.

Definite. I have been going, &c.

Prior-Past, indefinite. I had gone, &c.

Definite. I had been going, &c.
Future Tense, indefinite. I shall or will go, &c.
Definite. I shall or will be going, &c.
Prior-Future, indefinite. I shall have been gone, &c.
Definite. I shall have been going, &c.

In like manner, teachers may give their pupils any other verb, and particularly irregular verbs, and oblige them to form all the tenses and persons. The past tense and participles may be found in my Grammar p. 74, 75, 76.

The same may be done with verbs in the passive, interrogative and negative form.

LESSONS IN PARSING, AND RESOLUTION OF PHRASES.

LESSON I.

If the power of example *is* so great, care should be taken that the best examples only should be exhibited. *Rambler No.* 4.

If, a verb in the imperative mode, contracted from *give; the*, a definitive adjective agreeing with *power*, and expressing a particular power; *power*, a common noun, nominative to *is; of*, a preposition; *example*, a noun following *of* in the objective case; *is*, the substantive verb, intransitive, in the third person of the present tense, indicative mode, agreeing with *power; so*, an adverb or modifier of *great; great*, an adjective agreeing with *power; care*, a noun, the nominative to *should be; should*, an auxiliary verb, past tense of *shall*, but in this conditional sentence, the time or tense is indefinite; *be*, an intransitive verb, and with *should* is indefinite in time; *taken*, a passive participle, from *take*, an irregular, but transitive verb; and *should be taken* are the passive form of the verb *take*, indefinite tense. See *Improved Grammar*, p. 68, 69. *That*, a pronoun or substitute for the following member of the sentence; *the*, a definitive adjective agreeing with *examples; best*, an adjective in the superlative degree, agreeing with *examples; examples*, a noun in the plural number, the nominative to *should be exhibited; only*, an adverb or modifier of *examples* and limiting the word to the *best; should*, an auxiliary verb as before; *be*, an intransitive verb, as before; *exhibited*, the participle passive of the verb *exhibit*, and these forming the passive form of the verb, in time indefinite. Gram. p. 56.

RESOLUTION.

Give the fact, viz. the power of example is so great, then care should be taken *that*, viz. the best examples only should be exhibited. The verb *give* introduces the condition, or supposition, which being admitted or granted, the consequence follows.

LESSON II.

If her ladyship therefore designs to continue her assembly, I would advise her to shun such dangerous experiments.—
Rambler No. 10.

If, a verb. Imp. for *give*, introducing a condition; *her*, a pronominal adjective agreeing with *ladyship*, which is a common noun, nom. to *designs; therefore*, a compound of *there* and *for*, (*there* originally a pronoun signifying *that*, and *for* a preposition, the word then is equivalent to *for that*, that is, for *that reason*, referring to something preceding,) *designs*, a regular verb transitive, ind. mode; pr. tense; 3d person sing., agreeing with *ladyship; to*, a preposition; *continue*, a transitive verb, preceded by *to*, in the infinitive mode, following *designs;* Gram. Rule xxxi: *her*, pronominal adj. agreeing with *assembly*, which is a common noun, sing. num. obj. case, governed by *continue; I*, a personal pronoun, sing. num. nom. case to *would advise; would*, an auxiliary verb, past time of *will*, but indefinite; *advise*, a regular verb transitive, with the auxiliary *would*, in the indefinite tense, and agreeing with *I; her*, a personal pronoun of feminine gender, in the objective case following *advise; to shun*, a transitive regular verb in the infinitive mode, following *her* or *advise; such*, an adjective agreeing with *experiments; dangerous*, an adjective agreeing with *experiments*, which is a common noun, in the plural number, governed by *shun* in the obj. case.

RESOLUTION.

Give, or grant the fact expressed in the words, *her ladyship designs to continue her assembly*, then I would advise her, &c.

Formerly this verb *if* was followed by *that*, as, "If *that* I may apprehend."—*Phil.* 3. 12. This is the proper phrase, the word *that*, a pronoun following the verb *if* in the objective case, and referring to the following clause of the sentence. In modern writings, *that* is usually omitted.

LESSON III.

But *though that* we, or an angel from heaven preach to you otherwise, than that which we have preached to you, let him be accursed.—*Gal.* 1. 8. *Bishop's Bible.*

But, a connective or conjunction, indicating some connection of the sense with the preceding sentence; *though*, a verb transitive, but defective, imp. mode, introducing a condition admitted, and governing the pronoun *that* in the objective case; *that*, a pronoun or substitute for the following clause of the sentence; *we*, a personal pronoun, nom. plu. to *preach; or*, a connective expressing an alternative or one of two things; *an*, an adjective, denoting *one* indefinitely; *angel*, a noun, sing. num. nominative to *preach; from*, a preposition; *heaven*, a noun sing. num. following *from; preach*, a regular verb transitive, in the future tense, for *shall preach*, or *should* preach, agreeing with *angel* the nom.; *to*, a preposition; *you*, a personal pronoun, obj. case plu. following *to; otherwise*, a compound of *other* and *wise*, used as a modifier of the sense, or manner of speaking; *than*, a connective; *that*, a pronoun following *than*. Rule 45; and referring to the following clause of the sentence; *which*, a pronoun of the neuter gender, obj. case, governed by *preach*. Rule 12; *we*, a personal pronoun, nom. plu. to *have preached; have*, an auxiliary verb; *preached*, a participle of the perfect tense, with the auxiliary *have*, forming the perfect tense, agreeing with *we* in the nom. case; *to*, a preposition; *you*, a pronoun, obj. case plu. following *to; let*, an irregular verb transitive, imp. mode, agreeing with the pronoun *thou* or *you; him*, a personal pronoun, in the obj. case, sing. following *let*, a transitive verb; *be*, intransitive verb, with *accursed*, the passive participle of *accurse*, constituting the passive form of the verb, following *let*, [or *let him be accursed*, may be classed together in the imperative mode.]

RESOLUTION.

But allow, [grant, admit] that [which follows] an angel from heaven preach to you otherwise, than that which we have preached to you, let him be accursed.

LESSON IV.

Though he was rich, yet for your sakes he became poor.
2 *Cor.* 8, 9.

Though, a verb defective, imp. mode, followed by the clause, *he was rich*, as the object: *he*, a personal pronoun, nom. case, to *was ; was*, the substantive verb, in the past tense, 3d person, sing. num. agreeing with *he ; rich*, an adjective agreeing with *he ; yet*, a connective ; *for*, a preposition ; *your*, a pronominal adjective, plu. agreeing with *sakes ; sakes*, a noun plu. numb. following the preposition *for ; he*, as before, nominative to *became ; became*, an intransitive verb, in the past tense, 3d person sing. agreeing with *he ; poor*, an adjective agreeing with *he*.

RESOLUTION.

Allow, or admit, that he was rich, yet for your sakes he became poor. The compound *although* has a like signification, and is to be parsed in like manner.

LESSON V.

His face was as *though* he would go to Jerusalem. *Luke* 9, 53.

His, an adjective agreeing with *face ; face*, a noun nom. to *was ; as*, an adverb ; *though*, a defective verb, imp. mode ; *he*, a personal pronoun, 3d person nom. to *would go ; would*, an auxiliary to *go* ; *go*, a verb intransitive, with *would* in the tense indefinite, 3d person, agreeing with *he ; to*, a preposition ; *Jerusalem*, a proper noun, following *to*.

RESOLUTION.

His face was, as, *allow* or admitting the fact that he intended actually to go to Jerusalem—as if the fact were admitted and real. The following may thus be resolved. "He says I must not go ; but I will *though*"—vulgar phraseology. Allow or admit that he says "I *must not go*, yet I will."

LESSON VI.

Provided it shall not rain, I will take a ride.

Provided, a passive participle of the verb provide, with the following clause constituting the clause independent. But there is an ellipsis of the word *that—provided that*, it shall not rain ; that fact *being provided. It*, the neuter pronoun, nom. case ; *shall*, an auxiliary to *rain ; not*, an adverb ; *rain*, a verb intransitive, in the third person, with *shall*, forming the future tense, agreeing with *it ; I*, a personal pronoun, first person, nom. to *will take ; will*, an auxiliary to *take*, a transitive verb, and with *will* forming the future tense, first person, agreeing with *I*; *a*, an adjective agreeing with *ride*; *ride*, a noun obj. case, following *take*.

LESSON VII.

The woman saith to him, Sir, I perceive that thou art a prophet.—*John* 4, 19.

The, a definitive adjective; *woman*, a noun feminine, nom. case to *saith*; *saith*, an irregular transitive verb, in the 3d person sing. num. agreeing with woman; *to*, a preposition; *him*, a personal pronoun, obj. case after *to*; *Sir*, a noun in the nominative case, used as an address; *I*, a personal pronoun first person, nom. to *perceive*; *perceive*, a regular transitive verb, in the first person, ind. mode, pr. tense, agreeing with *I*; *that*, a pronoun, or substitute for the following clause; *thou*, a personal pronoun, 2d person, sing. num. nom. to *art*; *art*, an intransitive verb, 2d person, ind. mode, pr. tense, agreeing with *thou*: *a*, definitive adjective, agreeing with *prophet*; *prophet*, a noun nominative case following *art*. Rule xxix.

RESOLUTION.

Thou art a prophet; I perceive *that*, [that fact, thou art a prophet.]

EXERCISES IN FALSE CONSTRUCTION.

SOLEMN STYLE.

Who *is* thou, O man, that *presume* on thy own wisdom? Thou *ought* to know thou *are* ignorant.

He that *confess* his sins and *forsake* them, shall find mercy.

A soft answer *turn* away wrath. Anger *rest* in the bosom of fools.

FAMILIAR STYLE.

Philadelphia *are* a beautiful city; it *stand* on the west bank of the Delaware; its streets *art* regular; its side-walks *is* well paved; it *containeth* people who *speaks* different languages; its mechanics *is* noted for good workmanship; its literary men *is* distinguished for science.

New York *are* a growing city; its harbor *art* large and of easy entrance; it *wilt* be a great emporium of trade. *Their* inhabitants *is* industrious and enterprising; they *is* distinguished for arts.

Boston *have* been lately incorporated into a city. The growth of the city *have* been very rapid. *Their* inhabitants *is* distinguished for enterprise and learning. Great improvements *has* been made recently in *their* streets, buildings and commercial conveniences.

New Haven *wast* incorporated in January in the year seventeen hundred and eighty four. *Their* streets *is* regular, and *it* are ornamented with trees, which *renders* the city most beautitiful. Yale College *presenteth* a noble view from the open square. The town *were* settled in 1638.

Hartford *standeth* on the west banks of the Connecticut; *their* surrounding country *consist* of most fertile land; and it *have* a great internal trade. The town was settled in the year sixteen hundred and thirty six, and incorporated in May, in the year seventeen hundred and eighty four.

New London, Norwich and Middletown *was* incorporated in May in the year seventeen hundred and eighty four. They *is* handsome cities. New London *have* one of the best harbors in the world.

His cattle *is* very large. Our constitution *were* formed in the year seventeen hundred and eighty seven. The church *are* often disgraced by hypocrites. A multitude *were* assembled.

That pens want mending. *This* books *is* torn. *These is* a fine day. I do not like *these* sort of clothes. *Those* kind of horses are excellent for the harness.

He *which* is not contented with the goods of fortune *whom* he now enjoys, might be unhappy with greater possessions.

He *which* delights in low tricks *want* dignity of mind.

He *which* is guilty of cheating must be rewarded with the infamy *whom* he deserves.

His sister *which* is much beloved by *his* acquaintance, for *its* virtue and good sense, is older than I am; *he* sings sweetly; and *he* charms by *their* modesty.

Virtue is *his* own reward; it *keep* conscience tranquil.

The states *who* lie on the east of the Alleghany mountains *is* called the Atlantic states.

The forest *are* full of birds *who* delight us with their songs.

The boys *who* I admire are those *which* are studious. The women *who* you saw are very handsome. The ladies *which* possess modesty and good sense are respected.

See that *boys* impudence. The *ladys* bonnet is awry. John *his* book is lost.

It was proposed to *he* and *I*, that we should study in the same room. The story was told to *we* and *they*. *I* and *you is* yet young; we are younger than *them*. The instructor taught *I* and *she*.

Him being sick, the physician was called.

Her being dressed, she wênt to church.

Them being convened, the business was begun.

I did *not* hear *nothing* about the affair. He did *not* hear *not* one word. They do *not* care *nothing* about the war in Europe. We did *not* pay *nothing* for our dinner. We see the apples on the tree, but we can *not* get *none*.

A woman *which have* merit, improved by a refined and virtuous education, *retain*, in *his* decline, *a* influence over the men, more flattering than *those* of beauty.

Admirable would be the effects of such refined education, contributing no less to public good than to private happiness. *An* man, *which* at present must degrade *herself* to a fop or *an* coxcomb in order to please the women, would soon discover that their favor *are* not to be gained, but by exerting every manly *talents* in public and private life; and the two sexes instead of corrupting each other, would be rivals in the race of virtue. Mutual esteem would be to each a school of courtesy; and a mutual desire of pleasing would give politeness to their behavior, delicacy to their sentiments, and tenderness to their passions.